Recipes from an English Master Chef

John Burton-Race

Recipes from an English Master Chef

JOHN BURTON-RACE

HEADLINE

First published in 1994 by Headline Book Publishing

10 9 8 7 6 5 4 3 2 1

British Library Cataloguing in Publication Data

A catalogue record for this book is available from the British Library

Edited by Susan Fleming

Book interior designed by Design/Section
Printed and Bound in Great Britain by Butler & Tanner Ltd.

Headline Book Publishing
A division of Hodder Headline PLC
338 Euston Road
London NW1 3BH

CONTENTS

Dedication

*To the memory of Paul Mansfield, a promising
young chef who could have been great.*

Acknowledgements

*Thanks are due to a number of people – to Sir David Napley
who made it all possible, to Carl Wadsack who taught me,
to Raymond Blanc who doubled my already existing
enthusiasm and to Michael Taylor and Nigel Marriage, my
pastry chef and sous chef respectively, who make my
daily working life easier.*

*Behind every kitchen lunatic there must be someone to
stabilise and guide, to encourage and calm and that person
for me is my wife, Christine. Without her I'd be lost.*

INTRODUCTION

BY EGON RONAY

*J*ohn Burton-Race bears the cross of two curses: he is a perfectionist and a man obsessed.

These are, in my view, two of the four main prerequisites of a truly great chef. Intelligence is another; I have yet to meet a dullard who appreciates a good table. And, it goes without saying, superlative taste, in other words an exceptional palate, is a *sine qua non*. None of these are properties that can be acquired. It is axiomatic that truly great chefs cannot be made; they are born.

I have known many chefs toiling obsessively, trying to make it, but unable to do so. I have known perfectionists who could dexterously give a tomato the faultless shape of a rose but that pointless skill was their best. Others, amusing themselves at the stove, had intellect but lacked the gourmet's judgement. And I have seen cooks of gifted palates, with the divine spark of imagination, but without the devilish spark of obsessive application. I have seen very, very few, in whom all these gifts culminate, as they do in John Burton-Race.

'Hyperactive' is how one of our creator chefs once apostrophised to me this driven man for whom little, outside his cooking, can act as a magnet for long. In turn, Burton-Race said of the same chef: 'We are both lunatics for whom nothing is good enough and we keep looking for more difficult tasks.'

His wealthy, mathematician father thought that giving him his reins to join a hotel kitchen of all places, when he 'chucked it in [his school studies] because I was sick of books', would cure him of a teenager's whim. Instead it set him on the road to discover his vocation. It took years to acquire technical knowledge, like a carpenter to 'turn a leg, dovetail a joint', as he says in his perceptive Introduction, until he discovered his own divine spark when he worked in Raymond Blanc's kitchens. That's when his suspicion was awakened that he might be the 'carpenter' who 'might just develop into a Hepplewhite'.

When people comment on some of Burton-Race's dishes – so many of which I know well – I can form my own views whether they possess a really perceptive palate. This is because his creative gifts go far beyond a single constituent, say a gamey piece of baked red mullet, a marvellously light concoction of sautéed foie gras, or a refined caramel mousse, delectable as they are. The greatest dishes in his restaurant may look, at first, involved, giving the superficial impression that the constituent parts are perhaps too many and even, to the naked eye, not naturally congruous. His greatest achievement is that his vision can pre-assemble in his mind's eye (in his palate's imagination, if you like) the constituent parts, so that when you finally savour the result you are amazed how perfectly they fit, how faultlessly they hang together, how well they succeed as a whole. Anyone who talks about nothing but the constituents, observing the assembly of the parts but not the parcel, so to speak, betrays a lack of fine gastronomic judgement, blessedly ignorant of his or her shortcoming. This extremely rare gift of creating unexperienced tastes and flavours by instinctively bringing together ingredients in combinations that don't occur to anyone else, is what crowns this young man as one of the small handful of truly great chefs of this country.

All this is, of course, not enough, or rather it would be too much, in our homes. Kitchen shelves everywhere are groaning under ambitious, flamboyant and basically alienating cookery books. This is why I welcome John Burton-Race's book: it is absolutely practical, painstakingly attentive to details like measures, times and methods to a degree I have not seen before, wise to the home-cook's inexperience giving his revelatory 'Chef's Tips', and attempting to make artists of us by suggesting pretty ways of serving up our attempted imitations.

When I noticed grouse on one of his many judiciously chosen, seasonal menus it recalled the gaffe in my *Daily Telegraph* column many years ago when I described how Scotland's most famous hostess of the day roasted grouse. I quoted: 'Half-way through I lift the grouse by its hind legs...etc.', which the papers's sub-editors failed to notice. Next morning the growling Editor read it and phoned me: 'Which, pray, are the grouse's hind legs?' It's not the kind of 'Chef's Tip' you will find in this book, but a great number that throw a lifeline to the inexperienced and make a vital difference to the outcome. Typical of the trouble the book takes to help you, and symptomatic of the author's character I have described, is the overwhelming detail of preparing the said grouse. Seventeen stages in cooking grouse?! Unbelievable - until you see how sensibly the book guides you through three stages of preparation, six stages of cooking the bird, six of preparing the sauce, and two useful pointers how to dish it up.

You see what I mean by perfectionism and obsession? As for the other two ingredients with which I started this little pen picture, don't worry about the infallibility of your palate, nor, if I may say so, about your intelligence: they are built into the recipes. Extraordinarily well conceived, they bear the mark of exceptionally good recipes: if the dish doesn't succeed, it will most definitely be your fault.

FOREWORD

$\mathcal{M}$any chefs claim that cooking is an art. I disagree. I believe that cooking is a craft first and foremost. It's rather like being a cabinet-maker: first of all the individual craftsman learns the basics of how to prepare wood, turn a chair leg, dovetail a joint, then he can add his own vision, leave his own mark, when he just might develop into a Hepplewhite. At art school Dali's technical ability was probably no greater than the next man's: only after learning how to judge perspective, put paint on canvas, and blend and mix colours could he overturn all the accepted basic principles and allow his own uniquely lunatic imagination to take over.

In cookery, as in cabinet-making and painting, you can develop your own style only when you're confident of your technical ability. Only when you have perfected your craft can you then look at being an individual artist. In cooking today there are lots of brilliant technicians, but only a few whom I would consider creative and inventive enough to be called artists.

I've been seeking perfection in my own craft since I was seventeen, in a variety of places and under a variety of mentors. I'm pleased and proud that the majority of the restaurants and chefs I have encountered during my career have been French; as a result the food I cook is unashamedly influenced by classic French cuisine. However, artistic perfection is somewhat less easy to attain than a grasp of the basics; even if I live to be a hundred, I shall die knowing nothing, before I have mastered all that there is to know about food and cooking. It's such a huge subject, and I feel as yet, despite all the years of practice, that I am only just scratching the surface. I'm trying all the time, pushing my technical skills as far as they might go and, although most experiments are a success, I must admit to quite a few disasters in the privacy of my own kitchen. However, it keeps me entertained because, remember, I'm doing this twelve to fourteen hours a day, every day of the week, and I don't want to be bored!

The basics of my craft are exemplified in the book, as are many of my own culinary principles. These remain constant, whatever else I might be doing. First of all, food should always taste good. To a large extent the best flavour is reliant upon good ingredients: it is my belief that half the success of a good plate lies in the quality of its ingredients. In Great Britain we produce the finest beef, lamb, salmon and various fruits and vegetables, so there is no excuse for us producing anything less than the finest dishes.

The next step concerns what you *do* with these ingredients. Generally speaking, cookery is said to be an application and utilisation of heat. This is obviously so in the majority of cases, but I've tried to go beyond that, showing how some foods can be prepared in *other* ways, without heat. I think the recipes in the seasonal menus which follow are illustrative of all possible ways in which foods can be rendered not just palatable but delicious. These outline the techniques which every practitioner of my craft has to perfect when learning the basics.

Every food has its own flavour, texture and colour, and it is my third basic tenet that these characteristics should remain foremost in the mind. A sauce, a vinaigrette or a herb should be used to complement and enhance the main centre of interest, but never to overpower or complicate it. It is far better to mix only two sauces or two textures and tastes to achieve a pleasing result than it is to complicate the simple by adding a mass of flavours, textures and colours.

If all these are vitally important to me, so too are presentation and lightness. I'm not a devotee of the fancier flights of what became known as *nouvelle cuisine*, but basically what the `new cooking' did was to create and build fresh concepts on the rock-solid foundations of the classic craft. Those few great modern chefs who were responsible for the initial ideas and initial spread of *nouvelle cuisine* worked on the basis of their craft but re-emphasised that food should *look* good - which is of the essence so far as I am concerned - and decided that food should be lighter and healthier. This I heartily agree with too, as I believe people no longer judge a good meal by their bloated stomachs. I myself hate leaving the table feeling as though someone has driven a wheelbarrow into me!

Many critics say of British chefs that it is difficult for us to cook with the best in Europe because we have no tradition in our craft to fall back on. This, however, is simply not true. We have centuries of fine British cooking behind us, from a plain but essentially flavourful tradition. But we also have other influences, from the centuries during which Great Britain governed about one-third of the world. Then we could, and did, adopt and

adapt ideas from countries such as India, Pakistan and China and from the Far East, Africa and South America. These ideas, and lots of ingredients, have been absorbed into British culinary thinking for many years now, and can still be garnered for new and exciting dishes. This is a major part of my own cooking tradition, as I was brought up and learned to eat abroad, in the Far East. I firmly believe that we in Britain can stand up with the best of what Europe (and America and Australia) can offer!

In most of the recipes in the book I go into quite precise detail. This is in order to pass on what I have learned over the years because, of course, craft is based on experience which non-chefs may not necessarily possess. I hope that by reading through, and perhaps even cooking from, the recipes, you too can learn from and about my craft.

John Burton-Race
February 1994

Spring Recipes

Menu 1
GRILLED SALAD OF SCALLOPS WITH GAZPACHO

FILLET OF RED MULLET PAN-FRIED AND SERVED WITH
A PORT SAUCE

STRAWBERRY SHORTBREAD TARTLETS

Menu 2
ROASTED LAMB SWEETBREADS IN PUFF PASTRY CASE WITH
SPRING VEGETABLES

GRILLED SQUID STUFFED WITH A SCALLOP FORCEMEAT WITH
ITS INK SAUCE

BAKED EGG CUSTARD PEAR FLAN

Menu 3
PITHIVIERS OF GOATS' CHEESE WITH A WALNUT CREAM

BRAISED TURBOT IN SHERRY VINEGAR WITH
SHRIMPS AND BACON

GÂTEAU MARJOLAINE

Menu 4
PICKLED MACKEREL

BRAISED OXTAIL IN RED WINE WITH A MUSHROOM FARCE

LIGHT LEMON MOUSSES WRAPPED IN CANDIED LEMON

Menu 5
POTTED CRAB
BREAST OF DUCKLING WITH SHERRY VINEGAR AND HONEY
CARAMELISED APPLE TARTS WITH VANILLA ICE CREAM

Menu 6
SMOKED SALMON MOUSSE WITH CHIVE CREAM SAUCE
A FILO-WRAPPED PARCEL OF GUINEA FOWL
CHOCOLATE VACHERIN

Menu 7
CONSOMMÉ OF LANGOUSTINE
FILLET OF NEW SEASON'S LAMB WITH
A WHITE JUICE AND BROAD BEANS
A GRATIN OF MANGO, GUAVA AND PINK GRAPEFRUIT

Menu 8
DRY-GRILLED SALMON WITH RED CABBAGE AND CHICORY
LEG AND SADDLE OF RABBIT, BAYONNE HAM,
SWEETCORN AND PARSLEY
APPLE, SULTANA AND CALVADOS PANCAKES

Spring Menu 1

GRILLED SALAD OF SCALLOPS WITH GAZPACHO

FILLET OF RED MULLET PAN-FRIED AND SERVED WITH A PORT SAUCE

STRAWBERRY SHORTBREAD TARTLETS

GRILLED SALAD OF SCALLOPS WITH GAZPACHO

SERVES 6

This is a light, colourful dish with which to start any spring meal. Grilled scallops have an excellent flavour.

Although gazpacho is classically a cold Spanish soup, I have used it as a sauce in this dish. By putting together these two ingredients of different textures a new dimension is attained. This is just an example of one of the many uses of gazpacho which, in general, goes with most fish and shellfish.

Prepare and clean the scallops as explained in the Chef's Tip below. This dish requires you to marinate the scallops overnight before use. (The marinade can then be strained and used again.)

CHEF'S TIP

1. To open scallops, take a cloth in your left hand to hold the shell fast and place the scallop flat side up, the narrow part of the shell pointing away from you. With your right hand insert a small, strong palette knife between the two shells at the edge of the scallop, or where you find it most comfortable. With a flick of the wrist ease the shell open and carefully remove it and discard the top shell.

2. Again using the palette knife, ease out the scallop by

inserting the knife underneath the white flesh, cutting through the connecting muscle tissue. During this operation be careful not to damage or cut the white flesh of the scallop. Do not be alarmed if you notice a slight movement - the fish is still alive!

3. Turn the scallop out into a bowl and with the aid of a knife separate the white muscle and orange-coloured flesh from the other organs. Discard the latter. Keep the corals. Wash the white scallop flesh thoroughly and dry on a clean kitchen cloth. Discard the bottom shell.

24 large scallops, shelled (see Chef's Tip)	**40 ml (1½ fl oz) Tarragon Vinaigrette (see p.234)**
½ quantity Basic Fish Marinade (see p.224)	*Garnish*
Salad	**1 lemon**
½ curly endive or frisée	**1 large red pepper**
1 radicchio	**salt**
1 handful corn salad (or *mâche* or lamb's lettuce)	**30 g (1 oz) butter**
2 handfuls rocket leaves	**30 ml (1 fl oz) raspberry vinegar**
1 shallot	**a pinch of caster sugar**
1 bunch chives	**180 ml (6 fl oz) Gazpacho (see p.236)**
	a small bunch of fresh chervil

Marinating the scallops

1. Place the scallops in the fish marinade and cover with cling film. Refrigerate overnight, or for 12 hours.

Preparing the garnish

2. With the aid of a peeler, remove the zest of the lemon. With a knife, carefully slice off all the white pith. Blanch the zest in boiling water for 2 minutes to remove all the bitterness. Strain through a fine-mesh conical strainer, and repeat the blanching process until the zest is tender. Refresh in cold water, then drain and dry on kitchen paper. Lay the zest out on a chopping board and slice it lengthways into hair-thin strips (*julienne*). Reserve aside.

3. Skin the pepper (see Chef's Tip). In a pan of boiling salted water cook the pepper halves until tender. Drain and refresh in cold water. Remove and dry. Cut into small 1 cm (½ in) diamond shapes: you will require four per plate.

4. In a small frying pan melt the butter, turn up the flame and gently fry the pepper diamonds. Add the raspberry vinegar and sugar, and gently reduce the liquid until dry. Remove from the heat and reserve aside.

Preparing and assembling the salad

5. Wash and prepare the endive and radicchio, then dry them thoroughly in a lettuce basket. For the smaller leaves, such as the corn salad and rocket, I use a clean kitchen cloth as they bruise and damage easily. When dry, put into a large salad bowl.

6. Peel and chop the shallot. Chop the chives, and add both to the salad leaves. Pour in the tarragon vinaigrette and with the aid of two spoons carefully lift and mix the salad.

7. Lay out six hors-d'oeuvre plates. On each spoon 2 tablespoons of the prepared gazpacho, to cover the whole base of the plates with a thin even layer. In the centre of each plate build up a pyramid of your prepared salad, alternating the colours of the lettuce for maximum effect.

Cooking the scallops and serving

8. Take the scallops out of the marinade. On a very hot griddle or oven-top grill plate, grill the scallops and their corals. The cooking time is approximately 2 minutes per side, or until crisp and golden on the outside and soft inside. Do not over-cook the scallops or they will become tough and rubbery.

9. Arrange the scallops around the salad and top each one with a little strip of the prepared lemon zest and a red pepper diamond. Garnish each plate with a few tiny sprigs of chervil, and serve immediately.

CHEF'S TIP

To skin peppers, cut them into quarters lengthways and remove the core and seeds. Blanch in boiling water for 2 minutes, then remove, using a slotted spoon. Slip a sharp knife between flesh and skin and pull skin off. Then cook if required, and cut the pepper pieces to the required size and shape.

FILLET OF RED MULLET PAN-FRIED AND SERVED WITH A PORT SAUCE

SERVES 6

*R*ed mullet are at their best between April and October. When buying the fish check that they are a good red colour, and that they are firm to the touch with no scale damage. A lot of the red mullet you buy nowadays is trawled in massive nets and when caught in this fashion sustains a lot of damage: the scales get brushed off, the flesh is bruised and the fish lack a lot of the redness they should have.

6 x 225 g (7½ oz) red mullet	60 ml (2 fl oz) ruby port
salt and pepper	60 ml (2 fl oz) Fish Stock (see p.223)
30 ml (1 fl oz) clarified butter (see Chef's Tip)	60 ml (2 fl oz) whipping cream
Sauce	30 g (1 oz) unsalted butter
4 shallots	lemon juice
1 garlic clove	*Garlic croûtons*
1 sprig fresh tarragon	½ baguette or French stick loaf
110 g (3½ oz) tomatoes	30 ml (1 fl oz) clarified butter (see Chef's Tip)
30 ml (1 fl oz) sherry vinegar	½ garlic clove

Preparing the red mullet

1. Cut all the fins from the red mullet and place the fish in the sink. Using the back of a small filleting knife scrape off all the scales (tail to head) and discard. With a pair of fish scissors open the stomach of the mullet and discard all the entrails. Keep the livers, wash them under cold running water, dry and reserve aside in a bowl. Cut out the gills, wash the fish, and place on kitchen paper to dry.
2. Turn the mullet on its side and make an incision at the head, then, following the contours of the head, slice along its side, the knife angled towards the backbone. Cut off the first fillet. Turn the fish over and remove the second fillet in the same way. With a pair of fish pliers or tweezers remove the small bones running down the middle of the fillet. Repeat this process for the remaining mullet.
3. Season the fillets with salt and pepper and reserve aside on a baking tray.

Preparing the sauce ingredients

4. Peel and finely chop the shallots. Peel, crush and chop the garlic. Blanch the tarragon for 30 seconds. Strain and refresh it in cold water.

CHEF'S TIP
Blanching tarragon removes some of the herb's strength. If added to a sauce in its raw state it would be far too strong and bitter tasting.

CHEF'S TIP
To make clarified butter, gently melt butter on the side of the stove. As it melts, with the aid of a small ladle, remove and discard all the surfacing scum and milk. Strain and reserve aside in a clean jar. Keep refrigerated.

5. Blanch, skin and seed the tomatoes (see p.25), then cut the flesh into 5 mm (¼ in) dice.

Preparing the garlic croûtons

6. Preheat the oven to 180°C (350°F) Gas 4.
7. Slice six small pieces from the *baguette* and, using a 2 cm (¾ in) wide cutter cut out six croûtons. With a small pastry brush, brush a little of the clarified butter over both sides of the croûtons. Bake on a tray in the preheated oven for 5 minutes or until golden. Remove, and using the peeled half clove of garlic, rub both sides of the toasted croûton. Reserve aside in a bowl.

Cooking the red mullet

8. Heat the clarified butter in a shallow frying pan. As it begins to smoke put two of the red mullet fillets into the pan, skin-side down. Cook for 2 minutes then, using a palette knife, carefully turn them over and cook for a further minute. Remove the fish from the pan and place them on to a large serving dish. Keep them warm above the stove, and repeat the process for the remaining fish fillets.

Making the sauce

9. Add the chopped shallots to the mullet pan, and cook for about a minute without colouring.

10. Add the tarragon and garlic and pour in the sherry vinegar. Boil and reduce the vinegar until fully evaporated. Pour in the port, bring to the boil and boil to reduce by half its volume.

11. Add the fish stock, bring to the boil, and with the aid of a small ladle skim off any surfacing fat residue. Reduce the liquid by half its own volume and immediately pour in the cream. Boil and reduce to a consistency that will coat the back of a spoon.

12. Dice the butter into small 1 cm (½ in) pieces and, piece by piece, whisk this into the sauce. Check seasoning, and add salt and pepper to taste and a little lemon juice. Strain the finished sauce into a small pan, add the tomato dice and keep warm.

To finish and serve

13. Lay out the garlic croûtons on a tray and place in the oven to warm. Warm the fish fillets at the same time, no longer than a minute.

14. Season the reserved red mullet livers with salt and pepper. Heat a little extra clarified butter in a small pan and when hot flash-fry the livers to pink.

15. Remove the garlic croûtons from the oven and top each one with a liver.

16. Remove the red mullet fillets from the oven. Mask each plate with a little of the hot port sauce. Place two fillets on top of each puddle of sauce. Top six of the fillets with the garlic croûtons. Serve immediately.

As an option, I like to serve this dish with a little creamed mashed potato and buttered spinach.

Grilled Salad of Scallops with Gazpacho

Roasted lamb Sweetbreads in Puff Pastry Case with Spring Vegetables

Pithiviers of Goats' Cheese with a Walnut Cream

Pickled Mackerel

STRAWBERRY SHORTBREAD TARTLETS

SERVES 6

*E*verybody likes strawberry shortbread, and this is *my* interpretation of a very well-tried dish. It is a light crumbly tartlet filled with a mousseline of pastry cream and topped with glazed strawberries. The secret of the dish's success lies in the shortbread!

Shortbread tartlets
120 g (4 oz) unsalted butter, cut into 1 cm (½ in) cubes
120 g (4 oz) plain flour, sieved
75 g (2½ oz) caster sugar
1 egg yolk
Strawberry glaze
210 g (7 oz) ripe strawberries
150 g (5 oz) caster sugar
30 ml (1 fl oz) liquid glucose
Mousseline
150 g (5 oz) Pastry Cream (see p.249)

1 vanilla pod
150 ml (5 fl oz) whipping cream
Sauce and garnish
510 ml (17 fl oz) Vanilla Egg Custard Sauce (see p.250)
2 teaspoons Kirsch
6 x 6 cm (2½ in) rounds Biscuit Sponge (see p.245)
30 uniform-sized strawberries, washed and hulled
30 g (1 oz) shelled pistachio nuts, skinned (see Chef's Tip) and finely chopped
6 sprigs fresh mint

Preparing and cooking the shortbread

1. Put the butter dice, plain flour and caster sugar into a bowl. Rub together using your fingertips until the mixture resembles fine breadcrumbs, then add the egg yolk to bind the shortbread together. Lightly mould into a ball and wrap in cling film. Place into the refrigerator and chill for 1 hour.

2. Line a baking tray with greaseproof paper and place on to this six ring moulds, 7.5 cm (3 in) in diameter, 3 cm (1½ in) high. Lightly grease the inside of each mould with a little extra butter.

3. Divide the shortbread into six equal pieces and roll each one out on a floured surface to approximately 1 cm (½ in) thick. Carefully line the ring moulds with the shortbread. Cut away any excess shortbread from the top of the moulds. Place the lined moulds into the refrigerator to chill for 20 minutes.

4. Preheat the oven to 200°C (400°F) Gas 6. Cut six 7.5 cm (3 in) squares of greaseproof paper, place a square into the middle of each shortbread tartlet and then fill with baking beans. Bake for 15 minutes, then carefully remove the paper and beans, and place the moulds back into the oven for a further 8

minutes to dry out. When thoroughly baked remove from the oven and leave to cool. Do not remove the ring moulds. Reserve aside.

Preparing and cooking the strawberry glaze

5. Wash the strawberries, and hull them. Place them into a liquidiser and liquidise to a smooth pulp. Strain through a fine sieve, forcing all the juice through with the back of a ladle, into a saucepan. Discard the seeds.

6. Add 110 g (3½ oz) of the caster sugar and the liquid glucose to the strawberry juice. Place on to the stove and bring to the boil. Remove any surfacing froth and impurities with a ladle. Reduce until it becomes thick and syrupy. Remove from the heat and reserve aside.

CHEF'S TIP
To skin pistachios, place them in boiling water for 2 minutes. Pour into a sieve and refresh under cold running water, then rub them in a clean tea towel to remove the skins.

Preparing the mousseline

7. Place the pastry cream in a bowl and whisk until smooth. Split the vanilla pod lengthways

and scrape the seeds out, using the point of a knife. Mix the seeds into the pastry cream.

8. In another bowl whisk the whipping cream until firm. Fold the cream into the pastry cream. Reserve in the refrigerator.

To garnish and serve

9. Preheat the oven to 220°C (425°F) Gas 7.

10. Fill each shortbread tartlet with the mousseline.

11. Pour 110 ml (3½ fl oz) of the vanilla egg custard into a bowl and stir in the Kirsch. Dip each sponge biscuit disc into the custard to soak, and place on top of the mousseline.

12. Lay out six plates and spoon the remaining vanilla egg custard on to each plate.

13. Bring the strawberry glaze to the boil. Add the prepared garnish strawberries, gently mix them into the glaze, then remove from the heat. Using a fork, stand five strawberries on top of each tartlet.

14. Place the tartlets into the preheated oven for 1 minute only to enable you to remove the ring moulds more easily. Remove from the oven and carefully lift off the ring moulds.

15. Sprinkle the tarts with the chopped pistachios and place them on the sauced plates. Decorate with a sprig of mint on top of each tartlet and serve.

Spring Menu 2

ROASTED LAMB SWEETBREADS IN PUFF PASTRY CASE WITH SPRING VEGETABLES

GRILLED SQUID STUFFED WITH A SCALLOP FORCEMEAT AND SERVED WITH ITS INK SAUCE

BAKED EGG CUSTARD PEAR FLAN

ROASTED LAMB SWEETBREADS IN PUFF PASTRY CASE WITH SPRING VEGETABLES

SERVES 6

The best time for lamb is in the early spring, therefore this is probably the best time for lamb offal. New season lamb is always more delicate and it is for that reason that I have included this dish as a start to a spring menu.

Connoisseurs of offal dishes would probably rate veal sweetbreads as the best, and they can easily be substituted in this dish. However, they are at least six times the price!

700 g (1½ lb) fresh lambs' sweetbreads
6 cooked Puff Pastry Boxes, 8 x 5 cm (3 x 2 in) (see p.242)
salt and pepper
60 g (2 oz) clarified butter (see Chef's Tip, p.15)
Sauce
500 g (18 oz) lamb bones
1 onion
1 leek
½ celery stalk
3 garlic cloves
1 litre (1¾ pints) Chicken Stock (see p.225)

1 bay leaf
1 sprig fresh thyme
Mushroom duxelles
120 g (4 oz) white button mushrooms
2 shallots
1 garlic clove
1 sprig fresh tarragon
30 g (1 oz) unsalted butter
120 ml (4 fl oz) white wine
240 ml (8 fl oz) double cream
Basil butter
90 g (3 oz) unsalted butter

1 sprig fresh basil
a little lemon juice
Garnish
6 tomatoes
120 g (4 oz) baby spring vegetables (choose from broad beans, peas, turnip, spinach,

leek, carrots, broccoli)
60 ml (2 fl oz) Vegetable Stock (see p.222)
2 tablespoons double cream
a little lemon juice
½ garlic clove, peeled

Preparing and cooking the sauce

1. Chop up the lamb bones and in a large saucepan cover them with cold water and bring to the boil. Skim off the scum and refresh under cold water. Clean out the pan and vigorously clean the bones, washing off all the blood and fat particles that adhere to them.

2. Peel and coarsely chop the onion, leek and celery. Peel the garlic.

3. Place the bones back in the pan and cover with the chicken stock. Add the coarsely chopped onion, leek and celery, two of the garlic cloves, the bay leaf and thyme. Bring to the boil, skim and simmer for 1½ hours.

Preparing the sweetbreads

4. Meanwhile, plunge the washed lambs' sweetbreads into a large pan of boiling salted water, bring back to the boil and simmer for 5 minutes or until they have stiffened. Refresh under cold water and then strain.

5. With a small knife remove all fat, gristle and membrane. Press between kitchen paper and a heavy weight to extract the water.

Preparing the garnish and basil butter

6. Blanch, refresh, skin and seed the tomatoes (see Chef's Tip), then cut the flesh into 5 mm (¼ in) dice.

7. Carefully cook the spring vegetables individually in boiling salted water - for minutes only - strain, and allow to cool naturally.

8. For the basil butter, soften the butter and beat until white in a food processor or bowl. Chop the basil finely and add to the butter with a squeeze of lemon juice, and a pinch of salt and pepper. Place in a container and chill.

Making the mushroom *duxelles*

9. Wash the mushrooms and dice the flesh, including the stalk, into 5 mm (¼ in) dice. Peel and finely chop the shallots and garlic; blanch and chop the tarragon.

10. Melt the butter in a hot pan, and quickly sauté the mushrooms, shallots and tarragon, turning all the time until coated with butter. Pour in the white wine and reduce until dry. Add the cream, bring to the boil, season with salt and pepper and keep warm.

Finishing the sauce and cooking the sweetbreads

11. Strain off the lamb stock when ready and set to reduce in a large flat pan, with the remaining clove of garlic, chopped. You want to reduce it by about two-thirds.

12. Preheat the oven to 200°C (400°F) Gas 6.

13. When the sauce is nearly ready, in a large ovenproof skillet pan heat the clarified butter. When smoking hot, add the seasoned sweetbreads. Brown evenly on all sides, then roast in the preheated oven for 4 minutes.

To finish and serve

14. Heat through the *duxelles* and warm the pastry boxes. Reheat the spring vegetables in the vegetable stock and cream, with the ½ garlic clove. Bring to the boil and reduce to thicken, then whisk in the basil butter, a little at a time, until the desired flavour is achieved. Season if necessary with salt, pepper and lemon juice. Remove the garlic.

15. Place a hot pastry box in the centre of each plate and half fill with the *duxelles*. Around the box sprinkle the hot glazed vegetables and the diced tomatoes. Place two or three sweetbreads in each box and place the remainder around the outside. Quickly spoon over the hot sauce.

Place the box lid on top and serve
immediately.

CHEF'S TIP

*To skin tomatoes, first remove the stalks and cores
(coloured flesh beneath the stalks). With the point of a
sharp knife, make a cross at their top. Submerge them in
boiling water for 10 seconds, then immediately refresh in
cold water. Drain them, peel off the skins, and cut into
quarters. Spoon out the seeds and discard. Cut the flesh
into the size of cubes required in the dish.*

GRILLED SQUID STUFFED WITH A SCALLOP FORCEMEAT AND SERVED WITH ITS INK SAUCE

SERVES 6

Squid is probably most common and therefore most popular in countries which border the
Mediterranean. The classic recipe for squid in Spain uses the ink to make the sauce, and although
somewhat off-putting in appearance, it is a delicious way of serving an otherwise bland
ingredient. Squid is usually available through the spring and summer months at the larger
fishmonger's. When buying it, a general rule of thumb is, the smaller they are the more tender
they are, so buy them small!

If you want to simplify the recipe a little, the squid don't have to be stuffed. In this case, grill
for only 3 minutes per side.

600 g (1 lb, 5 oz) baby squid (about 30 fish)

30 ml (1 fl oz) clarified lemon and garlic butter
(see Chef's Tip)

salt and pepper

Scallop forcemeat

150 g (5 oz) fresh scallop meat (6 fresh
scallops)

1 sprig fresh tarragon

½ teaspoon salt

cayenne pepper

1 egg

60 ml (2 fl oz) whipping cream

juice of ½ lemon

Ink sauce

1 fennel bulb

2 shallots

3 garlic cloves

60 g (2 oz) unsalted butter

1 sprig fresh lemon thyme

¼ bay leaf

60 ml (2 fl oz) dry white wine

210 ml (7 fl oz) Fish Stock (see p.223)

60 ml (2 fl oz) whipping cream

juice of ½ lemon

1 tablespoon squid ink

Tomato sauce and garnish

180 g (6 oz) tomatoes

½ garlic clove

2 basil leaves

110 ml (3½ fl oz) Tomato Sauce (see p.232)

10 g (¾ oz) unsalted butter

Preparing the squid

1. Pull off the squid heads and reserve in a bowl. Pull out the exposed, clear backbone and remove and discard all the entrails. Inside the squid sac is a small pouch containing a little ink. Squeeze this pouch between your forefinger and thumb to remove all the ink. Reserve aside in a bowl for the sauce. Wash the squid under cold running water, and discard all the skin and membranes.

CHEF'S TIP

The squid has a darker skin on the outside and two inner membranes. If the squid is small enough these should be quite easy to remove with your hands. Use a small knife for any difficult pieces.

If there is not a sufficient amount of ink within the squid, some fishmongers sell the ink separately in small sachets.

2. Remove the tentacles from the squid heads. Discard the heads and clean the tentacles, removing the outer skin. Once cleaned, dry the squid thoroughly on a kitchen towel and reserve aside on a tray.

Preparing the scallop forcemeat

This forcemeat differs from a mousseline or quenelle. Because the squid is grilled under intense heat very little cream is used in its make-up.

3. Open, cut out and clean the scallops (see Chef's Tip, p.13). Separate the coral from the flesh, and dry the meat thoroughly on kitchen paper.

4. Blanch the tarragon.

5. Put the scallop flesh and blanched tarragon into a food processor and cut the scallops to a fine paste. Be careful at this stage: if the bowl starts to feel warm to the touch, stop the machine and refrigerate the scallop meat until cold. If you allow the scallops to get hot they will start to cook and the forcemeat will be ruined.

6. Add some salt and a little cayenne. Continue to cut the scallops for a further minute and then add the egg.

7. Stop the machine and with a palette knife clean the scallop meat from around the edge of the bowl and from underneath the blades. Replace the top and gradually add the cream. When thoroughly mixed, add a little lemon juice for acidity. With the aid of a plastic scraper push the scallop forcemeat through a fine-mesh sieve into a bowl. Refrigerate until cold.

8. When cold, fill a piping bag with a 1 cm (½ in) plain nozzle with the prepared forcemeat. Carefully fill all the cleaned squid pouches with the forcemeat and again reserve aside on a tray. Brush the squid with clarified lemon and garlic butter, season with salt and pepper and refrigerate until ready to cook.

CHEF'S TIP

To achieve 30 ml (1 fl oz) clarified lemon and garlic butter, melt 75 g (2½ oz) of butter with 1 crushed garlic clove, the juice of ½ lemon and a pinch each of cayenne and salt. When the butter has melted remove the surface scum and milk with a small ladle and discard. Strain the butter through a clean, dry muslin cloth into a bowl.

Preparing and cooking the sauce

9. Top and tail the fennel. Peel off the outside leaves and cut the bulb in two. Cut out the inner stalk. Separate the leaves and dice the fennel into 5 mm (¼ in) cubes. In a pan half-filled with boiling water, cook the diced fennel for 3 minutes. Strain and refresh in cold water, then cool. Strain again and reserve aside in a bowl.

10. Peel and finely chop the shallots and garlic.

11. In a shallow pan melt half of the butter and add the shallots. Cook over a gentle flame until opaque. Add the garlic, lemon thyme and bay leaf and continue cooking for 2 minutes. Be careful not to colour the shallots.

12. Pour in the dry white wine and boil to reduce until fully evaporated. Add the fish stock and bring the liquid to the boil. Continue boiling until reduced by half.

13. Add the cream and boil to thicken. The sauce must have the consistency which will coat the back of a spoon. Strain in the lemon juice.

14. Dice the remaining butter into small cubes and, piece by piece, whisk this into the sauce until completely dissolved. Finally, stir in the squid ink. Check the seasoning, and add salt and pepper to taste.

15. Strain the finished ink sauce through a fine-mesh conical strainer into a smaller pan, add the fennel dice and reserve aside until serving.

Preparing the tomato sauce and garnish

16. Blanch, skin, seed and cut the tomato flesh into 5 mm (¼ in) dice (see Chef's Tip, p.25). Peel the garlic, and shred the basil leaves.

17. Pour the tomato sauce base into a pan and heat. Check seasoning.

18. In another pan, place 30 ml (1 fl oz) water, the garlic and shredded fresh basil. Season to taste. Add the butter and warm the emulsion until the butter has melted. Add to this the diced tomato flesh. Keep warm on the side of the stove.

Cooking the squid

19. Remove the squid from the fridge and place it under a preheated *hot* grill. Grill for 5 minutes on one side. Turn the squid over and grill the other side for 3 minutes, along with the tentacles.

To serve

20. Reheat the ink sauce but do not boil it, or it will crack or separate.

21. As an option I like to serve herb or plain vermicelli noodles or pasta (see p.240) with this dish. If using, place a spiral of the prepared buttered pasta in the centre of six hot plates.

22. Around this pour a large tablespoonful of hot tomato sauce. With a fork remove the tomato dice from the basil emulsion and sprinkle it over the tomato sauce. Around the outer rim of the tomato sauce carefully spoon the squid ink sauce.

23. Between these two sauces place the grilled squid, five per portion. Between the squid place the grilled tentacles. Serve immediately.

Serve six small bowls of mixed salad leaves in a tarragon vinaigrette (see p.234) with the addition of a little diced wild garlic strands for added flavour.

BAKED EGG CUSTARD PEAR FLAN

SERVES 6

*P*ears baked in the custard give the flan a delicious taste. It can be prepared and cooked well in advance of serving.

250 g (9 oz) Sweet Pastry (see p.244)	1 egg yolk
60 g (2 oz) ground almonds	80 g (2¾ oz) caster sugar
3 ripe pears	*To finish*
Custard	30 g (1 oz) flaked almonds
1 vanilla pod	icing sugar to dust
270 ml (9 fl oz) milk	30 g (1 oz) apricot jam
2 whole eggs	270 ml (9 fl oz) Egg Custard Sauce (see p.250)

Preparing the pastry case

1. Lightly grease an 18 cm (7 in) flan ring with butter, place on a greased baking sheet, and line it with the rolled-out sweet pastry. Trim off any surplus pastry. Place into the refrigerator to chill and relax.

2. Sprinkle the ground almonds into the base of the pastry case.

3. Peel the pears, cut them into two lengthways and remove the core. Lay them

flat, and with a sharp knife make a cut from the fat end down towards the thin end, but do not cut all the way through the thin end. Make several more parallel cuts in the same way, so that the fat end can fan out. Place the pears, thin or stalk ends pointing to the centre, into the pastry base. Fan out as much as possible.

Preparing the custard

4. Split the vanilla pod in half lengthways. Pour the milk into a saucepan, add the vanilla and warm through on the stove.
5. Preheat the oven to 220°C (425°F) Gas 7.
6. Place the eggs, egg yolk and 60 g (2 oz) of the caster sugar in a bowl, and beat together. Pour the warmed milk over this and whisk until smooth. Remove the vanilla pod halves and strain the custard over the pears in the flan. Sprinkle the remaining caster sugar over the pears. Place into the preheated oven and bake for 40 minutes. Remove from the oven and when cold remove the flan ring.

To finish and serve

7. While the oven is still hot, place the flaked almonds on to a baking tray and sprinkle with icing sugar. Cook until golden, about 5 minutes, but keep looking. Remove and reserve aside.
8. Put the apricot jam and 30 ml (1 fl oz) water into a saucepan and bring to the boil. Boil for 1 minute and remove from the heat. Whilst still hot brush the jam over the pear flan. Press the sugared almonds around the outside of the flan covering the pastry edge. Chill before serving.
9. Lay out six plates, and pour equal amounts of the vanilla egg custard on each.
10. Cut the flan into six equal portions (one pear half per person). Place into the centre of each plate and serve.

Spring Menu 3

PITHIVIERS OF GOATS' CHEESE WITH A WALNUT CREAM

BRAISED TURBOT IN SHERRY VINEGAR WITH SHRIMPS AND BACON

GÂTEAU MARJOLAINE

PITHIVIERS OF GOATS' CHEESE WITH A WALNUT CREAM

SERVES 6

*F*or this dish I use a Crottin de Chavignol from France, but a good English alternative can work just as well. Serve this as an hors-d'oeuvre or as a hot cheese course at the end of a meal.

6 x 80 g (2¾ oz) goats' cheeses (unpeeled weight)	*Salad*
12 medium spinach leaves	180 g (6 oz) assorted lettuce leaves
120 g (4 oz) shelled walnuts	30 g (1 oz) chives
plain flour for dusting	2 shallots
550 g (1¼ lb) Puff Pastry trimmings (see p.242)	a handful of small croûtons (see p.138)
	Walnut cream
1 egg mixed with 30 ml (1 fl oz) milk (egg wash)	1 garlic clove
	110 ml (3¾ fl oz) Chicken Stock (see p.225)
60 ml (2 fl oz) Walnut Vinaigrette (see p.233)	60 ml (2 fl oz) whipping cream
	juice of ½ lemon
	salt and pepper

CHEF'S TIP
For this dish it is not necessary to use virgin puff pastry because it is not essential for the pastry to rise, therefore trimmings from another dish will do.

Preparing the *pithiviers*
1. Pick and discard the stalks from the spinach leaves and carefully wash the leaves in a sink of cold water. Blanch them in boiling salted

water for 60 seconds, then remove and refresh in cold water. When cold, carefully lay them flat on a clean kitchen cloth to dry. During this process, take the utmost care not to rip or damage the leaves.

2. With a peeler remove all the outside crust and hard, discoloured skin from the goats' cheeses and discard. Wrap the goats' cheeses in the spinach leaves, two per cheese, and reserve aside on a tray.

CHEF'S TIP

It is important to remove the cheese crust and skin for two reasons: firstly, it's bitter to the taste, and secondly, it will allow the cheese to melt far more easily inside the pastry.

Preparing the walnuts

3. Cook the walnuts in boiling water for approximately 3 minutes, then remove the pan from the heat. Do not refresh in cold water. Peel the walnuts with a small knife whilst they are still hot and reserve aside in a bowl. Half will be used for the salad, half for the walnut cream.

Preparing the salad

4. Wash and prepare your salad leaves. For this dish, as with any salad base, choose your lettuce variety for colour and flavour. I like to use oakleaf, corn salad or *mâche*, yellow frisée, chicory and peppercress or American land cress (or a good peppery watercress). Most of the larger supermarkets now do a range of mixed, pre-washed lettuces - this is quite suitable. Allow 30 g (1 oz) per person, and place in a bowl.

5. Chop the chives, and peel and chop the shallots. Add these to the salad.

Making the *pithiviers*

6. Dust your work surface with a liberal amount of plain flour. Cut six 40 g (1½ oz) pieces of pastry and with a rolling pin roll them out to form six 15 cm (6 in) square pieces about 3 mm (⅛ in) thick. This is for the bottom of the *pithiviers*. In the middle of these, place the goats' cheeses.

7. For the top of the *pithiviers*, divide the remaining pastry into six pieces and roll these out to 3 mm (⅛ in) thick to form six 16 cm (6½ in) pieces.

8. With a brush baste the egg wash on to the pastry around the edge of the goats' cheeses. Lay the pastry tops on top of the cheese and gently press and shape the two pieces of pastry together. Be careful not to trap any air between the pastries when you are doing this, and ensure the edges of the pastry are completely sealed.

9. Using an 11 cm (4½ in) round cutter placed over each *pithivier*, cut away the excess pastry. Make sure they are still well sealed, then place them on to a baking tray lined with greaseproof paper. Decorate the tops lightly by scoring, then allow the pastry to relax for about 15 minutes before cooking.

10. Preheat your oven as high as it will go (250°C), baste the *pithiviers* with more egg wash and cook for 12 minutes until golden brown.

Preparing the walnut cream

11. Peel and chop the garlic. In a shallow saucepan boil the chicken stock, add the garlic and boil to reduce the volume by half. Whisk in the cream and stir in the strained lemon juice. Re-boil and check the seasoning. Season to taste with salt and pepper.

12. Remove the walnut cream from the stove and whisk in half of the walnut vinaigrette. When completely smooth add half of the peeled walnuts. Reserve aside and keep warm.

To serve

13. Mix the remainder of the walnuts and walnut vinaigrette into the salad.

14. Lay out six plates, and at the head of each plate place a mound of dressed walnut salad. Scatter with a few croûtons.

15. Remove the cooked *pithiviers* from the oven and lay these down in front of the salad.

16. Over a fierce flame whisk the walnut cream until smooth - do not boil though - and spoon a dessertspoon of the finished sauce either side of the *pithiviers*. Serve.

BRAISED TURBOT IN SHERRY VINEGAR WITH SHRIMPS AND BACON

SERVES 6

*T*urbot is one of the nicest fish available in European waters. Large turbot are always best poached in a *court bouillon*, braised or simply steamed. Baby turbot or chicken turbot (*turbotin*) are nicer grilled, fried or roasted, having a very close texture but a somewhat milder flavour than the larger ones. Turbot is available all year round, but is best from March to August.

For this dish you will require a large fillet of turbot, off the bone, skin removed.

approx. 1 kg (2¼ lb) turbot fillet or 6 x 150g (5 oz) pieces	60 ml (2 fl oz) sherry vinegar
salt and pepper	210 ml (7 fl oz) Fish Stock (see p.223)
Braising liquor	*Sauce*
90 g (3 oz) smoked bacon	15 g (½ oz) parsley
60 g (2 oz) shallots	2 ripe plum tomatoes
2 garlic cloves	180 g (6 oz) grey shrimps
30 ml (1 fl oz) olive oil	30 ml (1 fl oz) whipping cream
60 g (2 oz) unsalted butter	60 g (2 oz) unsalted butter
1 sprig fresh thyme	lemon juice

Preparing the turbot and braising liquor ingredients

1. Cut the turbot fillet into six equal pieces and season them with salt and pepper. Reserve aside.
2. Rind the bacon, and cut into rashers 5 mm (¼ in) thick. Slicing across the rashers, cut them into small strips. Put them in a small saucepan, cover with cold water and bring to the boil. As it boils it will throw a scum or froth: remove this with a ladle and discard. Boil for 2 minutes, strain through a fine-mesh conical strainer and reserve aside.
3. Peel and very finely chop the shallots. Peel, crush and chop the garlic cloves.

Preparing the sauce ingredients

4. Pick the parsley leaves from the stalks, then wash, dry and chop them. (Use a flat or wild parsley variety - they have the most flavour.) Reserve aside.
5. Blanch, skin and seed the tomatoes (see Chef's Tip on p.25), then dice the flesh into 5 mm (¼ in) cubes. Reserve aside.
6. Cook and peel the shrimps (see Chef's Tip).

Braising the turbot

7. Preheat the oven to 160°C (325°F) Gas 3.
8. In a shallow ovenproof pan heat the olive oil and add the butter. As soon as the butter has melted add the chopped shallot and cook for about 2 minutes or until tender but with *no colour*. Add the thyme and stir in the blanched bacon strips. Cook for a further 2 minutes.
9. Pour in the sherry vinegar and boil to reduce its volume by two-thirds, or until syrupy.
10. Add the garlic and stir in the fish stock. Bring the stock back up to the boil and remove all the surfacing fat with a small ladle.
11. Turn down the heat to achieve a gentle simmer, and carefully place the turbot (flat or skin-side down) into the pan. Cover with butter paper, place a lid on the pan and cook in the preheated oven for 10 minutes.
12. When cooked remove the turbot from the braising liquor to a tray. Cover with butter papers and keep warm above the stove.

Making the sauce

13. Strain the braising liquor through a fine-mesh conical strainer into another pan and, on

the stove, bring the liquid to the boil. Reduce by half its volume. Add the cream and re-boil.
14. Dice the remaining butter and, piece by piece, whisk into the sauce. When the butter has been fully incorporated, strain the sauce into another pan. Check the seasoning, adding some salt, pepper and lemon juice to taste.
15. Add the peeled shrimps, chopped parsley and tomato dice. The cooked turbot above the stove should now be fully relaxed. As it relaxes and cools it will give a little more juice. Pour and stir this into the finished sauce for added flavour. Keep the sauce hot but do not re-boil it.

CHEF'S TIP
In most cases you can buy grey shrimps cooked fresh from the ports. (Because they are small they do not

travel to the fishmonger's very successfully.) If buying live shrimps, wash them in cold water and cook them in boiling salt water, **nage** *or* **court bouillon** *(see p.224) for 3 minutes. Strain and reserve on a tray to cool, then peel. If buying peeled, cooked shrimps, buy a third of the weight listed in this recipe: two-thirds of the shrimp's body-weight is lost when it is peeled and the head is removed.*

To serve
I like to serve this dish on a bed of buttered spinach leaves, but this is entirely optional.
16. Lay out six hot plates. In the centre of each place a heaped tablespoon of buttered spinach. Place the turbot on top and mask the fish with the finished sauce. Serve immediately.

A good accompaniment to this dish is some creamed mashed potato or fresh pasta.

GÂTEAU MARJOLAINE

SERVES 16

*T*his is a classic French dessert usually made with butter cream. I prefer to substitute the butter filling with light mousses layered between a crisp nut meringue. The three flavours I prefer in its construction are white chocolate, praline and bitter chocolate. You could add a little Kirsch to the white chocolate mousse if so desired.

You need one large terrine, 30 cm long x 10 cm wide x 10 cm high (12 x 4 x 4 in).

Nut meringue
75 g (2½ oz) hazelnuts
110 g (3½ oz) nibbed almonds
150 g (5 oz) caster sugar
10 g (⅓ oz) plain flour
4 egg whites
White chocolate mousse
240 g (8 oz) white chocolate
300 ml (10 fl oz) whipping cream
1 egg yolk
Praline mousse
2 gelatine leaves
90 g (3 oz) caster sugar
110 g (3½ oz) egg yolks (approx. 4 egg yolks)
270 ml (9 fl oz) whipping cream
60 g (2 oz) praline paste (see Chef's Tip)
30 ml (1 fl oz) Stock Syrup (see p.249)

30g (1 oz) Nougatine, crushed (see p.248)
Dark chocolate mousse
120 g (4 oz) bitter dark chocolate
2 egg yolks
60 ml (2 fl oz) Stock Syrup (see p.249)
270 ml (9 fl oz) whipping cream
Sauces
270 ml (9 fl oz) Coffee Egg Custard Sauce (see p.250)
270 ml (9 fl oz) Egg Custard Sauce (see p.250)
270 ml (9 fl oz) Chocolate Sauce (see p.250)
icing sugar to dust

CHEF'S TIP
Praline paste is available in good delicatessens and supermarkets. A product called Nutella, a hazelnut paste, would also be acceptable.

Preparing and cooking the nut meringue

1. Preheat the oven to as high as it will go (250°C). Place the hazelnuts and almonds on to separate baking trays and roast in the oven until golden brown, about 3-4 minutes only. Remove from the oven and rub the hazelnuts in a cloth to remove the skins.

2. Place the hazelnuts, the almonds, the caster sugar and plain flour into a liquidiser, and blend together until the mixture resembles fine breadcrumbs. Reserve aside.

3. In a mixing bowl whisk the egg whites until firm and peaked. Fold the liquidised nuts and sugar into the egg whites.

4. Spread the nut meringue 5 mm (¼ in) thick on to a square or rectangular tray lined with greaseproof paper. This should be 40 x 30 cm (16 x 12 in) if your oven can accommodate that size. Place into the slightly cooler oven at 230°C (450°F) Gas 8 until golden brown, about 15 minutes. Remove from the oven when baked. Allow to cool slightly then cut four strips of meringue the length and width of your terrine mould. (These are used as layers to separate the mousses in the terrine.) Leave to cool before removing the paper from all but one slice. Reserve aside.

For the white chocolate mousse

5. Chop the white chocolate into small pieces and place it in a bowl. Place the bowl over a pan half-filled with simmering water. Stir to melt, then reserve aside.

6. Pour 60 ml (2 fl oz) of the whipping cream into a saucepan and bring to the boil. Pour this on to the melted chocolate and stir in until smooth. Add the egg yolk, stir until incorporated, and reserve aside.

7. Place the remaining whipping cream in another bowl. Whisk until thick and peaked. Fold this into the melted chocolate. Place the mousse into the refrigerator whilst you line the terrine with the meringue.

8. Place one of the nut meringue slices, paper-side down, into the terrine. (Leave the paper on this slice as it helps when turning the mousse out - the paper can be removed later.)

Pour the white chocolate mousse on top of the meringue. Gently tap the terrine on to your work surface to achieve a smooth surface. Place the terrine into the freezer to set.

For the praline mousse

9. Soak the gelatine leaves in cold water to soften.

10. Put the sugar and 60 ml (2 fl oz) water in a saucepan. Mix together with a spoon, then boil and reduce until a thick syrup has been achieved. *Do not caramelise.*

11. Place the egg yolks in a mixing bowl. Pour in the hot reduced syrup and whisk to a thick white sabayon. Reserve aside.

12. Put the cream and praline paste into a bowl, and whisk together until thick and peaked, but not granular. Reserve aside.

13. Place the stock syrup in a saucepan and warm. Remove from the heat and whisk in the softened gelatine. Fold this into the sabayon. Then gently fold in the whipped cream and praline mixture. Lastly, fold in the crushed nougatine.

14. Remove the terrine from the freezer and place a slice of nut meringue on top of the white chocolate mousse. Pour on top of this the praline mousse. Again tap the terrine down on to your work surface and place the terrine back into the freezer to set.

For the dark chocolate mousse

15. Chop the dark chocolate, and melt as for the white chocolate. Mix until smooth and reserve aside.

16. Place the egg yolks into a mixing bowl, and whisk together. Put the stock syrup into a saucepan and place on to the stove to boil. When boiling pour it over the yolks, whisking continuously until a thick and white sabayon. Reserve aside.

17. In a bowl, lightly whisk the whipping cream until thick but not peaked. Fold the melted chocolate into the sabayon then fold this into the lightly whipped cream.

18. Remove the terrine from the freezer, and place a slice of nut meringue on top of the

praline mousse. Pour the chocolate mousse on top of this. Fill to the top of the terrine mould. Again tap the terrine down to gain a level surface. Place the remaining nut meringue on top. Cover with cling film and place in the freezer to set, approximately 4 hours.

To finish and serve

19. Make the coffee, vanilla and chocolate sauces, and chill in the fridge.
20. Lay out the required number of dinner plates, and spoon 3 dessertspoons of coffee sauce, vanilla sauce and chocolate sauce around the borders of each plate, alternating each spoon of sauce. Using the tip of a knife, swirl the sauces into each other, giving a marbled effect.
21. Remove the terrine from the freezer, and remove the cling film. Dip a thin knife into boiling water and run it round inside the edge of the terrine. Turn the terrine over and gently tap the terrine to free the cake. Turn out on to a board. Dust the top of the meringue with icing sugar.
22. With a warmed knife, cut the required number of slices from the terrine, and lay each down on to the centre of a plate. (A slice 1.5 cm/½-¾ in wide should be sufficient per serving.) Serve immediately.

Spring Menu 4

PICKLED MACKEREL

BRAISED OXTAIL IN RED WINE WITH A MUSHROOM FARCE

LIGHT LEMON MOUSSES WRAPPED IN CANDIED LEMON

PICKLED MACKEREL

SERVES 6

I think mackerel is one of the tastiest and certainly one of the cheapest fish in our waters. They are available all year round, but are best in the months of April, May and June. When choosing mackerel at the fishmonger's they should be fairly stiff, bright in colour with clear eyes and bright red gills.

This dish is an excellent alternative to a cooked fish dish, and is easy to do. Prepare it the night before and serve it for lunch.

6 x 225 g (7½ oz) mackerel	1 large leek
Marinade or pickling vinegar	2 celery stalks
1 litre (1¾ pints) white distilled vinegar	1 fennel bulb
30 g (1 oz) fresh parsley	90 g (3 oz) caster sugar
2 garlic cloves	30 g (1 oz) salt
15 g (½ oz) black peppercorns	1 sprig fresh thyme
6 juniper berries	1 bay leaf
zest and juice of 1 lemon	15 g (½ oz) dried fennel seeds
1 large onion	1 star anise
1 large carrot	90 ml (3 fl oz) virgin olive oil

Preparing the mackerel

1. With some fish scissors cut off all the fins. Working in the sink, with the heel of a knife, tail to head, scrape off all the scales. Turn the

fish over and repeat the process.
2. Again with the scissors, carefully cut open the stomach. Remove all the entrails, cut out the gills, and discard. Wash the fish under cold

running water. Dry on a kitchen cloth.

3. With a very sharp filleting knife remove the fillets. Make an incision just behind the head of the fish following the contours of the skull. Cut along the back of the mackerel, head to tail, and carefully slice down (knife angled towards the backbone), removing the first fillet. Again turn the fish over and repeat this process. Discard the bones.

4. Once the fillets are removed lay them flat on a tray. The next step is to remove the bones running down the middle of each fillet. In the case of mackerel it is easier just to slice lengthways either side of these bones, being careful not to waste any flesh. If you attempt to remove these small bones individually with fish pliers or tweezers you might break up the flesh. Each fillet is now divided into two, so you have 24 narrow fillets.

5. Roll each quartered fillet into a coil, skin-side out, and spike with a cocktail stick. This will keep its shape during pickling. Repeat this process for the other mackerel pieces. Reserve aside on a tray.

Preparing the marinade or pickling vinegar

6. Pick the leaves off the parsley, wash and dry. Peel and chop the garlic, crush the peppercorns and juniper berries, keeping them separate. Blanch the lemon zest for about 3 minutes, then dry well; cut into very fine strips.

7. Peel and very finely slice the onion. Peel the carrot and with a canelle knife cut grooves along its length. Cut into as fine rings as possible. Peel the celery and slice across the grain into thin strips. Wash the leek, remove the outside leaves, cut off all its green top and slice the white of leek in the same way. Top and tail the fennel; cut it into four; remove core, separate the leaves, and finely slice.

8. Into a large stainless-steel bowl pour your white distilled vinegar. Add the sugar and salt, peppercorns, thyme and bay leaf.

9. Add the parsley, garlic, juniper berries, fennel seeds and star anise. Stir with a large whisk, ensuring that the sugar and salt are completely dissolved.

10. Add the lemon zest strips, the strained lemon juice and olive oil. Whisk and reserve aside.

11. Add all the vegetables and the mackerel. Ensure that the liquid completely covers the fish. With a spoon stir bottom to top, then cover the bowl with cling film.

CHEF'S TIP
Do not use aluminium foil to cover any vinegar mixture as the acid will eat through this and taint the fish. Use a plastic or stainless-steel bowl for the same reasons.

---

12. Leave the fish to marinate overnight, or for at least 12 hours.

To serve

13. Lay out six plates. With a spoon carefully remove the mackerel pieces to a tray. Pull out the cocktail sticks and discard them.

14. Place two or four fillets of fish in the centre of each plate and top these with the pickled vegetable garnish. Spoon a little of the pickling liquor around the outside of this and serve.

Braised Oxtail in Red Wine with a Mushroom Farce

Caramelised Apple Tarts with Vanilla Ice Cream

Leg and Saddle of Rabbit, Bayonne Ham, Sweetcorn and Parsley

Terrine of Artichokes

BRAISED OXTAIL IN RED WINE WITH A MUSHROOM FARCE

SERVES 6

*O*xtail is a very tasty meat, and although it takes quite a while to cook it is well worth the wait! The tails need to be soaked in water overnight to remove excess blood. In this recipe only the thicker end of the tail is used. The thin end has not much meat and can be shredded up into the sauce or served whole. We sometimes fill the tail with wild mushrooms and sweetbreads, but in this recipe I have replaced them with button mushrooms.

1 whole oxtail
salt and pepper
60 ml (2 fl oz) vegetable oil
240 g (8 oz) *Mirepoix* (see p.239)
½ bottle red wine
1.2 litres (2 pints) Chicken Stock (see p.225)
1 whole garlic bulb
1 sprig fresh thyme
1 bay leaf

90 ml (3 fl oz) Meat Glaze (optional)
vegetables for garnish (6 each of small potatoes, small carrots, broccoli florets, courgette pieces, see Chef's Tip)
Filling
¾ quantity Chicken Mousse (see p.239)
120 g (4 oz) button mushrooms
60 g (2 oz) pig's caul (*crépinette*), soaked in cold water for 24 hours (see Chef's Tip on p.62)

Preparing and cooking the oxtail

1. Trim the oxtail, removing excess fat from the thicker end. Counting down the vertebrae, cut the tail in half, right through the joint. The knife should cut through with no trouble at all if on the correct side of the bone. If not, resistance will be met and you should try again on the other side of the vertebrae. Immerse the tail in cold water and leave for 24 hours.
2. Remove the tail from the water and dry with a cloth or paper towel. Season with salt and pepper.
3. In a roasting tray, heat the oil and when hot gently place in the thick piece of tail, taking care not to splash the oil. Brown evenly all over, then transfer to a casserole.
4. In the same roasting tray, add the *mirepoix* vegetables and sauté until golden brown. Remove with a slotted spoon to the casserole.
5. Tip off the oil from the roasting tray, return the tray to the heat and pour in the red wine. Boil and scrape off any sediment with a wooden spoon. Reduce by half then add the liquid to the casserole.
6. Add the chicken stock to the casserole,

bring to the boil and skim. Add the garlic, thyme and bay leaf and set to simmer. Depending on the thickness of the tail, cooking time can vary between 3 and 5 hours. The tail is cooked when the meat is seen to be coming away from the bones and is quite tender.
7. When cooked, carefully remove from the liquid and allow to cool. Strain the stock and wait for the fat to rise to the top.

Preparing and cooking the oxtail 'package'

8. With a small sharp knife, place the tail on its back and gently ease away the meat from the bones. If the tail is cooked properly this should be quite easy. The result should be a rectangular piece of meat that is quite boneless. With a flat spatula, lift the tail on to a large sheet of cling film, still keeping it flat.
9. Dice the mushrooms and mix into the chicken mousse.
10. Carefully, where the bone once was, place the chicken mousse mixture along the whole length of the tail, down the centre only. The mousse strip should be only 3 cm (1½ in) wide. Re-form the tail using the cling film to

hold the tail in place, and twist each end of the film, sealing it from the air. Re-wrap in another sheet of film, exactly the same way.

11. Poach the wrapped tail in simmering hot water for 30 minutes. When cooked, remove and allow to cool.

12. When cold, cut through the cling film and the tail, into six equal pieces. The pieces should be round and about 4 cm (1½ in) high. Remove the cling film carefully.

13. Place each piece flat side down and put a tablespoonful of the remaining mousse on each.

14. Cut the soaked caul into six pieces. Open out one piece of caul, stretch it over the quenelle and down the sides and pull it tight around the tail. The tail is now ready for reheating.

To finish and serve

15. Preheat the oven to 200°C (400°F) Gas 6.

16. Skim the fat from the oxtail stock and place the stock in a large reducing pan. Bring to the boil, skim and reduce rapidly by half. At this stage the meat glaze should be added if used.

17. Place the oxtail in a deep ovenproof pan and add a little of the stock – about 150 ml (5 fl oz). Bring to the boil, place in the preheated oven, and cook for about 15 minutes, removing every now and again to spoon the stock over the oxtail. This stock will reduce and become sticky while the mousse cooks. Be careful not to *over*cook the topping.

18. Meanwhile lightly cook the vegetables in boiling salted water, and drain well. Arrange on six plates, leaving room for the oxtail in the centre.

19. Place the oxtail on the plates. Taste the sauce for seasoning and correct if necessary, then strain over the top of the oxtail. Serve at once.

CHEF'S TIP

Use any vegetables available - baby spinach leaves, turned parsnips, small Brussels sprouts are all suitable as well.

LIGHT LEMON MOUSSES WRAPPED IN CANDIED LEMON

SERVES 6

*L*emons are cheap and always available. They are a very versatile product. This dish consists of a lemon mousse wrapped in lemon slices, served with a lemon egg custard sauce.

90 ml (3 fl oz) whipping cream	*Candied lemon slices*
150 ml (5 fl oz) lemon juice, or juice of	**2 lemons**
3 lemons	**270 ml (9 fl oz) Stock Syrup (see p.249)**
1 gelatine leaf	*Candied lemon zest*
3 eggs, separated	**1 lemon**
120 g (4 oz) caster sugar	**80 g (2½ oz) caster sugar**
10 g (⅓ oz) cornflour	*To serve*
6 x 4 cm (1¾ in) discs Biscuit Sponge	**270 ml (9 fl oz) Lemon Egg Custard Sauce**
(see p.245)	**(see p.250)**
	6 sprigs fresh mint

Preparing the candied lemon slices

1. Do this the day before making the lemon mousses. Slice the lemons as thinly as possible, into rounds, keeping them whole. Place them

into a bowl. Pour boiling water over them and leave to cool. When cool refresh under cold water and drain (this removes some of the acidity in the lemons).

2. Place the stock syrup into a saucepan and bring to the boil. Pour the boiling syrup over the lemon slices. Cover with cling film and leave to cool. This process has to be repeated at least six times, straining off the syrup from the lemons and re-boiling.

Making the lemon mousses

3. Bring the whipping cream to the boil, and add the lemon juice. Reserve.
4. Soak the gelatine leaf in cold water to soften.
5. Whisk the egg yolks and half the sugar together in a bowl until smooth and white. Add the cornflour and whisk until smooth. Reserve aside.
6. Place the cream and lemon juice back on to the stove to re-boil. When boiling pour on to the whisked yolks, sugar and cornflour. Mix the ingredients together and place all the mixture back into the saucepan. Again, re-boil, whisking all the time.
7. Remove from the heat and whisk in the softened gelatine leaf. Using a plastic spatula pour the finished lemon base into a large stainless-steel bowl and reserve aside.
8. Whisk the egg whites to a soft peak, by hand or in a machine. Slowly add the remaining caster sugar and continue whisking until a smooth meringue is formed. Immediately fold this meringue into the lemon base until fully incorporated and reserve aside.

Lining the moulds

9. Place six ring moulds – 6 cm (2½ in) in diameter, 3.5 cm (1½ in) high – on a tray lined with greaseproof paper.
10. Strain off the syrup from the candied lemon slices and reserve aside. Place a lemon slice into the centre of each ring mould.
11. Cut the remaining slices in half and line the inside of the ring moulds, the round edge of the lemon slice facing downwards. Fill the lined moulds with the lemon mousse.
12. Dip the biscuit discs into the reserved syrup and gently press them on top of the moulds - this will be the base of the mousse when turning them out. Place the mousses into a refrigerator and chill for 4 hours to set.

Preparing the candied lemon zest

13. Peel the lemon using a peeler, and with a knife carefully cut away all the white pith from the rind. Slice the rind into *julienne* (thin sticks) lengthways, and as fine as possible.
14. Boil a saucepan of water, add the *julienne* of lemon and bring to the boil for 2 minutes. Refresh in cold water, strain and repeat the process twice. This will ensure that the lemon is tender and all the bitterness removed.
15. Place 100 ml (3½ fl oz) water and the caster sugar in a saucepan, and bring to the boil. Add the lemon zest *julienne*, reduce the heat and gently cook for 10 minutes. Pour the syrup and zest into a small container and reserve.

To serve

16. Prepare the lemon egg custard sauce and chill.
17. Lay out six plates, and pour a little lemon sauce into the centre of each – leaving a 3 cm (1¼ in) border of plate showing.
18. To turn out the lemon mousses; warm a small thin knife in boiling water and carefully cut around the inner edge of the ring moulds. Lift off the moulds and using a fish slice lift the mousses, and turn them, biscuit sponge side down, into the centre of the lemon sauce.
19. Place a little of the candied lemon zest on top of each mousse. Pour a little of the remaining syrup around the border of the plate. Place a sprig of mint into the side of each mousse, and serve immediately.

I recommend serving a little lemon sorbet and *langues de chat* (cigarettes, see p.246) as an added accompaniment.

Spring Menu 5

POTTED CRAB

BREAST OF DUCKLING WITH SHERRY VINEGAR AND HONEY

CARAMELISED APPLE TARTS WITH VANILLA ICE CREAM

POTTED CRAB

SERVES 6

Crabs are available all the year round. The male or cock crab is the best as it has the highest yield of white claw meat. Where possible buy your crab alive, but it would obviously be simpler (if more expensive!) to buy it ready cooked. Again, to simplify, you could use all fish stock instead of the consommé.

Make this dish the night before you wish to serve.

1 x 1.3 kg (3 lb) crab	1 tablespoon lemon juice
2 litres (3½ pints) *Court Bouillon* or *Nage* (see p.224)	2 gelatine leaves, soaked in cold water to soften
salt and cayenne pepper	210 ml (7 fl oz) whipping cream
Crab mousse	*Sauce or crab butter* (optional)
1 garlic clove	1 garlic clove
2 sprigs fresh tarragon	2 sprigs fresh tarragon
2 sprigs fresh parsley	150 ml (5 fl oz) Crab Consommé (see above)
90 ml (3 fl oz) Fish Stock (see p.223)	1 tablespoon Cognac
110 ml (3½ fl oz) Crab Consommé	150 ml (5 fl oz) whipping cream
(see Consommé of Langoustine, p.55)	1 gelatine leaf, soaked in cold water to soften
30 ml (1 fl oz) Cognac	1 tablespoon lemon juice

Preparing and cooking the crab

1. Cook the crab for 12 minutes in the prepared boiling *court bouillon* or *nage*. Remove to a tray and allow to cool.

2. When cold enough to touch, pull off its claws. With a meat bat crack them open and carefully remove the white meat. Reserve aside in a bowl. Repeat the process for the legs.

3. Turn the crab shell flat-side down, exposing the lower shell, and pull this out from the main shell or box. Remove any exposed white meat.

4. Remove the intestines and stomach bag near the head and discard. With a spoon clean out all the dark meat which is to be found either side of the main shell, and reserve aside in another bowl.

Preparing the crab mousse

5. Peel and crush the garlic; blanch the tarragon; wash the parsley leaves, dry and chop.

6. In a shallow pan boil the fish stock and crab consommé together over a fierce flame, and begin to reduce the liquid. Add the garlic and tarragon. With a small whisk stir in the dark crab meat and reduce the flame. Add the Cognac, lemon juice, and a little salt and cayenne.

7. Continue reducing until most of the liquid has evaporated, and you're left with a sticky syrup. Add the soaked gelatine and remove from the stove.

8. Over a bowl and using a plastic scraper, pass the dark crab-meat base through a sieve and reserve aside to cool. Discard the trapped sediments.

9. In another bowl, whip the cream to soft peaks. Do so lightly, as over-whipping will give the crab meat a granular texture.

10. When cold but not set, stir the chopped parsley into the dark crab-meat base. Add the white claw meat to this and with a spatula gently fold in the cream.

11. Immediately fill six small 7.5 cm (3 in) ramekins or dariole moulds. Tap them down on to your work surface to ensure no air bubbles are trapped. Refrigerate overnight to set and for the flavours to mature.

12. When set, dip the ramekins into a bowl of boiling water for a few seconds. Run a small knife around the upper edge of the ramekin and turn the crab shapes out on to a clean tray. Refrigerate again.

Preparing the sauce or crab butter (optional)

13. Peel and crush the garlic; blanch the tarragon.

14. Pour the crab consommé into a saucepan, and add the garlic, tarragon, Cognac, and a little cayenne and salt. Bring to the boil, removing all surfacing scum with a ladle.

15. Boil and reduce the consommé by half its volume, then pour in the cream. Continue boiling and reducing the sauce.

16. Stir the soaked gelatine into the reducing sauce, and add the lemon juice. Skim off any surfacing froth, and whisk the sauce: as it reduces it thickens, and has a tendency to stick and burn on the bottom of the pan.

17. When the sauce has reached a fairly syrupy texture, quickly strain it into a bowl through a fine-mesh conical strainer. Place this bowl over a bowl of ice, stirring from time to time. As it cools it will thicken further.

18. When cool but not set, remove the sauce from the ice. Take the potted crab shapes from the fridge and with the aid of a tablespoon carefully mask them with the finished sauce. Ensure that this is done as quickly as possible, for as soon as the sauce comes into contact with the cold potted crab it will set immediately. Be sure all the crab shapes are covered with an even layer of sauce. Put the finished crab shapes back in the fridge until ready to serve.

To serve

I like to serve this dish with a little salad bound in a tarragon vinaigrette (see p.234) with chives and chopped shallots, and a little pile of skinned diced tomato sprinkled with lemon juice. Brown toast is essential.

19. Remove the potted crab from the fridge. Lay out your plates and with the aid of a fish slice carefully lift each potted crab and place slightly off centre on the plates.

20. Opposite the crab place a little mound of prepared salad leaves and opposite that a teaspoon of tomato dice.

If you are feeling rich, or really want to impress your guests, top each crab shape with a little caviare and lay a tiny sprig of dill over that to maximise the effect.

BREAST OF DUCKLING WITH SHERRY VINEGAR AND HONEY

SERVES 6

In this recipe we only use breasts of duck. These are easily available but, if a whole duck is purchased, then the legs can be casseroled for another dish at a later date. The sauce is best made with duck bones, which give a much rounder taste, so ask your butcher for those wings and back bones he cuts out!

6 x 150 g (5 oz) duck breasts (supremes)	**30 ml (1 fl oz) sherry vinegar**
salt and pepper	**60 g (2 oz) honey**
Sauce	**1 litre (1¾ pints) Chicken Stock (see p.225)**
450 g (1 lb) duck bones	**1 sprig fresh thyme**
1 onion	**1 bay leaf**
6 shallots	**juice of ½ lemon**
½ carrot	*Garnish*
1 leek	**350 g (12 oz) fine yellow or green beans**
1 celery stalk	**½ garlic clove**
4 garlic cloves	**2 shallots**
60 ml (2 fl oz) vegetable oil	**60 ml (2 fl oz) whipping cream**

Preparing the duck breasts

1. First remove and discard any excess fat from the duck breasts. Reserve the breasts aside. Remove the wing bones if any and keep. Chop these and the bones for the sauce roughly.

Making the sauce

2. Peel, trim and wash the onion, shallots, carrot, leek, celery and garlic as appropriate. Chop them all roughly.
3. Heat the oil in a heavy tray and cook the bones until golden brown, about 5 minutes.
4. Heat a large saucepan and pour in the vinegar. Add the honey and reduce carefully until the mixture becomes sticky. Be careful not to reduce it too far as the honey can burn. Lift the roasted bones from the tray, add to the honey mixture, and turn them over and over on a low heat, until glazed.
5. Meanwhile, reheat the oil and cook the chopped vegetables - *not* the garlic - until golden brown, a few minutes. Add to the bones, and cover with the stock. Bring to the boil, add the chopped garlic, the thyme and bay leaf, skim, and simmer for 1 hour.

6. Strain off the stock, discarding the bones etc, and reduce the stock rapidly by two-thirds to concentrate the flavours. Frequently skim off the resulting fat and scum, as this can cloud the ultimate sauce.

Preparing the garnish

7. Top and tail the beans, removing any strings, and cook rapidly in boiling salted water until tender, about 3 minutes. Refresh under cold water and drain. Reserve aside. Peel the garlic and shallots, and chop the latter finely.

Cooking the duck breasts and garnish

8. Preheat the oven to 220°C (425°F) Gas 7.
9. Season the duck breasts with salt and pepper and in a hot pan place them, skin-side down, to colour. When golden, turn and seal the other side. This should take only 1–2 minutes.
10. When brown on both sides, place skin-side down on a tray and bake in the preheated oven for 10 minutes for pink flesh, a little longer for well done.
11. Meanwhile heat up the cream with the garlic and finely chopped shallots. Season with salt and pepper and keep warm.

12. When the breasts are cooked to your liking, remove from the oven and allow them to rest for 5 minutes. The skin should be crisp and a lot of the fat should be rendered down. (Drain this off and keep for frying.)

To serve
13. Remove the garlic from the cream mixture. Add the beans, and turn them over and over until coated and hot. Spoon a large pyramid on to each warm plate.
14. Carve the duck breasts into slices and prop up round the beans, skin-side uppermost.
15. Quickly taste the sauce, add a few drops of lemon juice if necessary, and spoon round the plate. Serve at once.

CARAMELISED APPLE TARTS WITH VANILLA ICE CREAM

SERVES 6

*W*e seem particularly to like French apple tarts in this country, although we have a great fruit pie tradition of our own. I like to make individual tarts – much more dramatic than a slice or wedge.
    You can use puff pastry trimmings for the tarts, as the pastry doesn't need to rise.

600 g (1 lb, 5 oz) Puff Pastry (see p.242)	juice of 1 lemon
1 egg, beaten with 1 teaspoon caster sugar (egg wash)	110 g (3½ oz) unsalted butter
	120 g (4 oz) ground almonds
Filling	*To serve*
6 large dessert apples (preferably Cox's)	6 scoops Vanilla Ice Cream (see p.248)
180 g (6 oz) caster sugar	6 large mint leaves or shreds of vanilla pod
20 ml (⅔ fl oz) Calvados	

Preparing the tart bases
1. Cut the puff pastry into twelve 50 g (1¾ oz) pieces, and roll each out into 15 cm (6 in) squares, 3 mm (⅛ in) thick. Lay these on to a tray and place in the refrigerator to chill for 20 minutes.
2. Line two baking trays with greaseproof paper.
3. When the pastry has chilled, cut each square into 14 cm (5¼ in) discs using a plain cutter. Lay six of these discs on to the prepared trays.
4. Brush a little of the egg wash around the outside edges of the puff pastry bases.
5. Using a 12 cm (4¼ in) plain pastry cutter, cut out the centre of each of the remaining six discs. Place these rings on top of the pastry bases to make the border of the tarts. Gently press down the edges. (Wrap the pastry trimmings in cling film and keep them in the freezer for another dish.)
6. Carefully brush the top border with a little egg wash, and place the tart cases back into the refrigerator.

Preparing the filling
7. Peel the apples and cut them into halves. Cut each half into quarters and remove the core using a small knife. Place into a bowl of cold water until ready to use.
8. In a saucepan bring the sugar, Calvados and lemon juice to the boil. Dice the butter and whisk it into the boiling sugar, piece by piece. When all the butter has dissolved, remove from the heat and reserve aside.

Constructing and cooking the apple tarts
9. Preheat the oven as high as it will go (250°C).
10. Lengthways slice each drained and dried

quarter of apple into five equal slices. Use a whole apple per tart.

11. Remove the tart cases from the refrigerator and divide the ground almonds between them. This will absorb the apple juice when cooking, and adds another flavour. Place three slices of apple on top of the almonds and place the other slices, slightly overlapping, around the middle of the pastry tart base. Finish by placing two slices of apple in the centre for maximum height (core sides facing each other). Brush the apple slices with plenty of the Calvados and butter syrup. Repeat for the other tarts.

12. Place the tarts into the preheated oven and bake for 15 minutes. Remove from the oven and brush the apple slices with more Calvados and butter syrup. Return them to the oven and bake for a further 10 minutes until golden and caramelised.

CHEF'S TIP

The alcohol and water in the Calvados and butter syrup will evaporate off while it is baked in the oven to form a sugar crust over the apples.

To serve

13. Lay out six plates, and place a hot caramelised apple tart into the centre of each.

14. Scoop out a ball of the prepared vanilla ice cream, shape into a quenelle, and place it on top of the apple tarts. Put a leaf of mint on to the ice cream for added effect – or shreds of vanilla pod – and serve immediately.

CHEF'S TIP

These apple tarts can be baked in advance to the first stage – 15 minutes – then warmed through in a hot oven at the same temperature as before for 10 minutes before serving.

Spring Menu 6

SMOKED SALMON MOUSSE WITH CHIVE CREAM SAUCE

A FILO-WRAPPED PARCEL OF GUINEA FOWL

CHOCOLATE VACHERIN

SMOKED SALMON MOUSSE WITH CHIVE CREAM SAUCE

SERVES 6

This is a very simple but always popular start to any meal. Use this recipe and nine times out of ten you will please all of your guests - it's the safe-bet hors-d'oeuvre!

The best smoked salmon comes from Scotland. Try to buy, when affordable, a whole side on the bone for the best-quality product. For this dish the actual mousse is made from the trimmings of the salmon, slices from a side are used to line the moulds.

at least 450 g (1 lb) smoked salmon in the piece	300 ml (10 fl oz) whipping cream
30 ml (1 fl oz) olive oil	juice of 1 lemon
Mousse	cayenne pepper
150 g (5 oz) smoked salmon trimmings	**Garnish**
60 ml (2 fl oz) Noilly Prat	120 ml (4 fl oz) Chive Cream Sauce (optional, see p.231)
60 ml (2 fl oz) Fish Stock (see p.223)	30 g (1 oz) Keta caviare (salmon eggs)
1½ gelatine leaves, soaked in cold water to soften	6 tiny sprigs fresh dill
	2 tomatoes

Cutting the salmon and preparing the ramekins

1. With a long thin filleting knife, cut off all the hard, dry outer skin of the smoked salmon side. Reserve aside in a bowl to make the mousse. Using a small pair of fish pliers remove the bones which run down the middle of the salmon and discard.

2. Have ready six ramekins, 6.5 cm (2½ in) in diameter, 3.5 cm (1½ in) deep. Using a small pastry brush, line the insides of the ramekins with the olive oil. This will help when turning out the finished mousses.

3. Slice carefully, as thin and as long as possible, six even slices of smoked salmon, and lay these out flat on a tray.

4. Using a ramekin dish as a stencil, turn upside-down and cut six smoked salmon discs from the pre-sliced salmon. Take these and carefully lay them in the bottom of the ramekins. These will form the top of the mousses. Cut the remaining smoked salmon into deep enough strips to line the sides of the ramekins. Press them tight against the sides of the moulds and with a small, sharp knife cut off any overlapping edges. (These trimmings can be added to the bowl of salmon trimmings to make the mousse.) Cover the lined moulds with greaseproof paper and refrigerate.

Making the mousse

5. In a food processor, cut the smoked salmon trimmings to a fine paste or purée. Take off the bowl and refrigerate to cool.

6. Pour the Noilly Prat into a shallow pan and over a fierce flame boil and reduce until the liquid becomes syrupy but not burnt. Add the fish stock and reduce the stock by half of its volume. Add the gelatine and remove from the stove. Pour into a small bowl to cool.

7. Divide the cream equally between two bowls. With the aid of a whisk beat half to form a peak. Do not over-beat the cream or the texture of the mousse will become granular and split. Refrigerate.

8. Take the smoked salmon trimmings from the fridge. Back on the machine, re-beat the mixture for about 30 seconds to ensure that as

fine a paste as possible has been attained. Add the now cool fish stock and gelatine. Beat for a further minute, then add the lemon juice.

9. Pass this mixture through a fine-mesh sieve into another bowl. Do this as quickly as possible, as if the mixture sets it is ruined.

10. Quickly add the liquid cream and with the aid of a whisk stir vigorously to a smooth consistency. Season with a pinch of cayenne. Gently fold in the whipped cream.

11. Remove the pre-lined moulds from the fridge, and with a ladle fill the moulds to the top. Level off the mousses with a palette knife and refrigerate for at least 4 hours.

To serve

This is purely optional, but I like to dress this dish with a little chive cream sauce.

12. When set remove the mousses from the fridge. To turn them out just run a small knife around the edge of the moulds to free the sides. They should ease out without a problem. Be careful not to cut the smoked salmon or dent the mousses.

13. Position the mousses in the centre of each plate and with the aid of a small brush carefully brush a little more olive oil over the outside of the smoked salmon.

14. Top the mousses with ½ teaspoon Keta caviare and on top of this lay a small sprig of dill.

15. Skin, seed and dice the tomatoes. Spoon 2 dessertspoons of chive cream sauce around the mousses and decorate with three piles of tomato dice evenly spaced around the plate. (Squeeze a little lemon juice on the tomatoes for added flavour.)

Serve this dish with sliced toasted brioche. Melba toast is also a good accompaniment.

A FILO-WRAPPED PARCEL OF GUINEA FOWL

SERVES 6

The guinea fowl or African hen (*Gallina africana*) is a rather splendid and very underestimated bird. Its flavour is that of a gamey chicken, slightly less gamey than a pheasant. There are a lot of inferior Continental birds on the market, though, which should be avoided. The nicest birds we have used were grown for us by a breeder in Kent but sadly she had to desist due to European legislation. Now we buy a corn-fed bird reared in France.

There is little fat on a guinea fowl apart from two small pockets either side of the breast meat above the wings. For this recipe try to buy the bird with the giblets included. *Foie gras* is purely optional!

3 x 1 kg (2¼ lb) young guinea fowl	***Cabbage and filling***
salt and pepper	**1 Savoy cabbage**
cooking oil	**150 g (5 oz) button mushrooms**
Sauce	**2 shallots**
1 onion	**60 g (2 oz) clarified butter (see Chef's Tip, p.15)**
½ carrot	**120 g (4 oz) *foie gras* (optional)**
1 leek	**15 g (½ oz) mint leaves**
1 celery stalk	**30 g (1 oz) parsley leaves**
6 garlic cloves	**cayenne pepper**
110 ml (3½ fl oz) sherry vinegar	**a few caraway seeds**
110 ml (3½ fl oz) Madeira	***To finish and serve***
1.2 litres (2 pints) Chicken Stock (see p.225)	**6 sheets filo pastry**
1 sprig fresh thyme	**a little butter**
1 bay leaf	**1 egg**
	60 g (2 oz) fresh shelled peas

Preparing and cooking the guinea fowl

1. Remove the legs and breast meat from the carcass, leaving them whole. Remove all the skin and cut out the leg bones and wing bones. Keep the leg and breast meat plus the giblets aside.
2. Season the breast and leg meat and seal in hot oil until golden brown. The legs should take longer, leaving the breast still pink and moist in the middle. Reserve aside.
3. Cut the heart and liver into 5 mm (¼ in) dice, season and seal in a little hot oil. This should take only 1 minute. Cool on kitchen paper.

Preparing and cooking the sauce

4. Chop up the carcasses, bones and trimmings coarsely. Peel the onion, and coarsely chop it, the carrot, leek and celery. Peel the garlic.

5. Brown the chopped bones quickly in hot oil in a saucepan. Remove with a slotted spoon to a casserole. Tip off the fat from the saucepan (keep it) and add the sherry vinegar. Bring to the boil, scraping off all sediments with a wooden or plastic spoon, and reduce until nearly dry.
6. Add the Madeira to the saucepan and bring to the boil before adding to the bones along with the chicken stock, thyme, bay leaf and peeled garlic.
7. Brown the roughly chopped vegetables in a little hot oil and add to the stock. Bring to the boil, skim and simmer for 1 hour.

Preparing the cabbage and filling

8. Remove from the cabbage six large leaves but not the tough outside ones. Carefully trim down the large central rib, but do not cut out

entirely. Plunge the leaves into boiling salted water and cook until pliable but not too soft or else they will tear. Drain on a clean cloth or kitchen paper. Allow to cool.

9. Cook the remaining cabbage as *choucroûte* (see p.237). Cool.

10. Wash and slice the mushrooms quite thickly, about four slices per mushroom. Peel and finely chop the shallots and add to the mushrooms with a little salt and pepper.

11. Fry the mushrooms and shallot in hot clarified butter and allow the mushrooms to give off all their water before removing from the heat to cool.

12. If using the *foie gras*, cut it into six equal pieces and season. Seal in a hot pan without fat for 10 seconds on each side.

13. Wash, dry and chop the mint and parsley leaves.

Assembling the cabbage 'parcels'

14. Place the six blanched cabbage leaves on a clean table and pat completely dry.

15. Place a small pile of *choucroûte* in the centre of each leaf. On top place some mushrooms.

16. Slowly building up layers, put on top of the mushrooms a guinea fowl leg. Then the diced cooked heart and liver. If using *foie gras* it should be added at this stage.

17. If the guinea fowl breast is rather pointed I cut the point off and put it in where it will not protrude quite so much. The breast is placed on top of the pile.

18. Finally sprinkle on top the chopped mint and parsley, a pinch of cayenne pepper and a few caraway seeds. This sounds like a huge pile but if assembled correctly the cabbage leaf should be large enough to wrap round the filling. Hold together with two or three cocktail sticks.

To cook and serve

19. Preheat the oven to 200°C (400°F) Gas 6.

20. Open out the filo, one sheet at a time (to stop them all drying out), and brush with clarified butter. Place each cabbage parcel in the centre and remove the cocktail sticks. Invert the parcel and filo, and tightly wrap the filo underneath the cabbage. Place on a baking sheet with the join underneath and brush with egg wash. Reserve aside.

21. Strain off the stock and quickly reduce by half, skimming off all fat and scum. You need about 600 ml (1 pint).

22. Cook the shelled peas in boiling salted water.

23. Bake the filo parcels in the preheated oven until crisp and golden brown – 15-20 minutes. A small knob of butter may be rubbed over the filo during cooking to give the pastry a glaze.

24. When cooked remove from the oven and carefully, using a sawing action, cut out a wedge to show the filling and layers. Pour the sauce around and sprinkle the hot peas into the sauce.

CHOCOLATE VACHERIN

SERVES 6

I, like me, you are addicted to chocolate, this is an excellent way to die! It is a light, rich-tasting chocolate mousse, layered between crisp chocolate meringue and wrapped in dark chocolate. The 'wrapping' can be quite complicated, I must admit, and the mousses are perfectly delicious without it.

Chocolate meringue
150 g (5 oz) egg whites
150 g (5 oz) caster sugar
130 g (4¼ oz) icing sugar
20 g (⅔ oz) cocoa powder
Chocolate mousse
120 g (4 oz) bitter dark chocolate
30 g (1 oz) unsalted butter

120 g (4 oz) egg whites
60 g (2 oz) caster sugar
1 egg yolk
Garnish
75 g (2½ oz) bitter dark chocolate
1 quantity Coffee Egg Custard Sauce (see p.250)
110 ml (3½ fl oz) Chocolate Sauce (see p.250)
cocoa powder and icing sugar to dust

Making the chocolate meringue

1. Line two baking trays with greaseproof paper, and preheat the oven to 120°C (250°F) Gas ½.
2. In a mixing bowl whisk the egg whites to a firm peak. Add the caster sugar, a little at a time until fully incorporated. Whisk to a stiff meringue.
3. Sieve together the icing sugar and cocoa powder. Using a spatula, fold this into the meringue.
4. Put the meringue into a piping bag, fitted with a 1 cm (½ in) plain nozzle, and pipe twelve 5 cm (2 in) round discs on to one of the lined trays. With the remaining meringue, pipe on to the other tray 48 sticks 3 cm (1¼ in) long by 1 cm (½ in) wide.
5. Place the trays into the preheated oven, and leave the door slightly open to help dry the meringue. Bake the discs for 45-60 minutes, the sticks for 30 minutes. If cooked, the meringue will lift cleanly away from the paper. Remove from the oven and reserve.

Making the chocolate mousse

6. Line a tray with greaseproof paper, and place on it six ring moulds, 7.5 cm (3 in) in diameter, and 3 cm (1¼ in) tall.
7. Chop the dark chocolate and dice the butter and place them into a stainless-steel bowl over

a pan of simmering water. Stir the mixture until melted. Reserve aside and keep warm.
8. In a mixing bowl whisk the egg whites to a smooth peak, then whisk in the caster sugar.
9. Add the egg yolk to the warm chocolate, and mix thoroughly. Using a spatula, carefully fold in the whisked egg whites until fully incorporated.
10. Fill a piping bag fitted with a 1 cm (½ in) plain nozzle with the chocolate mousse. Pipe a little of the chocolate mousse into the base of each ring mould, about 5 mm (¼ in) deep.
11. Gently press a chocolate meringue disc into the mousse. Repeat for the other moulds.
12. Pipe another layer, 1 cm (½ in) deep, of chocolate mousse on top of each meringue disc, and gently press another chocolate meringue disc on top.
13. Fill the moulds to the top with the chocolate mousse, level with a spatula and place into the freezer for 1 hour to set.

'Wrapping' the chocolate mousses

14. Chop the dark chocolate finely and place in a bowl over a pan of simmering water to melt, stirring all the time.
15. Cut six pieces of flexible plastic 4 cm (1¾ in) wide by 24 cm (9½ in) long.
16. Remove the chocolate mousses from the freezer and rub each ring mould in the palm of

your hands. Gently push the mousses out on to the work surface.

17. Using a palette knife, spread a little of the melted chocolate over each plastic strip. Carefully pick up the chocolate-covered strip and wrap it, chocolate inside, around the outside of the chocolate mousse, leaving a little of the chocolate plastic overlapping. Repeat for the other mousses. Place on to a tray and refrigerate for a further 2 hours.

To serve

18. Make the coffee egg custard, and the chocolate sauce. Leave them to cool then place into the refrigerator.

19. Lay out six plates, and spoon on to them the coffee custard. Using a teaspoon trickle lines of chocolate sauce in an abstract way across the coffee custard.

20. Remove the chocolate vacherins from the refrigerator, and place eight 'sticks' of meringue on top of each. Lightly dust with icing sugar and a little cocoa powder.

21. Carefully peel away the plastic from each mousse, and place the mousses into the centre of each plate. Serve immediately.

Spring Menu 7

CONSOMMÉ OF LANGOUSTINE

FILLET OF NEW SEASON'S LAMB WITH A WHITE JUICE AND BROAD BEANS

A GRATIN OF MANGO, GUAVA AND PINK GRAPEFRUIT

CONSOMMÉ OF LANGOUSTINE

SERVES 6

Langoustines (Dublin Bay prawns) are deep, cold-water shellfish. I buy mine directly from Scotland but increasingly they seem to be available at the best fishmonger's. They are a fairly fragile shellfish and do not travel very well from the ports, especially during the warmer summer months. It is probably better to buy the ones which are cooked directly after landing at the ports. The only drawback after that is that you will have to rely on the fishmonger to sell you fresh ones and not some which have been hanging around the shop for three days.

All the langoustines I buy come to me alive, and for the above reasons, I only include them on my menus in the winter months or early spring.

When preparing and cooking langoustines for other dishes, always remove their heads and all the tail shells, and store them in the freezer. When you have enough, they will make an excellent consommé which can be served as a light starter to a spring lunch. The consommé can also be used as a sauce when serving ravioli or, cold, mixed in equal proportions with gazpacho (see p.236) as a lovely summer soup.

This method of preparing the consommé can be adapted to suit any shellfish: it's the shells which will determine the flavour. Try crab, prawn, etc.

2 kg (4¼ lb) langoustine shells (if possible, reserve some of the tail flesh as garnish)	outside leaves from 2 fennel bulbs
	5 garlic cloves
2 large onions	225 g (7½ oz) ripe tomatoes (plum tomatoes are the best)
1 large carrot	
1 celery stalk	120 ml (4 fl oz) olive oil
1 leek	60 ml (2 fl oz) Cognac

2 sprigs fresh thyme

1 bay leaf

parsley stalks

60 g (2 oz) tomato paste

150 ml (5 fl oz) dry white wine

3 sprigs fresh tarragon

2 litres (3½ pints) Fish Stock (see p.223)

cayenne pepper

a little lemon juice if needed

Clarification

2 shallots

1 celery stalk

1 leek

2 garlic cloves

1 sprig fresh tarragon

6 egg whites

CHEF'S TIP

If using fresh, live langoustines cook them for 5 minutes in a good **court bouillon** *(see p.224). Refresh in cold water and drain in a colander. Pull off the heads from the tails. With a pair of kitchen scissors cut the shell from the tail meat, and reserve for use in another dish.*

Preparing the consommé ingredients

1. Put all the shells in a colander and wash and drain them thoroughly.

2. Peel and cut the onions into 1.5 cm (¾ in) dice. Peel, wash and dice the carrot and celery, and trim and dice the leek. Dice the outside leaves of the fennel. Peel the garlic cloves and reserve aside.

3. Cut the tomatoes in half, and squeeze out and discard the seeds. Reserve the flesh.

4. Heat a large, thick-bottomed saucepan over a fierce flame. Add the olive oil and when it begins to smoke add the drained langoustine shells. Avoid stirring too often as you will lose too much heat in the pan. The idea is to seal and fry the bones, not to boil them in oil. Cook for about 10 minutes.

5. Pour in the Cognac and ignite it. When the flame has gone out, stir the langoustine shells.

6. Add all the vegetables except for the tomatoes, stir, and continue to cook for a further 5 minutes.

7. Add the thyme, bay leaf, parsley stalks and tomato paste. Cook for a further 3 minutes, not allowing the tomato paste to catch or burn on the bottom of the pan. Moisten with the white wine and reduce until fully evaporated.

8. Add the garlic, tomato halves and tarragon, and cover with the fish stock. Stir, bring the liquid to the boil and skim off any of the surfacing fat and scum. Turn down the flame and simmer for 1 hour.

Preparing the clarification

9. Meanwhile, peel and finely chop the shallots. Chop the celery, wash and chop the leek, and cut into tiny 5 mm (¼ in) dice. Peel the garlic cloves and cut them in two. Blanch the tarragon. Put the vegetables, garlic and tarragon, with a little cayenne, into a bowl.

10. Pour on the egg whites and with a whisk beat them together. Do not add any salt to the clarification because this tends to break down the albumen in the egg whites. I use three large, fresh egg whites per litre (1¾ pints) of stock. Use a little more if the egg whites are not fresh.

Clarifying the consommé

11. When the consommé is ready, remove the saucepan from the stove. Ladle the shells and liquid into a colander, with another saucepan underneath to trap the liquids, and with the aid of a kitchen spoon crush the shells into the colander. This is very important as you must not leave any liquid in the colander. Crush the shells as small and as dry as you can.

12. Take the saucepan with the strained liquid and sediments back to the stove and bring back to the boil. As it does so, a layer of clear red oil should begin to surface on the liquid. Remove this with a ladle. (Keep it, it is excellent for use in fish salads or as a garnish to a fish plate.)

13. Once the oil has been removed a frothy scum will appear. This you skim off and discard. Boil the stock for a further 5 minutes and then strain it through a conical fine-mesh strainer into another pan. Bring the somewhat

thinner liquid back to the boil and again remove all the surfacing scum.

14. Turn down the heat and all at once add the prepared clarification. Whisk vigorously, turn the heat back up and continue whisking until the consommé shows signs of boiling. Just as it is about to boil, turn down the flame and gently simmer the liquid for a further 15 minutes.

15. Place a conical strainer over a bowl, and line this with a clean muslin cloth. Remove the consommé from the stove. Gently, break the crust on top of the consommé and ladle the clear liquid into the muslin. This will trap any loose sediments. The consommé is now ready.

To serve

16. Take the clarified consommé back to the stove and keep warm. Taste it, and if it is too sweet, add a little lemon juice.

17. Lay out six soup bowls. If you have them, place three langoustine tails in each bowl. (Ensure that there is no shell on the tails and that the black line running along the middle is removed.) Pour on the consommé and serve immediately.

As an optional garnish to the consommé, I add a little skinned diced tomato and shredded fresh coriander.

FILLET OF NEW SEASON'S LAMB WITH A WHITE JUICE AND BROAD BEANS

SERVES 6

This is a delightfully light dish after all those heavy winter casseroles. It combines the new sweet lamb with fresh spring broad beans. It has colour, taste and texture, and is relatively inexpensive.

3.5 kg (7½ lb) best end of lamb on the bone	1 bay leaf
salt and pepper	*Sauce*
30 ml (1 fl oz) cooking oil	2–2.25 kg (4–5 lb) broad beans
Stock	2 shallots
½ whole garlic bulb	30 g (1 oz) mixed chives and chervil
1 onion	4 tomatoes
5 shallots	a little lemon juice
1 leek	*Garnish*
1 celery stalk	3 shallots
1.75 litres (3 pints) good white Chicken Stock (see p.225)	½ whole garlic bulb
	60 g (2 oz) butter
1 sprig fresh thyme	90 g (3 oz) basmati rice

Preparing the lamb and stock

1. Remove the fillets of lamb from the bone, or ask your butcher to do it. Cut out the silvery membrane, being careful not to cut into the flesh. Refrigerate the fillets until you need them. Keep all the trimmings, but discard any fat. Chop up the bones.

2. Peel the garlic, onion and shallots. Roughly chop the onion, leek, celery and shallots.

3. Place the chopped bones in a large pan with the trimmings, cover with cold water and boil. Skim off all impurities, then tip the water away.

4. Clean the pan and run cold water over the bones and wash to remove any coagulated pieces. Return to the pan and cover with the

chicken stock. Bring to the boil and skim.
5. Add the herbs, the garlic and the roughly chopped vegetables. Skim the stock and simmer for 1 hour. (No carrot is used in this stock as the lamb is already sweet and the carrot would only make it sweeter.)

Preparing and cooking the garnish

6. Peel and chop the shallots and garlic. In a small, heavy pan melt the butter and add the shallots and allow to cook slowly, without colour. Half-way through cooking add the garlic. Cook all the contents to a softened pulp gently, but not colouring. Stir often. When cooked put in a liquidiser and blend until a smooth paste is obtained. Season to taste and reserve aside.
7. Boil 600 ml (1 pint) salted water and cook the washed basmati rice, about 15 minutes. Rinse and keep hot.

Preparing the sauce ingredients

8. Pod the broad beans and dip the grey-green beans in hot salted water. Plunge into cold water and when cold strain. Pick off the hard outer shell to reveal an emerald-green bean. Reserve aside in a small pan. You need about 180 g (6 oz).
9. Peel and finely chop the shallots. Chop the chervil and chives. Skin and seed the tomatoes and cut into 5 mm (¼ in) dice. Add to the pan with the beans.

Finishing the sauce and cooking the lamb

10. Preheat the oven to 220°C (425°F) Gas 7.
11. Strain the lamb stock and re-boil to reduce by half. (At this stage more chopped garlic may be added to improve the taste.) Skim often and *do not* let the edges burn or turn brown as this can discolour the stock. You want it to be white.
12. When the sauce is nearly ready, season the lamb fillets and brown all over quickly in hot oil. Tip off any excess oil, then place in the preheated oven for 6 minutes only. New season's lamb is best eaten cooked pink and the fillet should give slightly when touched. Remove from the oven and allow to rest.

To serve

13. Heat up the shallot purée and mix it into the hot rice, a little at a time, until the rice is bound together and soft. Taste for seasoning and alter if necessary. Press into six dariole moulds, and invert on to the top of six hot plates. Keep covered.
14. Season the reduced lamb juice and strain over the bean mixture in the small pan. Keep hot but do not boil or the tomatoes will start to disintegrate.
15. Slice the lamb fillets into five or six pieces each, and place in a crescent at the base of the plate.
16. Add two or three drops of fresh lemon juice to the sauce to add a little sharpness and quickly spoon it around the pink lamb. Remove the moulds from the rice and serve at once.

A Gratin of Mango, Guava and Pink Grapefruit

SERVES 6

*S*pring is an awkward season for interesting local fruits. None of the berried fruits are available at this time, but tropical fruits make a delicious conclusion to any spring menu.

2 ripe guavas
210 ml (7 fl oz) Stock Syrup (see p.249)
3 pink grapefruits
4 ripe mangoes
icing sugar to dust

Sabayon
6 egg yolks
2 teaspoons Malibu (a coconut and rum liqueur)
2 teaspoons white rum
30 g (1 oz) caster sugar

Preparing the fruits

1. Peel the guavas and slice them into eight pieces. Place them into a stainless-steel saucepan and add 110 ml (3½ fl oz) of the stock syrup. Poach them over a gentle heat until the flesh is soft. Remove them from the heat and pour into a liquidiser. Liquidise until smooth, then strain through a fine-mesh sieve into a bowl. Discard the seeds and reserve the pulp.

2. Top and tail the grapefruits using a small knife, then cut away the skins and white pith. Over a bowl to catch the juice, carefully remove the grapefruit segments. Slice each segment into half lengthways. Reserve in the bowl.

3. Again top and tail the mangoes, then use a peeler to remove the skin. Stand the mango up and slice downwards each side of the stone. Slice the mango widthways 5 mm (¼ in) thick. Reserve aside.

CHEF'S TIP
The stone is approximately a third of the mango and the same shape as the fruit. Cut away the flesh as close to the stone as possible.

4. Line a tray with cling film and place on to this six 7.5 cm (3 in) ring moulds. Place the mango slices into the moulds, packing them down slice upon slice, until all the mango is used.

5. Place the grapefruit segments on top of the mango, arranging them neatly into a spiral. Place into the refrigerator.

Making the sabayon

6. In a stainless-steel bowl whisk the egg yolks together until blended, then add the remaining stock syrup. Whisk together well. Add the Malibu and white rum. Pour the sabayon through a sieve into a clean bowl. Reserve.

To serve

7. Lay out six dinner plates, and spoon the guava pulp into the centre of each.

8. Using a wide palette knife pick up the moulds holding the mango and grapefruit, and place into the centre of each plate. Remove the ring moulds.

9. Half fill a saucepan with hot water, place on to the stove and bring to the simmer. Preheat the grill to its maximum temperature.

10. Place the sabayon mixture over the simmering water, add the caster sugar and whisk continuously for about 5 minutes until the sabayon thickens and peaks. It will become pale in colour.

11. Spoon the sabayon over the grapefruit and mango. Lightly sprinkle icing sugar over the sabayon and place each plate under the preheated grill until the sabayon has a golden glaze. Serve immediately.

Spring Menu 8

DRY-GRILLED SALMON
WITH RED CABBAGE AND CHICORY

LEG AND SADDLE OF RABBIT,
BAYONNE HAM, SWEETCORN AND PARSLEY

APPLE, SULTANA AND CALVADOS PANCAKES

DRY-GRILLED SALMON WITH RED CABBAGE AND CHICORY

SERVES 6

This dish is special, because it is one in which the skin is consumed with the salmon. The texture of the fish is quite unique, and the flavour, because of the Chinese spices, is very unusual. The salmon needs to be marinated for at least 24 hours in advance of cooking.

800 g (1¾ lb) wild salmon

salt and pepper

a little olive oil

Marinade

2 garlic cloves

2 sprigs fresh coriander

½ teaspoon each of ground coriander, Chinese five-spice powder, ground mace, ground cinnamon, caster sugar and table salt

juice of 1 lemon

Red wine vinaigrette

½ garlic clove

20 ml (⅔ fl oz) red wine

20 ml (⅔ fl oz) red wine vinegar

½ teaspoon sugar

1 egg yolk

½ teaspoon Dijon mustard

120 ml (4 fl oz) light olive oil

lemon juice to taste

Salad

½ small red cabbage (about 150 g/5 oz)

2 heads white chicory

1 shallot

½ bunch chives

Garnish

1 quantity Butter Sauce for Fish (see p.231)

2 large tomatoes

Preparing the salmon and marinade

1. Place the fillet of salmon on a board, skin-side up, and, with the back of a knife, scrape off all the scales. Turn the salmon over and, using a pair of fish pliers, remove all the fine bones. Reserve aside on a tray. Clean the work surface and then cut the salmon into six equal pieces.

2. Peel and finely slice the garlic. Wash, dry and shred the fresh coriander.

3. In a bowl combine the spices, sugar and salt. Add the lemon juice and whisk to a smooth paste.

4. Scrape out on to a stainless-steel or plastic tray, and add the fresh coriander.

5. Lay the salmon pieces, skin-side down, on to the marinade in the tray. Cover with cling film and weight down the top with another tray. Refrigerate for 24 hours.

CHEF'S TIP
During marination the salt will pull all the moisture out of the salmon skin and the skin in turn will absorb the spices through the lemon juice.

6. After 24 hours, remove the salmon (you will notice a crust has formed on its skin) and transfer it to a clean tray basted with a thin layer of olive oil. Refrigerate again until it is time to cook it.

Preparing the vinaigrette

7. Peel and finely chop the garlic.

8. Place the red wine, red wine vinegar and sugar in a small saucepan, and warm over a gentle flame. Do not boil. Reserve aside.

9. In a stainless-steel bowl, stir the egg yolk and Dijon mustard together with a whisk, then add the red wine mixture and the garlic.

10. Pour the oil into another pan and gently warm it over the stove (just to room temperature). Gradually pour the oil into the base and vigorously whisk to emulsify. If, during this process, the vinaigrette appears to be too thick, just add a little water.

11. Check the seasoning and season with salt and pepper. Squeeze in a little lemon juice for acidity. Reserve aside for the salad.

Preparing the salad and garnish

12. Remove the outside leaves of the cabbage, cut out the core and discard. Wash and carefully drain the cabbage and dry with a clean kitchen towel. Shred into long, thin strands and place them in a bowl.

13. Cut off the bottoms from the chicory heads. Remove twelve outside leaves and reserve aside in a bowl for presentation of the dish. Shred the remainder and add it to the cabbage.

14. Peel and finely chop the shallot, chop the chives, and add to the salad. Season with salt and pepper. Do not add the vinaigrette until the last minute, just before the salmon is cooked.

15. Skin, seed and dice the tomatoes. Reserve aside.

To cook and serve

16. Preheat a solid oven-top grill to medium. Unlike most grilled fish, this dish calls for a moderate heat. The idea is to cook the salmon gently from the skin upwards, but not to burn the skin in the process.

17. Pour the oil from the salmon tray on to the grill and, as quickly as possible, place the salmon, skin-side down, on to the grill to cook. It takes at least 7 minutes.

18. Warm through the butter sauce and, separately, the tomato dice.

19. While the salmon is cooking, spoon 3 dessertspoons of the vinaigrette into the salad and mix thoroughly. Spoon a little more red wine vinaigrette on to the chicory leaves.

20. In the centre of your serving plates lay down two chicory leaves to form a V shape and spoon a large dessertspoon of salad between them.

21. With a fish slice remove the salmon and lay it down on top of the salad, skin-side up.

22. Spoon a little warm butter sauce around the salmon and garnish the plates with a little of the warmed tomato dice.

If you feel it is necessary to serve anything with this dish, a few first-crop Jersey potatoes is a good option.

LEG AND SADDLE OF RABBIT, BAYONNE HAM, SWEETCORN AND PARSLEY

SERVES 6

*T*his dish may seem fairly complex but once all the ingredients are in place it is comparatively straightforward. The sweetcorn acts as a good foil for the saltiness of the ham, and the recipe makes clever use of the leg meat of a rabbit which can sometimes be a bit tough.

We have used wild rabbits which have been soaked in milk overnight to extract the blood and to whiten the flesh. This dish uses only the leg and saddle meat. The rib cage and trimmings go to make the sauce.

3 rabbits, cut into joints	**120 g (4 oz) Chicken Mousse (see p.239)**
salt and pepper	***Sauce***
cooking oil	**2 litres (3½ pints) Chicken Stock (see p.225)**
1 quantity Green Herb Pasta (see p.240), cut into noodles	**1 onion**
Rabbit 'parcels'	**½ carrot**
3 thin slices Bayonne, Parma or East Denhay ham	**1 leek**
	1 celery stalk
1 bunch fresh parsley	**1 sprig fresh thyme**
60 g (2 oz) sweetcorn	**1 bay leaf**
60 g (2 oz) cooked ham	**6 garlic cloves**
120 g (4 oz) *crépinette* or pig's caul, soaked in cold water for 24 hours	**1 bunch fresh tarragon**
	lemon juice

CHEF'S TIP

The only way to preserve pig's caul - the veil-like membrane from the stomach lining - is to salt it. This salt must be washed off by soaking. Some butchers can supply it pre-soaked.

Preparing the rabbit

1. Remove all sinews from the leg and saddle meat, then, carefully, following the contours of the saddle bone, remove the fillets. From three saddles there will be six fillets.
2. Carefully, with a sharp knife, remove the thigh bone from the leg, keeping the leg as intact as possible.
3. Between two sheets of cling film or plastic, beat the now half-boneless rabbit leg with a meat bat, making the leg twice as large but half as thin. Do not bash holes in it.

Assembling the rabbit 'parcels'

4. Season the saddle fillets and in a little hot oil quickly seal them on all sides. This should take only 1–2 minutes. Allow to cool, then roll each up tightly in half a slice of the Bayonne, Parma or East Denhay ham.
5. Wash, dry and chop the parsley. Cook the sweetcorn in salted water for a few minutes, then drain well, dry and leave to cool. Chop the cooked ham into 5 mm (¼ in) dice. Cut the pig's caul into six equal-sized pieces.
6. Mix the chicken mousse, chopped parsley, corn and diced cooked ham in a bowl. Taste for seasoning and adjust if necessary.
7. Remove the plastic from the leg meat and season the legs. Place a small spoonful of the chicken mixture along the leg and press into it the ham-wrapped fillet.
8. Add more mousse to cover the fillet totally, but do not put in too much as it may ooze out on cooking. Gather up the overlapping side of the leg meat and cover the filling.
9. Spread a piece of pig's caul out on a clean

surface and put the leg in the centre. Wrap it up tightly, leaving the leg bone protruding. Tie with string in two places just to hold the caul in place. Do the same with the other legs. Reserve aside in a cool place.

Making the sauce

10. Chop up the remaining rabbit bones, and in hot oil sauté in a cast-iron pan until golden brown, about 5 minutes. Lift out with a slotted spoon to a saucepan and cover with the chicken stock.

11. Peel the onion, and coarsely chop along with the other vegetables. Roast them in the same pan until they are golden brown, another 5 minutes, then add them to the rabbit bones.

12. Add the thyme, bay leaf, peeled garlic and tarragon. Bring to the boil and skim, then allow to simmer for 1 hour.

To cook and serve

13. Strain the sauce stock and set to reduce by half. Preheat the oven to 220°C (425°F) Gas 7.

14. When the sauce is nearly ready, season the finished rabbit 'parcels' and in a shallow pan brown all over in a little hot oil.

15. Place in the preheated oven and roast for about 12 minutes or until firm to the touch, turning often so as not to get too dark on one side. Allow to rest for 4 minutes.

16. Cook and drain the pasta. Taste the finished sauce, and season if required with salt, pepper and a touch of lemon juice. Reheat the rabbit if necessary.

17. At the top of each plate place a swirl of hot pasta. Carve the rabbit leg diagonally into three or four pieces and place down, fanning it out below the pasta and showing off all the beautiful colours and work involved. Strain around the finished rabbit sauce and serve at once.

   I sometimes arrange the rabbit leg slices on blanched baby spinach, and decorate the plate with tomato dice.

APPLE, SULTANA AND CALVADOS PANCAKES

SERVES 6

*T*his is an interesting way of serving pancakes. They are filled with a custard bound with diced apple and almonds, and flavoured with sultanas soaked in Calvados.

Pancake batter	1 vanilla pod
3 eggs	60 g (2 oz) caster sugar
150 g (5 oz) plain flour	60 ml (2 fl oz) Calvados
510 ml (17 fl oz) milk	60 g (2 oz) sultanas
30 g (1 oz) caster sugar	60 g (2 oz) flaked almonds
30 g (1 oz) unsalted butter	icing sugar
90 g (3 oz) clarified butter	6 sprigs fresh mint
(see Chef's Tip, p.15)	*To serve*
Filling	510 ml (17 fl oz) Vanilla Egg Custard Sauce
300 g (10 oz) Pastry Cream (see p.249)	(see p.250)
6 eating apples	icing sugar
60 g (2 oz) unsalted butter	6 sprigs fresh mint

Preparing and cooking the pancakes

1. Beat the eggs together in a bowl, then beat in the flour. Whisk in the milk a little at a time, then add the caster sugar. Melt the unsalted butter over a low heat until it becomes nut brown in colour. Beat this into the batter and reserve aside.

CHEF'S TIP

It is essential to only use clarified butter when cooking the pancakes otherwise the milk (or sediment) of non-clarified butter will burn on to the pan and cause your pancakes to stick.

2. Place a 20 cm (8 in) frying pan on to the stove to heat. Melt a small quantity of the clarified butter, then pour in sufficient pancake batter to cover the base of the pan.
3. Cook for 2 minutes until golden then, using a palette knife, turn the pancake over and cook the other side. Turn the pancake out on to a cooling rack. Repeat the process until you have twelve pancakes in total. Reserve aside.

Filling the pancakes

4. Prepare and make the pastry cream.
5. Peel four of the apples, cut into two and remove the cores. Dice roughly into 1 cm (½ in) cubes.
6. Melt the butter in a saucepan. Split the vanilla pod lengthways in two, and add to the butter. Add the diced apples and sugar. Put a lid on top of the saucepan and cook over a gentle heat, stirring occasionally, until the apple has completely softened, approximately 10 minutes. When cooked remove from the heat. Remove the vanilla pod.
7. Liquidise the apple to a smooth pulp, then pour back into the saucepan.
8. Peel and core the remaining two apples and dice into 1 cm (½ in) cubes. Add these to the apple purée and warm over a low heat to part-cook the apple cubes. Cook for 3 minutes. Reserve aside to cool.
9. In a small saucepan warm the Calvados.

Add the sultanas. Remove from the heat and cling film the surface. Leave to cool.
10. Preheat the oven to 230°C (450°F) Gas 8. Dust the almonds liberally with icing sugar and moisten with 2 teaspoons of water. Mix together and lay them on a baking sheet. Cook in the oven for approximately 10 minutes until golden and crisp. Reserve aside to cool.
11. In another bowl, whisk the pastry cream until smooth, then stir in the soaked sultanas and the sugared almonds.
12. Lay out the pancakes. Place a tablespoon of apple into the centre of each pancake. On top of this place a tablespoon of the pastry cream filling. Fold the edges of the pancake into the centre to form a parcel, completely enveloping the filling. Turn the pancake over on to a buttered baking tray. Refrigerate until serving.

To finish and serve

13. Make the vanilla egg custard sauce, and reserve aside.
14. Preheat the oven to the highest it will go (250°C). Preheat the grill to its highest setting as well.
15. Remove the pancakes from the refrigerator and place into the oven for 5 minutes to warm through.
16. Lay out six plates, and divide the vanilla custard between them.
17. Remove the pancakes from the oven and dust the tops with icing sugar. Place them under the hot grill to caramelise. Repeat this process to achieve an even glaze.
18. Using a fish slice, carefully place two pancakes into the centre of each plate, one slightly overlapping the other. Place a sprig of mint in the centre. Serve immediately.

CHEF'S TIP

As an alternative, these pancakes may be served in a large dish and flamed at the table with Calvados. You can serve the vanilla egg custard sauce separately, or offer double cream instead if so desired.

Summer Recipes

Menu 1

TERRINE OF ARTICHOKES

LOBSTER BRAISED IN BASIL AND TOMATO

WILD STRAWBERRY AND RHUBARB BISCUIT

Menu 2

POTTED DUCKS LEGS AND A MADEIRA JELLY

FILLET OF STEAMED WILD SALMON WITH A
CHIVE BUTTER SAUCE

TARTLETS OF QUEEN OF PUDDINGS

Menu 3

MARINATED QUAIL ROASTED WITH SPICES AND
GARNISHED WITH PEANUTS

SEA BASS IN A SALT CRUST WITH TOMATO AND
ANCHOVY SAUCE

VACHERIN OF APRICOTS AND RASPBERRIES

Menu 4

SALAD OF SKATE IN A SOYA VINAIGRETTE

BABY CHICKEN FILLED WITH TRIPE AND LEEKS

A MOUSSE OF CREAM CHEESE WITH RED FRUITS

Menu 5

RAVIOLI OF LOBSTER

FILLET OF WELSH LAMB WITH A HERB AND PASTRY CRUST

WHITE CHOCOLATE MOUSSE WRAPPED IN
DARK CHOCOLATE TOPPED WITH GLAZED RASPBERRIES

Menu 6

AVOCADO PEAR SALAD WITH CRAB AND PINK GRAPEFRUIT

ROAST SQUAB PIGEON WITH PUY LENTILS AND A HONEY SAUCE

L'ORTOLAN'S STRAWBERRY CREAM CHEESECAKE

Menu 7

RATATOUILLE

RUMP STEAK WITH CAFÉ DE PARIS BUTTER

AN ICED HONEYED NOUGAT WITH DRIED APPLE
AND RASPBERRIES

Menu 8

BREAST OF GUINEA FOWL WITH A LIME GLAZE

PAN-FRIED VEAL KIDNEYS IN A PORT, TARRAGON
AND MUSTARD SAUCE

CHARLOTTE OF BLUEBERRIES

Summer Menu 1

TERRINE OF ARTICHOKES

LOBSTER BRAISED IN BASIL AND TOMATO

WILD STRAWBERRY AND RHUBARB BISCUIT

TERRINE OF ARTICHOKES

SERVES 10 OR 20

This makes an excellent vegetarian dish and a light hors-d'oeuvre for a summer luncheon. Alternatively, serve as a main course. The best artichokes come from France, namely Brittany, or California, and the season loosely runs from June to September.

Whole cooked artichokes can be served on their own, cold with vinaigrette, or hot with warm butter. Eating them this way is one of my wife's favourite pastimes and one which drives me mad! Nibbling away for what seems like hours, at what seems to be nothing, is not for me. In this recipe we cut away all but the best part of the artichoke – the artichoke heart.

The recipe here is for one large terrine, using twenty artichoke hearts cooked in a *blanc* (see p.238). It keeps well in the fridge if you have any left over.

20 large Artichoke Hearts (see p.238), still in their *blanc*

210 g (7 oz) artichoke trimmings (from trimming the artichokes after cooking, including the inner edible leaves)

1 small garlic clove

2 sprigs fresh tarragon

10 eggs

10 egg yolks

210 ml (7 fl oz) whipping cream

salt and pepper

60 g (2 oz) unsalted butter

To finish (optional)

34 medium spinach leaves

60 ml (2 fl oz) clarified butter (see Chef's Tip, p.15)

To serve

1 quantity Tomato Sauce (see p.232)

4 tomatoes, skinned, seeded and diced (or enough flesh to equal the tomato sauce in volume)

1 quantity Chive Cream Sauce (see p.231)

a few chopped chives

1. Line a 30 x 7.5 cm (12 x 3 in) terrine mould with cling film that will withstand oven cooking. Preheat the oven to 140°C (275°F) Gas 1.

Making the artichoke cream

2. Dry the artichoke trimmings on a kitchen cloth and reserve aside in a bowl. Peel the garlic. Blanch the tarragon.
3. Crack the eggs into a liquidiser bowl and add the egg yolks. Add the cream, artichoke trimmings, garlic and blanched tarragon. Liquidise for 2–3 minutes to a smooth cream. Add salt and pepper, and liquidise for a further 10 seconds to mix in the seasonings.
4. Melt the butter in a small saucepan over a fierce flame. When it begins to froth and turn nut brown, take to the liquidiser and very carefully add this to the cream. Re-mix.
5. Strain the cream through a fine-mesh conical strainer into a clean bowl. With the aid of a ladle skim off any surfacing scum and froth, and discard.

Layering the terrine

6. Remove the artichoke hearts from the *blanc* and place on a tray. Dry them thoroughly with a kitchen cloth.
7. Using a ladle, carefully pour enough of the cream mixture to line the bottom of the terrine mould to a depth of about 2 cm (¾ in). On top of this place four artichoke hearts face down. Cover with another layer of cream, taking care that none are showing above the cream. Repeat the process until the terrine is full.
8. Cover the terrine with another sheet of cling film and then with a sheet of foil.

Cooking the terrine

9. Put a shallow tray of water on the stove, and bring it to the boil. When boiling, place the terrine into the bain-marie, making sure that the level of the water is as high up the terrine as possible. This will ensure even cooking. Place the bain-marie into the preheated low oven and cook for 1 hour.

10. Turn the oven temperature down to 110°C (225°F) Gas ¼ and gently cook on for a further 1½ hours.
11. When the terrine is cooked or has set, remove from the oven and take the dish out of the water. Place the terrine in another shallow tray, surround it with ice and refrigerate when cold.

To finish

Purely as an option, to achieve the maximum effect on presentation, I like to wrap my terrine in blanched spinach leaves. This is a fairly simple operation.
12. First turn out the terrine. To do this, gently lift the sides of the cling film used to line the terrine. Run a small knife around the top edge of the terrine, between the cling film and the mould, to ensure that it is completely free. Fill a shallow tray with water and bring it to the boil. Place the terrine in this for 30 seconds then remove immediately. Turn the artichoke terrine upside-down and carefully remove the film.
13. Wash, pick over and re-wash the spinach leaves, then blanch briefly and refresh in cold water.
14. Strain well, and carefully, leaf by leaf, open up the spinach and place on kitchen paper to dry.
15. Wash the empty terrine mould and brush it with a little clarified butter. Leaf by leaf, line the terrine mould, overlapping the leaves to cover the inside completely. Ensure that you leave enough to give a good overlap of spinach at the top. Refrigerate to set the spinach to the butter.
16. When set, carefully place the terrine mould over the artichoke terrine and turn it over. Brush the top of the terrine with a little more clarified butter and fold over the overlapping spinach leaves. Now return it, completely sealed, to the fridge until required.

To serve

17. Turn the terrine out on to a clean chopping board. Over a flame warm a sharp filleting

knife and slice off the end of the terrine. Wipe the blade clean and again over a flame re-warm the knife and cut a slice 2 cm (½ in) thick. Lay this down in the centre of a large plate. Cut and arrange other slices in the same way.

18. Mix the tomato sauce and most of the diced tomato flesh together. Liquidise and pass through a conical strainer.

19. Alternate the two sauces around the outside of your terrine slices on the plates, decorate with reserved tomato dice and chopped chives, and serve.

LOBSTER BRAISED IN BASIL AND TOMATO

SERVES 6

This is a very simple light dish, ideal for a summer's lunch. Use only live lobsters for this dish, not ready-cooked ones. For the photograph, I garnished the plate with a little mould of lobster mousse: this is made from the filling of the lobster ravioli (see p.97), and poached in a bain-marie.

6 x 500 g (18 oz) lobsters
2 litres (3½ pints) *Court Bouillon* or *Nage* (see p.224)
salt and pepper
lemon juice
Vegetable garnish
1 large carrot, about 180 g (6 oz)
2 courgettes, about 180 g (6 oz)
1 large potato, about 180 g (6 oz)
18 asparagus spears, about 240 g (8 oz)
10 g (⅓ oz) baby spinach leaves
75 ml (2½ fl oz) Vegetable Stock (see p.222)
30 g (1 oz) unsalted butter
a few sprigs of fresh chervil
Basil sauce

2 shallots
2 garlic cloves
150 g (5 oz) plum tomatoes
120 g (4 oz) unsalted butter
about 10 basil leaves
30 ml (1 fl oz) Noilly Prat
30 ml (1 fl oz) dry white wine
210 ml (7 fl oz) Fish Stock (see p.223)
Lobster cream (optional)
110 ml (3½ fl oz) Lobster Consommé (see Consommé of Langoustine, p.55)
1 sprig fresh tarragon
a pinch of cayenne pepper
1 teaspoon Cognac
60 ml (2 fl oz) whipping cream

Preparing the lobsters

1. Kill the lobsters by inserting the point of a knife quickly into the air vent and making an incision about 2.5 cm (1 in) across.

2. Pull the claws from the lobsters and crack them with a meat bat. Be careful during this process just to crack the shell, but not so severely that you crush the claw flesh. Pull the head shell from the tail (see Chef's Tip). Reserve the claws and tails in separate bowls until ready for cooking.

3. Put the *court bouillon* in a large saucepan, and when it is boiling throw in the claws and cook them for 60 seconds. Remove and refresh in cold water. When cold, strain them and reserve aside on a clean tray.

4. Cook the lobster tails in the boiling *court bouillon* for just 30 seconds. Again, refresh in cold water and strain.

5. Carefully remove the claw meat intact from the shells. Cut the tail flesh from the shells as well. Make a small incision along the middle of the tails and remove the entrail lines and discard. Put the tail meat with the claw meat, and refrigerate until ready to cook.

Preparing the vegetable garnish

6. Peel and wash the carrot, courgettes and potato. With a small Parisian scoop, cut out as many balls as possible from all the vegetables. Reserve the carrot and courgette aside in a small bowl. Reserve the potato balls in a small bowl, covered with cold water.
7. Cut the asparagus tips from the stalks. Just the tops are used as garnish.

8. In a pan of boiling salted water cook the carrot balls for 3 minutes, just until *al dente*. Strain and refresh in cold water. Strain again and reserve aside. Repeat this process for the potato balls and asparagus spears, but leave the courgettes raw.
9. Pick the stalks from the baby spinach leaves. Wash the leaves in a liberal amount of cold water and drain. Reserve aside.

Cooking the lobster and sauce

10. Preheat the oven to 180°C (350°F) Gas 4.
11. Peel and finely chop the shallots. Peel, crush and chop the garlic. Blanch, skin and seed the tomatoes, then dice the flesh into 5 mm (¼ in) dice. Reserve aside.
12. In a large shallow saucepan, melt 60 g (2 oz) of the unsalted butter, then add the shallots. Gently cook them for 3 minutes or until tender; they should not colour.
13. Add the tomato dice and five of the basil leaves. Continue cooking for a minute or so, then add the Noilly Prat. Boil and reduce until a syrup and then add the white wine. Boil and reduce by half.
14. Pour in the clear fish stock. Bring up to the boil and with a small ladle remove and discard all the surfacing scum.
15. Turn the heat down to a gentle simmer

and carefully add the lobster flesh and garlic. Cover with butter papers and the lid. Cook in the preheated oven for 7 minutes.

Preparing the lobster cream (optional)

16. Put the lobster consommé in a separate pan with the tarragon, which you have blanched first, the cayenne and the Cognac. Boil to reduce the liquid by half. Add the whipping cream, a little salt to taste and a few drops of lemon juice. Boil again until the sauce thickens enough to coat the back of a spoon. Pass the lobster cream through a fine-mesh conical strainer into another pan and reserve aside. Keep warm on the side of the stove until ready to serve.

To finish

17. Once the lobster is cooked, remove the lid and butter papers. Carefully, using a fork and spoon, lift the lobster flesh out on to a clean tray. Cover again with the butter papers and reserve aside. Keep warm.
18. Put the pan with the lobster sauce back on the stove, and boil to reduce by half.
19. Strain the reduced lobster sauce through a fine-mesh conical strainer into another pan. Cut the remaining butter into 1 cm (½ in) dice and whisk this into the sauce. Check the seasoning. Add a little lemon juice for extra acidity – lobsters always give a sweet stock.
20. Finely shred or slice the remaining basil leaves and add these to the sauce. Reserve to one side on the stove.

To serve

21. Put the vegetable garnish stock and the unsalted butter in a pan. Boil and whisk until the butter has dissolved. Season with salt and pepper. Add the vegetable garnish – the carrot, potato and courgette balls, and asparagus tips. Heat them through quickly, then lastly add the

baby spinach leaves. Cook these until tender – seconds only – and reserve aside.

22. Lay out six warmed main-course plates and, using a spoon, sprinkle a thin border of the prepared vegetables around the outer rims of the plates. In the centre, place the lobster – the meat from one tail and both claws per plate.

23. Re-boil the lobster cream (if using) and strain a little between the vegetables and the lobster.

24. Pour the hot basil sauce over the lobster, garnish with chervil, and serve immediately.

WILD STRAWBERRY AND RHUBARB BISCUIT

SERVES 8

This dessert uses the tiny wild strawberries which have a delicious flavour and aroma. The plants can easily be grown in this country, and can produce an abundance of fruit throughout the summer.

400 g (14 oz) wild strawberries
icing sugar
Lime parfaits
2 limes
120 ml (4 fl oz) Stock Syrup (see p.249)
60 g (2 oz) egg yolks (usually about 3)
270 ml (9 fl oz) whipping cream

Sauce
270 g (9 oz) pink (forced) rhubarb
110 g (3½ oz) caster sugar
To serve
150 ml (5 fl oz) whipping cream
32 Glucose Biscuits, 6 cm (2½ in) in diameter (see p.246)
8 sprigs fresh mint

Preparing the strawberries

1. Carefully wash the wild strawberries in cold water, then drain. Place on to a tray and sieve 60 g (2 oz) of the icing sugar over them. Gently shake the strawberries to roll them into the sugar, then place in the fridge and reserve.

Preparing the lime parfaits

2. Line a tray with greaseproof paper and place on it eight x 6 cm (2¼ in) ring moulds, 2 cm (¾ in) high.

3. Remove the zest from the limes and in a small saucepan of water, boil it for 1 minute, then refresh in cold water. Strain and repeat the process three times in total, or until the zest is tender. With a knife, cut out the zest into fine strips.

4. In another saucepan, bring the stock syrup to the boil, then turn down the heat and add the lime zest strips. Gently poach for 10 minutes. Strain off the syrup and reserve. Put half the lime zest into a small container and reserve; on a chopping board finely chop the remainder. Reserve.

5. Squeeze the juice from one of the denuded limes, and reserve.

6. In a saucepan place 110 ml (3½ fl oz) of the syrup used in the cooking of the lime zest, and bring to the boil.

7. Beat the egg yolks in a mixing bowl, then pour in the boiling syrup and whisk on maximum speed until a thick and white sabayon.

8. Whisk the whipping cream in a bowl until softly peaked. Add the lime juice and fold it in using a spatula. Gently fold the cream into the sabayon. Fold in the finely chopped lime zest.

9. Spoon the mixture into the ring moulds, dividing it evenly, and place into the freezer for 3 hours before using.

Making the rhubarb sauce

10. Wash the rhubarb, and top and tail with a sharp knife. Cut the pinkest rhubarb into four 5 cm (2 in) lengths. Peel the outside skin off these pieces 3 mm (⅛ in) thick lengthways, and cut this into fine *julienne* strips. Reserve in a bowl. Cut the rest of the rhubarb into baton-sized pieces, about 5 cm (2 in) long, and reserve aside in another bowl.

11. In a large saucepan bring 150 ml (5 fl oz) water and the caster sugar to the boil. Pour 60 ml (2 fl oz) of this boiling syrup over the rhubarb *julienne*, then cling film the top tightly. Reserve to cool.

12. Place the syrup saucepan back on the stove and add the remaining baton-sized pieces of rhubarb. Over a gentle heat poach until the rhubarb is tender and begins to break up, about 6-8 minutes. Remove from the stove.

13. Pour the cooked rhubarb into a liquidiser and liquidise until smooth. Pass through a fine-mesh sieve into a bowl. Leave to cool, then place into the refrigerator.

To serve

14. In a bowl whisk the whipping cream to soft peaks. Refrigerate and reserve.

15. Lay out eight plates, and divide the rhubarb sauce between them. Place a disc of glucose biscuit into the centre of each pool of sauce.

16. Remove the *julienne* of rhubarb from the syrup and lay on a piece of kitchen paper to drain. Place five sticks of rhubarb on to the edges of the sauce at equal distances from each other. Lay another five sticks of rhubarb on top so that you have five crosses at equal distances from each other around the plate. Repeat this process for the other plates.

17. Place a little of the cooked lime zest between each of the rhubarb crosses.

18. Remove the lime parfaits from the freezer. Press them out of the moulds on top of the glucose biscuits.

19. Lay another glucose biscuit on top of the parfait, and spoon a layer of wild strawberries on top of this.

20. Spoon a little whipped cream on top of the strawberries and place another biscuit on top. Build on another layer of wild strawberries and cream and finally lightly dust half the top of each glucose biscuit with icing sugar, and lay this on top. Repeat this process for the other plates. Any remaining strawberries can be dotted around the sauced plates. Place a sprig of mint on the top of each 'tower' and serve immediately.

Lobster Braised in Basil and Tomato

Sea Bass in a Salt Crust with Tomato and Anchovy Sauce

Salad of Skate in a Soya Vinaigrette

White Chocolate Mousse Wrapped in Dark Chocolate Topped with Glazed Raspberries

Summer Menu 2

POTTED DUCK LEGS AND A MADEIRA JELLY

FILLET OF STEAMED WILD SALMON WITH A CHIVE BUTTER SAUCE

TARTLETS OF QUEEN OF PUDDINGS

POTTED DUCK LEGS AND A MADEIRA JELLY

SERVES 6

*T*his needs to be made well in advance. It can keep in the refrigerator for up to two weeks, and as it matures it gets better.

In France a similar dish called *rillettes* is traditionally made with pork alone, and originates from the Loire region. In this recipe we use not only pork but also duck legs. They can readily be bought at any supermarket; but if not, buy a whole duck, use the breasts as a main course and cook the legs in the following way, to be used at a future dinner party. (In fact you need carcasses of ducks to make the jelly.)

4 large duck legs
240 g (8 oz) belly pork
120 g (4 oz) pork back fat
6 garlic cloves
1 onion
½ carrot
1 leek
1 celery stalk
450 ml (15 fl oz) Vouvray wine
1 sprig fresh thyme
1 bay leaf
6 black peppercorns, crushed
salt and pepper
60 g (2 oz) fresh parsley, chopped

60 g (2 oz) clarified butter (see Chef's Tip, p.15)
Jelly
2 duck carcasses
90 ml (3 fl oz) cooking oil
600 ml (1 pint) Chicken Stock (see p.225)
1 quantity *Mirepoix* (see p.239)
30 ml (1 fl oz) sherry vinegar
120 ml (4 fl oz) dry Madeira
1 sprig fresh thyme
1 bay leaf
6 garlic cloves
Clarification
2 shallots
2 garlic cloves

¼ carrot
½ leek
½ celery stalk
3 egg whites
salt
2 gelatine leaves (optional), soaked in cold water to soften

To serve
180 g (6 oz) mixed salad leaves
60 ml (2 fl oz) Walnut Vinaigrette (see p.233)
12 cocktail gherkins
6 slices Melba toast

Preparing the potted duck

1. Preheat the oven to 110°C (225°F) Gas ¼.
2. Place the untrimmed duck legs in a large, thick-bottomed, ovenproof pan with a lid.
3. Remove and discard the skin of the belly pork. Dice the pork and the back fat coarsely. Add to the legs.
4. Peel the garlic and the onion. Chop the onion, carrot, leek and celery. Add to the legs, along with the garlic.
5. Pour in the wine and add the thyme, bay leaf and crushed peppercorns, along with 150 ml (5 fl oz) water.
6. Place in the preheated low oven, cover with foil and then the lid, and cook for 3-5 hours, until the pork and the duck legs are tender and the duck is falling off the bones.
7. Remove the duck legs from the pan with a slotted spoon. Strain the remaining fat and vegetables through a colander. Reserve both the liquid and the vegetables.
8. Pick through the vegetables, and remove and retain all the pork and back fat cubes. Discard the vegetables.
9. Remove the skin from the duck legs and pull off the flesh. Keep the bones. Shred the leg meat finely with a sharp knife, then place in a clean bowl and reserve.
10. Place the pork and back fat in a food processor and purée. If it is too thick, add some of the fat from the cooking liquor until the puréed pork is quite moist. Mix with the shredded duck meat.
11. Reduce the remaining stock, having first removed the fat from the top, then add a little – a dessertspoon perhaps – to the duck if it appears too dry. Season the duck mixture with salt and pepper and the chopped parsley.
12. Press the duck mixture into six 6.5 cm

(2½ in) ramekins or moulds, leave to cool, then chill in the refrigerator.
13. When cold and firm, spoon over some melted clarified butter to seal them, and leave to mature for seven days or more.

Preparing the jelly

14. Heat the cooking oil in a large roasting tray and add the chopped duck carcasses and the leg bones from the *rillettes*. Sauté until brown, about 6–7 minutes. Transfer to a casserole pan and cover with the stock.
15. Place the *mirepoix* in the oil in the tray and sauté until golden brown, about 6–7 minutes, then add to the stock.
16. Discard the oil from the roasting tray and pour in the sherry vinegar. Boil to reduce until a syrup, then add the Madeira. Bring to the boil and add to the bones and stock.
17. Bring the stock to the boil, skim and add the thyme, bay leaf and garlic. Simmer for 1 hour, then strain through a fine strainer. Allow to cool.

Clarifying the jelly

18. Peel the shallots and garlic. Dice the shallots, carrot, leek and celery. Chop the garlic.
19. Place the diced vegetables, egg whites and chopped garlic in a tall pan. Add the jelly stock and return to the stove. Bring to the boil, stirring often to stop the egg whites from sticking, and as soon as it boils reduce to a simmer. Cook for 15 minutes only.
20. Strain through a fine-mesh sieve lined with a muslin cloth, taste for seasoning and add salt alone if necessary (pepper would show in the jelly).
21. Whether gelatine is used or not depends on

the strength of the initial chicken stock. If the stock was thin and liquid when cold, gelatine should be used. If the stock was set to a jelly it should not be required. Add the gelatine if necessary, stir to dissolve, then allow to cool. Freeze until needed.

To serve

22. At least an hour before serving, remove the duck ramekins from the refrigerator and the jelly from the freezer. Bring the jelly to the boil. Lift off any impurities and allow to cool. Leave both at room temperature. Chill six plates.

23. Carefully flood each chilled plate with the cool jelly, and leave to set.

24. Wash and spin the salad leaves and toss in the vinaigrette. Arrange around each plate, leaving room for the duck in the centre.

25. Remove the duck from the moulds (or leave if presentable), and place in the centre of each plate.

26. Slice the gherkins several times lengthways, but only about three-quarters of the length. You want them to be joined still at one end. Fan these out on top of the *rillettes*, and serve at once with hot Melba toast.

FILLET OF STEAMED WILD SALMON WITH A CHIVE BUTTER SAUCE

SERVES 6

This makes a light dish for the warmer summer months. When buying the salmon ask the fishmonger for a piece from the front of the fish, a thick cut off the bone, skin removed.

I cook this dish in a bag or parcel made from aluminium foil. If this is not available, a strong piece of greaseproof paper or a bag will do the job just as well.

This dish is very simple, but there are several stages in its make-up.

800 g (1¾ lb) wild salmon, all skin and bones removed
salt and pepper
90 g (3 oz) baby spinach leaves
(about 40 small leaves)
6 sorrel leaves
1 quantity Butter Sauce for Fish (see p.231), made with chives
Lemon and garlic butter
30 g (1 oz) butter
½ garlic clove
juice of ½ lemon
a pinch of cayenne pepper
Vegetable garnish
1 large leek
1 celery stalk

1 fennel bulb
2 courgettes
1 large carrot
210 ml (7 fl oz) Vegetable Stock (see p.222)
Concentrated fish stock
6 shallots
1½ garlic cloves
1 sprig fresh tarragon
120 g (4 oz) unsalted butter
1 sprig fresh thyme
¼ bay leaf
½ teaspoon dried fennel seeds
60 ml (2 fl oz) Noilly Prat
60 ml (2 fl oz) white wine
150 ml (5 fl oz) Fish Stock (see p.223)
juice of ½ lemon

Preparing the vegetable garnish

1. Top, tail and trim the leek, cutting off most of the green, bitter top and outside leaf. Wash the leek, cut it in two and separate the leaves. Discard any silver or shiny leaves – these are tough and unpleasant to eat. Cut the leek into long thin strips, 9 cm x 3 mm (3½ x ⅛ in). Reserve aside on a tray.

2. Peel and wash the celery, cut in two and slice into thin pieces as for the leek. Cut off the tops of the fennel, and peel the outside leaves. Cut the bulb in two and remove the stalk. Cut into fine strips as for the other vegetables.

3. Top, tail and wash the courgettes. Slice lengthways into pieces 3 mm (⅛ in) thick, and cut into thin strips as above. Peel and wash the carrot and cut as above.

4. Lay all the vegetable strips on a tray but separately. They all have different cooking times and must be cooked in order of these times.

5. Bring the vegetable stock to the boil in a saucepan, and throw the carrots in first. Cook for 2 minutes and then add the fennel. Cook this for a further 60 seconds and then add the celery. Bring the stock back to the boil and add the leek for seconds only. The courgettes are not blanched.

6. Strain the vegetables into a colander or through a fine-mesh sieve, trapping the vegetable stock in a bowl.

7. Sprinkle the cooked vegetables over the raw courgettes on the tray while still hot. Season with salt and pepper and allow to cool. Keep the remaining vegetable stock as this will be incorporated into the fish stock.

Preparing the concentrated fish stock

8. Peel and slice the shallots. Peel and crush the garlic. Blanch the tarragon.

9. Melt 30 g (1 oz) of the butter in a shallow saucepan and add the sliced shallots. Gently cook these until soft but not coloured. Add the blanched tarragon, thyme, bay leaf and fennel seeds. Cook for a further 2 minutes.

10. Pour in the Noilly Prat, and boil to reduce the liquid until it has completely evaporated. Add the white wine and reduce it by half of its volume, then pour in the fish stock. Bring to the boil and with the aid of a ladle remove the surfacing fats and froth. Add the crushed garlic to the liquid.

11. Pour the still boiling fish stock into the vegetable stock, re-boil and again remove all the surfacing sediment. Turn down the stock to a gentle simmer and cook the liquid for a further 5 minutes. Strain the stock into another saucepan and boil to reduce it by half its volume.

12. Dice the remaining butter and, while the stock is still boiling, piece by piece whisk it in. Add the lemon juice, season with salt and pepper and reserve aside in a bowl. You need 270 ml (9 fl oz) sauce for the six salmon 'packages'.

Making the lemon and garlic butter

13. Peel and crush the garlic. In a small pan, melt the butter, then add the garlic and lemon juice. Season with salt and a pinch of cayenne. Reserve aside.

Preparing the salmon 'packages'

14. Wash the baby spinach leaves and place on a cloth to dry. Remove the stalks from the sorrel leaves and reserve aside.

15. Slice the fillet of salmon into six equal pieces and brush the tops of these with a little of the lemon and garlic butter.

16. Cut out twelve sheets of aluminium foil, 44 x 29 cm (17½ x 11½ in), and lay six of these flat on the work surface. With the remaining lemon and garlic butter, brush an area twice the size of the salmon pieces in the centre of each piece of foil.

17. Divide the spinach leaves and the vegetable strips into six even portions.

18. Arrange one portion of spinach leaves on top of the butter on each piece of foil. On top of this, place half of each portion of vegetable strips. Place the salmon on top of this and cover with the remaining half of vegetables. Top each pile with a sorrel leaf. (As an option, some raw tarragon and chervil and/or sliced raw mushrooms can be sprinkled over the dish for added flavour.)

19. Spoon 3 tablespoons of concentrated fish

stock over each piece of salmon. Take care not to let any stock run over the edge of the foil. Place the remaining sheets of foil on top and carefully fold the edges over three times, crimping them flat. It is extremely important, when wrapping the salmon parcels, that you do not inadvertently puncture the foil. If the parcels are not completely airtight, the dish will be a disaster.

Cooking the salmon

20. Preheat the oven to 200°C (400°F) Gas 6.
21. With a fish slice carefully lift the salmon packages and place them on a baking sheet. Place in the preheated oven and cook for 7–8 minutes. Half-way through the cooking check the salmon: the bags should be beginning to rise.

To serve

22. Warm through the chive butter sauce and place in a sauceboat.
23. Preheat six large plates and place the salmon parcels on these. Serve immediately. The parcels can be cut at the table with a pair of scissors. This is the most exciting part of the dish - the first escape of scented steam as the parcels are opened is wonderful! Serve with the chive butter sauce.

New potatoes served with their skins on are a nice accompaniment.

TARTLETS OF QUEEN OF PUDDINGS

SERVES 6

Queen of puddings is a classic English dessert. There are many variations on the basic theme. This one is served in a pastry case.

300 g (10 oz) Sweet Pastry (see p.244)
60 g (2 oz) Biscuit Sponge trimmings (see p.245)
300 g (10 oz) raspberries
Custard
1 egg
1 egg yolk
30 g (1 oz) caster sugar
120 ml (4 fl oz) milk

Meringue
2 egg whites
80 g (2¾ oz) caster sugar
Sauces and garnish
150 ml (5 fl oz) Vanilla Egg Custard Sauce (see p.250)
icing sugar
6 sprigs fresh mint

Preparing and baking the tartlet cases

1. Line a baking tray with greaseproof paper. Grease six 7.5 cm (3 in) ring moulds with a little butter and arrange on the tray.
2. On a lightly floured surface, roll out the sweet pastry to about 5 mm (¼ in) thick, and cut into six 12 cm (4½ in) round discs. Line the inside of the ring moulds with the pastry, and trim away any overlapping pastry at the top. Refrigerate the tray for 20 minutes to rest the pastry.
3. Preheat the oven to 220°C (425°F) Gas 7.
4. Place a small piece of greaseproof paper inside the tartlet cases and fill to the top with baking beans. Cook in the preheated oven for 15 minutes. Remove and discard the baking beans and paper, then return the tartlets to the oven for a further 10 minutes just to colour them golden brown. Remove from the oven and place on to a cooling tray, still in the rings.

CHEF'S TIP
The pastry cases must not have any holes as they have to hold the liquid custard. Plug any holes with a little raw sweet pastry and return them to the oven for a few minutes to seal.

5. Finely dice the biscuit sponge trimmings and place them into the bottom of the cold tartlets. Put eight raspberries in each tartlet.

Making and baking the custard

6. Preheat the oven to 180°C (350°F) Gas 4.

7. In a bowl whisk the egg, egg yolk and sugar together, then whisk in the milk. Pass through a fine-mesh sieve into a bowl.

CHEF'S TIP

Because we use such a small quantity of custard in the tartlets, it is not necessary to boil the milk.

---

8. Spoon the custard into the tartlets, filling them to the top. Place the tray of tartlets into the preheated oven and bake for 20 minutes or until the custard has set. (You can test this by pressing your finger down on to the centre of the tarts: the custard will feel firm.) Remove from the oven and leave to cool completely before removing the ring moulds.

Making the sauces

9. Make the vanilla egg custard sauce, and reserve aside.

10. Keep six of the remaining raspberries for garnish, and place the rest of the berries into a liquidiser. Add 30 g (1 oz) of the icing sugar and liquidise until smooth. Pass the purée through a fine-mesh sieve into a bowl. Reserve aside.

Preparing the meringue

11. Preheat the oven to the highest it will go (250°C). Remove the rings from the tartlets using a knife, and place the tartlets on to a baking tray.

12. Put the egg whites in a mixing bowl, and whisk to a peak. Slowly add the caster sugar, whisking all the time until it has all been added. Whisk to a firm meringue.

13. Put the meringue into a piping bag fitted with a plain 1 cm (½ in) nozzle, and pipe a 2 cm (¾ in) thick circle of meringue to cover the surface of the tartlets completely. Use a palette knife dipped into hot water to smooth the sides. Pipe a border of small peaks around the top of each of the meringues (like a crown).

To finish and serve

14. Lay out six plates, and spoon some vanilla egg custard on to each.

15. Place the tartlets into the preheated oven to scorch the meringue. Be careful as the oven is very hot: this will take 2 minutes. Remove from the oven and dust with icing sugar. Place a tartlet into the centre of each plate.

16. Place a raspberry into the centre of the meringue and spoon the raspberry purée over it, filling the inside of each meringue crown. Place a sprig of mint on top. Serve immediately.

Summer Menu 3

Marinated Quail Roasted with Spices and Garnished with Peanuts

Sea Bass in a Salt Crust with Tomato and Anchovy Sauce

Vacherin of Apricots and Raspberries

Marinated Quail Roasted with Spices and Garnished with Peanuts

SERVES 6

The quails in this eastern-inspired recipe are marinated for over 24 hours in a lime and orange marinade which helps tenderise the flesh. The quail is served whole which enables the guest to tackle the bird with gusto!

6 quails
salt and pepper
150 ml (5 fl oz) groundnut oil
Marinade
1 lime
1 orange
1 small fresh green chilli
1 garlic clove
40 g (1½ oz) curry paste
30 ml (1 fl oz) soy sauce
30 ml (1 fl oz) tamari sauce
(Japanese soy sauce)
30 g (1 oz) demerara sugar
30 g (1 oz) fresh or desiccated coconut

15 g (½ oz) grated fresh ginger
30 g (1 oz) parsley stalks
Sauce
450 g (1 lb) chicken bones
3 shallots
3 garlic cloves
1 leek
1 celery stalk
40 g (1½ oz) curry paste
1 sprig fresh thyme
1 bay leaf
1.75 litres (3 pints) Chicken Stock (see p.225)
90 ml (3 fl oz) whipping cream
(or coconut milk, see p.216)

Garnish
1 bunch spring onions
2 tomatoes
60 g (2 oz) mangetouts

900 g (2 lb) roasted peanuts, shelled (you need 180 g/6 oz nut flesh)
180 g (6 oz) cooked basmati rice

Preparing the quails and marinade

1. Remove the breast bone from the quail, and all the quills.
2. Squeeze the juice from the lime and orange. Finely grate the rind of the lime. Seed the chilli, and chop roughly. Peel and chop the garlic.
3. In a tray that will hold the quails, mix both the juices and zest and add the chilli, garlic, curry paste, soy and tamari sauces, sugar, coconut, ginger, parsley stalks and 60 ml (2 fl oz) of the groundnut oil.
4. Immerse the quails, making sure the marinade is pushed well inside the cavities. Coat them well all over, cover with cling film and place in the refrigerator for 24 hours.

Preparing and cooking the sauce

5. Chop the chicken bones. Peel the shallots and garlic. Chop the shallots, leek and celery.
6. Brown the chicken bones evenly in a further 60 ml (2 fl oz) oil in a large saucepan, then drain off the oil. Add the curry paste and mix thoroughly over a low heat.
7. Meanwhile, in a separate pan, sauté the chopped shallot, leek and celery in the chicken oil until brown, about 15 minutes. Lift from the oil using a slotted spoon.
8. Add to the chicken bones along with the thyme and bay leaf, cover with the stock and bring to the boil. Skim and simmer for 1 hour. When cooked, strain through a fine sieve and again through a muslin to trap all the curry particles.
9. Place the sauce over high heat to reduce by half, adding the peeled garlic. At this stage the sauce should be tasted to see if it requires more curry paste. It should be quite well spiced, but not too much. To give it a more fruity background, a little of the marinade can be added also.
10. Add the cream and seasonings as required. Pass the finished sauce through a fine sieve and keep hot.

Preparing the garnishes

11. Trim and shred the spring onions. Skin and seed the tomatoes and cut into large dice. Top and tail and cook the mangetouts briefly in boiling salted water, then drain and cut into diamond or lozenge shapes. Keep hot.

Cooking the quails and garnish

12. Preheat the oven to 220°C (425°F) Gas 7.
13. Remove the quails from the marinade and season them with salt and pepper. In a hot pan seal them in the remaining oil, breast side down first, and finishing finally on the back.
14. Place on a baking tray and roast in the preheated oven for 5 minutes.
15. Remove 60 ml (2 fl oz) of the finished sauce to a smaller pan and bring to the boil. Put in the shredded garnish spring onions.
16. Take the quails out of the oven. With a fork lift out the spring onions, now coated in a sticky sauce, and gently pile them on top of each quail breast, pressing them down to ensure they adhere properly. Return the birds to the oven to finish, about another 2 minutes.

To serve

17. Heat up the diced tomatoes, roasted peanuts and the rice. Press the rice into six small dariole moulds.
18. When the spring onions on top of the quails have turned golden brown begin to assemble the plates. Place the rice at the crown of the plate. Sprinkle around the base the hot peanuts, the tomato dice and the mangetout lozenges.
19. Bring out the quail and place in the centre of each plate. Quickly spoon around the sauce, but not over the top as this would disturb the decoration. Remove the moulds from the rice and serve at once. A finger bowl is probably required.

SEA BASS IN A SALT CRUST WITH TOMATO AND ANCHOVY SAUCE

SERVES 6

*S*ea bass is one of my favourite species of fish. It is caught in the Mediterranean and is also imported from Spain and France. Our local bass is best in the months of May through to August. Buy small fish, if possible, for this dish. For me the baby bass is the most succulent.

Enclosing the fish in salt crust pastry is a very effective and nutritious way of cooking, but it must be remembered that the crust is not meant to be eaten.

6 x 500 g (18 oz) sea bass	1 red pepper
1 egg, mixed with 30 ml (1 fl oz) milk (egg wash)	1 courgette
	Sauce
a little melted butter	75 ml (2½ fl oz) Fish Stock (see p.223)
Salt crust pastry	75 ml (2½ fl oz) Tomato Sauce (see p.232)
1 kg (2¼ lb) plain flour	4 anchovy fillets
550 g (1¼ lb) table salt	1 large basil leaf
20 g (¾ oz) dried fennel seeds	a little lemon juice
300 ml (10 fl oz) egg whites	salt and pepper
Vegetable garnish	110 ml (3½ fl oz) Butter Sauce for Fish (see p.231)
½ fennel bulb	

Preparing the salt crust pastry

1. Sieve the flour into the bowl of a mixer with a dough hook. Add the salt and fennel seeds. Turn the machine on to its lowest speed.
2. Add the egg whites and mix for 3 minutes. Turn the speed up a little and slowly add 210 ml (7 fl oz) water. As the paste comes together again, turn down the speed and continue beating for a further 2 minutes. The crust is ready when the paste comes away cleanly from the sides of the bowl.
3. Gather up all the paste from the dough hook and the bowl. On a clean dry surface dusted with a little flour, roll the mixture into a tight ball. Wrap tightly in cling film and reserve aside to rest for 20 minutes.

Preparing the vegetable garnish

4. Cut the stalk from the fennel. Peel the separated leaves, dice into 3 mm (⅛ in) cubes and in a small saucepan of boiling water, cook for 3 minutes. Strain through a fine-mesh conical strainer and refresh under cold running water. Once cold, strain and turn out on to a clean kitchen cloth to dry. Reserve aside.
5. Cut the pepper in two. Remove the white core and seeds. Dice, blanch and dry as for the fennel.
6. Wash and cut the courgette as for the other vegetables but leave raw. Reserve aside.

Preparing and cooking the sea bass

7. Preheat the oven to 220°C (425°F) Gas 7.
8. With some fish scissors, cut off all the fins from the bass and trim the tail fin. With the back of a knife, tail to head, scrape off all the fish scales. Again using a pair of fish scissors, open the fish's stomach and discard all the entrails. Cut out the gills. Wash the fish thoroughly under cold water and dry on kitchen paper.
9. Dust a clean, dry work surface with flour. Cut the salt crust pastry into six equal pieces and, in turn, cut these in half.
10. With a rolling pin roll out one of the pieces of salt crust to a rectangle, 32 x 20 cm (12¾ x 8 in), approximately 7–8 mm (⅓ in) thick. Lay

one bass lengthways in the centre of the salt crust. Roll another piece of pastry out to a similar size.

11. Dip a small pastry brush in cold water and brush around the edge of the pastry, place the second piece of pastry over the fish and, gently, using the side of your hand, mould and shape the pastry until the contours of the fish are visible. Press down firmly at the edges to seal the pastry tightly.

12. Cut away all the overlapping excess pastry around the fish. When doing this, remodel the fins as much as possible, and cut out a tail. Between the fins, leave a border of 1 cm (½ in) of pastry to allow for shrinkage during cooking. With the back of a knife score the fins to give a more authentic appearance. With the excess pastry, roll out and cut another fin. With the pastry brush, brush a little more water just behind the gill and press this on to the pastry. Mould an eye and again, with a little water stick the eye in place.

13. Gently drag the point of your knife along the middle of the fish, stopping just at the back of the head. To mould some scales: starting at the tail of the fish, with just the rounded point of your knife, pit the pastry all the way up to the head. Repeat this process several times for maximum effect but be very careful not to puncture the pastry.

14. Brush the fish with egg wash and reserve aside. Repeat this process for the other bass, and arrange them on a baking tray. Bake in the preheated oven for 17 minutes.

Making the sauce

15. Meanwhile, pour the fish stock into a pan with the tomato sauce. Add the anchovy fillets and the basil leaf. Bring to the boil, and with a ladle remove and discard any surfacing froth. Cook for about 5 minutes on a high flame, then add the lemon juice and seasoning.

16. Pass through a fine-mesh conical strainer into the butter sauce. Stir in the prepared vegetable garnish and keep warm on the side of the stove.

To serve

17. Remove the bass from the oven and brush them with a little melted butter. Lift them from their tray and place them down on a chopping board or presentation tray. Garnish the board with decorative lemon halves and small bunches of clean watercress if you like. Pour the finished sauce into a sauceboat.

18. Remember this is not an edible crust. At the table, take a strong knife and cut around the outer edge of the crust of one of the fish. Peel off the top half of the crust (the top skin will automatically come away as well) and with a spoon and fork remove the top fillet to the serving plate. Remove and discard the exposed backbone and gently ease out the remaining fillet. Place on the serving plate and mask the fillets with a little tomato and anchovy sauce.

A good accompaniment to this dish is just a few plain boiled new potatoes or fresh pasta. Serve a few salad leaves in a tarragon vinaigrette (see p.234) with chopped chives and shallots.

VACHERIN OF APRICOTS AND RASPBERRIES

SERVES 6

The most recognisable combination of ingredients in a dessert would, I suppose, be good old peach melba, which uses peaches in various ways accompanied by a raspberry sauce.

I find that apricots, cooked or otherwise, have a far more distinctive flavour than peaches. This dish is just my reworked interpretation of a classic recipe.

500 g (18 oz) ripe apricots
390 ml (13 fl oz) Stock Syrup (see p.249)
375 g (13 oz) raspberries
120 ml (4 fl oz) whipping cream
6 x 6 cm (2¼ in) discs *Langue de Chat*
(see p.246)

18 fresh mint leaves
Meringue vacherin
110 ml (3½ fl oz) egg whites
110 g (3½ oz) caster sugar
icing sugar
30 g (1 oz) nibbed almonds

Making the meringues

1. Line a large baking tray with greaseproof paper, and preheat the oven to 110°C (225°F) Gas ¼.
2. Pour the egg whites into a machine bowl and whisk to a peak. Slowly incorporate the caster sugar, and continue whisking until the meringue is firm. Fold in 110 g (3½ oz) of the icing sugar with a spatula.
3. Put the meringue in a large piping bag fitted with a 1 cm (½ in) plain nozzle, and pipe twelve 6 cm (2¼ in) round meringue discs on to the greaseproof paper. Sprinkle six of these with the nibbed almonds and dust with a little icing sugar.
4. Place the vacherins into the oven, leaving the door slightly open to help dry the vacherins whilst baking. Bake for approximately 45–60 minutes: they will lift cleanly off the greaseproof paper when baked. Remove from the oven and reserve.

Making the apricot sauce and sorbet

5. Wash, cut in half, and stone the apricots. Place in a saucepan, add 110 ml (3½ fl oz) of the stock syrup, and cook over a gentle heat for 10 minutes.
6. Liquidise and pass through a fine sieve into a bowl. Add a further 225 ml (7½ fl oz) stock syrup to the apricot purée and mix together. When finished you should have 800 ml (about 27 fl oz) apricot liquid. Reserve 210 ml (7 fl oz) for the sauce.
7. Place the remaining apricot liquid into an ice-cream machine, and churn until frozen. Remove the sorbet from the machine, place in a suitable container, and reserve in the freezer.

Making the raspberry sauce

8. Wash all the raspberries carefully and drain in a colander. Reserve 180 g (6 oz) of the raspberries aside for assembling the dessert.
9. Liquidise the remaining raspberries with the remaining stock syrup. Strain through a fine-mesh sieve into a bowl, and reserve aside.

To serve

10. Whisk the cream until stiff, then reserve in the fridge until needed.
11. Lay out six 20 cm (8 in) plates, and spoon 3 dessertspoons of apricot sauce around each, leaving an equal distance between the pools of sauce. Spoon the same amount of raspberry sauce between the apricot sauce, thus making a border of alternating sauces. Place a plain meringue disc into the centre of each plate.
12. Add the reserved whole raspberries to the remaining raspberry sauce, and gently coat them using a spoon. Garnish each pool of apricot sauce with a dipped raspberry.
13. Remove the sorbet from the freezer and, using a palette knife, fill a 6 cm (2¼ in) plain pastry cutter with it. Place this on to the meringue disc, removing the cutter. Repeat for the other plates.
14. Place a disc of *langue de chat* biscuit on top of the apricot sorbet and repeat for the other plates. Spoon the remaining raspberries on top of the biscuit discs.
15. Top the raspberries with a little whipped cream, and top in turn with the remaining meringue discs, nibbed almonds side up.
16. Place a mint leaf on the three raspberries around each plate, and serve immediately.

Summer Menu 4

SALAD OF SKATE IN A SOYA VINAIGRETTE

BABY CHICKEN FILLED WITH TRIPE AND LEEKS

A MOUSSE OF CREAM CHEESE WITH RED FRUITS

SALAD OF SKATE IN A SOYA VINAIGRETTE

SERVES 6

Skate is the second most popular fish bought in Great Britain. It is readily available all year round, although connoisseurs will say it is best between October and April.

For this light salad dish I use only the wings of the skate. Ask the fishmonger for wings with the skin *on*: the dish is steamed, and the skin helps to keep the moisture in the fish.

6 small skate wings, approx. weight 240 g
(8 oz) each
2 garlic cloves
2 sprigs fresh tarragon
90 g (3 oz) butter
juice of ½ lemon
a pinch of cayenne pepper
salt and pepper
Vegetable garnish
2 medium carrots
2 celery stalks
2 leeks
1 fennel bulb
2 courgettes
270 ml (9 fl oz) Fish Stock (see p.223)

Salad
30 g (1 oz) baby spinach leaves
30 g (1 oz) small rocket leaves
30 g (1 oz) yellow frisée or curly endive
2 shallots
15 g (½ oz) chives
30 ml (1 fl oz) Tarragon Vinaigrette (see p.234)
a few drops of soy sauce
Sauce
1 shallot
2 garlic cloves
15 g (½ oz) chives
60 ml (2 fl oz) Tarragon Vinaigrette (see p.234)
1 tablespoon each of soy and tamari sauces
a little lemon juice

Preparing the skate wings

1. Wash the wings under cold running water. With the aid of a pair of fish scissors cut around the thin part of the wing (a piece of flesh 1 cm/½ in from the edge) and discard. Dry on a clean kitchen cloth.

Preparing and cooking the vegetable garnish

2. Wash, peel and re-wash the carrots. Slice them into thin strips along the length of the carrot, the thickness of a matchstick. Lay them flat on the board and cut, again lengthways, into long thin strips (*julienne*). Reserve aside on a tray.

3. Repeat this process for the celery, leeks and fennel. Lay them down in separate piles on the tray with the carrot *julienne*. Cut the courgettes in similar fashion and place them in a large bowl.

4. In a shallow pan boil the fish stock. When boiling, and in order of cooking times, add the vegetables. Add the carrot, and then, at 1-minute intervals thereafter, add the fennel, celery and leeks. Cover with a lid and cook for a further minute. Remove and strain the vegetables through a fine-mesh conical strainer, trapping the stock in another pan. Mix these vegetables into the raw courgettes.

5. Put the fish stock back on the stove and gently reduce its volume by half or until it thickens and becomes syrupy. This is the base for the sauce.

Cooking the skate wings

6. Peel and chop the garlic. Blanch the tarragon. In a small pan melt the butter, and add and stir in the lemon juice, tarragon, garlic, cayenne, salt and pepper. Reserve aside.

7. Put your steamer on. If not available, on the stove boil a large saucepan of water over which you can place two Chinese steamer baskets, one on top of the other. These are just as good.

8. Add half of the melted lemon and garlic butter to the prepared vegetable *julienne*. Season with salt and pepper and mix them thoroughly with a spoon.

9. Cut six pieces of cling film and carefully lay them down on your kitchen table. Brush the cling film with the remainder of the lemon and garlic butter, sprinkle with half the vegetable *julienne* and lay the skate wings down on top. Season the skate wings, sprinkle on the remaining vegetables and wrap the skate up into tight, completely airtight parcels.

10. Steam the skate for 6 minutes in the prepared steamer baskets. The water must be boiling vigorously throughout the cooking. When cooked, remove the skate and allow to cool on a cooling rack.

11. When cool enough to touch, unwrap the parcels and with a knife carefully pull off all the vegetable strips and place them into a bowl. Again with a knife, peel off the dark skin from the skate wings and discard. Carefully run your knife between the flesh of the skate and its fine bones, and remove the bones. Place the skate on a tray and cover with a butter paper. Strain any skate cooking juices into the reduced fish stock.

Preparing the salad

12. Wash and dry the salad leaves. Peel and finely chop the shallots. Chop the chives. Mix together in a bowl.

13. Add the tarragon vinaigrette and a few drops of soy sauce. With the aid of two serving spoons turn the salad over until thoroughly mixed. Season with a little salt and pepper.

Preparing the sauce

14. Peel and finely chop the shallot. Peel and slice the garlic cloves. Chop the chives.

15. Add the garlic to the reduced fish stock and skate juices. With a whisk, stirring all the time, add the tarragon vinaigrette, soy and tamari sauces. Stir until fully emulsified and strain the sauce through a conical strainer into another pan. Add the chopped shallot, the chives, and a little lemon juice. Keep warm.

To serve

16. In the centre of each plate, place a mound

of the vegetable strips. Carefully arrange the filleted skate against the vegetables to form a pyramid. Around the outside of the skate, arrange the salad. Finally, pour over the warm soy vinaigrette sauce, and serve immediately.

To add colour a little peeled, diced tomato is a good option.

BABY CHICKEN FILLED WITH TRIPE AND LEEKS

SERVES 6

*B*aby chicken or poussin can easily be bought, and when filled with tripe makes quite a substantial meal. The leg needs to be boned out, and if you are not feeling confident ask your butcher to do it but ask him to leave the leg whole. If you feel like tackling it, it is really quite simple. First of all, cut the legs off the body. Follow the thigh bone round with a small knife all the way down to the joint. Cut through the ligaments and remove the bone. Carefully cut around the knuckle piece and ease the thigh meat away with the knife. At this stage the flesh can be pulled off the bone down to the foot. Use scissors to cut the bone leaving the leg inside out with the `ankle' still attached. Turn the leg back to its original form and it is now ready for filling.

3 baby chickens	**2 garlic cloves**
salt and pepper	**240 g (8 oz) white mushrooms**
30 g (1 oz) butter	**60 g (2 oz) butter**
Leg stuffing	**1 sprig fresh thyme**
2 large leeks	**1 bay leaf**
1 black Perigord truffle, about 50 g (2 oz)	**150 ml (5 fl oz) white wine**
(optional)	**150 ml (5 fl oz) dry Madeira**
180 g (6 oz) tripe	**300 ml (10 fl oz) Chicken Stock (see p.225)**
90 g (3 oz) veal sweetbreads (optional)	**210 ml (7 fl oz) whipping cream**
Sauce	**lemon juice**
60 g (2 oz) shallots	

Preparing the chicken and stuffing

1. Having removed the legs from the chicken, and the bones from the legs (see above), proceed to remove the wishbones, using poultry scissors.

2. Dice the leeks into 5 mm (½ in) dice, discarding the tough silvery leaves. Boil in salted water until tender. Refresh. Dice the truffle, if using.

3. Cut the tripe into 1 cm (½ in) dice. Blanch, skin and dice the sweetbreads, if using.

4. Mix together the leeks and diced tripe, truffle and sweetbreads, and season well.

5. Push the mixture up into the chicken legs, bringing each thigh round to re-form itself. Half fill the thigh then, with a needle and thread, sew the skin together, bringing both sides of the thigh together and pushing in as much mixture as possible. The result should be a fat chicken leg with no bones in it.

Cooking the chicken

6. Preheat the oven to 220°C (425°F) Gas 7.

7. Season the chicken well, and in the hot butter seal both the legs and breast meat. Place in the preheated oven for 10 minutes.

Making the sauce

8. Peel the shallots and garlic; chop the former, slice the latter. Wash and slice the mushrooms.

9. Melt 30 g (1 oz) of the butter and slowly, without colouring, add the shallots, garlic, thyme, bay leaf and finally the mushrooms. Gently cook until the mushrooms give out a liquid. Increase the heat and drive off the moisture.

10. Add the white wine and boil to reduce by two-thirds, then add the Madeira. Bring to the boil and then cover with the chicken stock. Boil, skim and simmer for 15 minutes.

11. Strain and reduce by half over a high heat.

12. Add 150 ml (5 fl oz) of the cream, bring to the boil, then whisk in the remaining butter.

Season to taste with salt, pepper and lemon juice. Keep hot.

To serve

13. Whip the remaining cream.

14. When the chicken is cooked, remove the breasts from the bone and pull out the threads from the leg meat.

15. On six hot plates, place the breasts cut diagonally into two. Cut the legs into three pieces each, exposing the filling, and place round the breast.

16. Quickly whisk the whipped cream into the hot sauce to give a frothy texture, and spoon over the chicken. Serve immediately.

This can be garnished with fresh pasta or rice.

A MOUSSE OF CREAM CHEESE
WITH RED FRUITS

SERVES 6

*T*his is a light fresh dessert, combining all the red fruits of summer, topped with a crisp lattice tuile.

120 g (4 oz) each of redcurrants, blackcurrants and cherries
120 g (4 oz) each of raspberries, strawberries and wild strawberries
150 ml (5 fl oz) Stock Syrup (see p.249)
icing sugar
Lattice tuiles

110 g (3½ oz) unsalted butter
120 g (4 oz) caster sugar
40 g (1½ oz) plain flour
30 ml (1 fl oz) fresh orange juice
To serve
350 g (12 oz) fromage blanc
6 sprigs fresh mint

Preparing the fruits

1. Wash the redcurrants, blackcurrants and cherries. Remove the stones from the cherries. Place in a bowl.

2. Bring the stock syrup to the boil in a saucepan. Pour the hot syrup over the cherries, redcurrants and blackcurrants and cover with cling film. When the fruit is cold, strain off the syrup, reheat the syrup and cover the fruit again. Leave until cold.

CHEF'S TIP
I 'cook' fruit by pouring hot syrup over them. This ensures that the soft berries do not break up in cooking, but retain their natural shape.

3. Wash the remaining fruit. Hull the strawberries and slice them into quarters. Add the strawberries, raspberries and wild strawberries to the cold syrup and, using a spoon, mix all the fruits together to coat them well.

4. Strain the fruit, retaining the syrup. Liquidise half of the fruit with all the syrup to a smooth purée.

5. Taste the purée. If it is too sharp, add a little icing sugar until the desired sweetness is obtained. Pass the purée through a fine-mesh sieve into the bowl containing the remaining whole red fruits. Gently mix with a spoon and reserve in the refrigerator.

Making the lattice tuiles

6. Melt the butter over a gentle heat, then remove from the heat.

7. Put the caster sugar and plain flour in a bowl. Using a wooden spoon stir in the melted butter, then the orange juice. Refrigerate for an hour before using.

8. Lightly grease a non-stick baking tray, and preheat the oven to 230°C (450°F) Gas 8.

9. Place two balls of the tuile mixture about 4 cm (1½ in) in diameter on to the tray, leaving plenty of room for spreading: they will be approximately 16 cm (6½ in) round when baked. Dip your fingers in a little cold water and flatten the tuile mixture slightly. Place into the oven to bake until golden brown,

about 8 minutes.

10. Remove the tray and leave to cool slightly. Using a wide palette knife remove the tuiles from the tray and place them over upturned ramekins, 7.5 cm (3 in) in diameter. Gently mould the shape of the 'bonnet' around the ramekin and leave to cool. Repeat this baking and shaping process for the other tuiles.

CHEF'S TIP
These tuiles are very fragile, so be careful when handling them. Reserve in an airtight container.

To serve

11. Lay out six plates, place a 6 cm (2¼ in) plain round cutter into the centre of one of them, and spoon in 60 g (2 oz) fromage blanc. Carefully remove the cutter. Repeat this process for the other plates.

12. Spoon the red fruit purée and fruits around each fromage blanc shape.

13. Lightly dust the tuiles with icing sugar and carefully place them over the fromage blanc shapes to cover them like a cloche hat. Place a sprig of mint on to each tuile and serve immediately.

L'Ortolan's Strawberry Cream Cheesecake

An Iced Honeyed Nougat with Dried Apples and Raspberries

Pan-Fried Veal Kidneys in a Port, Tarragon and Mustard Sauce

Salad of Hot Calf's Tongue with Capers and Gherkins

Summer Menu 5

RAVIOLI OF LOBSTER

FILLET OF WELSH LAMB WITH A HERB AND PASTRY CRUST

WHITE CHOCOLATE MOUSSE WRAPPED IN DARK CHOCOLATE TOPPED WITH GLAZED RASPBERRIES

RAVIOLI OF LOBSTER

SERVES 6

The best lobsters are English or Scottish. Avoid buying the cheaper North American type, as they lack the flavour and texture of ours. American lobsters are brown in colour, with orangey feet and underside. British lobsters are blue before cooking. Buy the lobsters live for this dish: check that they are not damaged and do not show any scaling or barnacles on their shells.

CHEF'S TIP
There are two main schools of thought on the subject of killing lobsters. Some say immersing them in boiling court bouillon is the best. Others prefer to bring them gently to the boil, starting the liquid from cold. As we only need to blanch or scald the lobsters in this recipe, not cook them through, I prepare them as for grilling by inserting a knife through the air vent at the top of the head. (Take care not to split the shell.) This method, although unpleasant, must be the quickest and therefore the most humane way of killing them.

2 x 500 g (18 oz) lobsters, live weight (after blanching, shell removed, approx. 400 g/14 oz flesh)
1 quantity *Court Bouillon* or *Nage* (see p.224)
salt and cayenne pepper
lemon juice
240 g (8 oz) Pasta for Ravioli (see p.241)
6 sprigs fresh chervil
Lobster mousse
1 sprig fresh tarragon
110 ml (3½ fl oz) Lobster Consommé (see Consommé of Langoustine, p.55)
1 egg
1 egg yolk
110 ml (3½ fl oz) whipping cream

Lemon and garlic butter

30 g (1 oz) unsalted butter

1 garlic clove

1 sprig fresh tarragon

1 teaspoon lemon juice

Sauce

2 tomatoes

1 fennel bulb

210 ml (7 fl oz) Fish Stock (see p.223)

60 ml (2 fl oz) Tarragon Vinaigrette (see p.234)

Preparing the lobster

1. Pull off the claws and crack them with a meat bat. Cook in boiling *court bouillon* for 60 seconds. Take them out and plunge them directly into cold water. Cook the tail in the same fashion but only for 30 seconds. (The tail shell is half as thick as the claw, thus the cooking time is halved.) When cold, strain off the water.

2. Break open the claws and remove the flesh. Reserve aside in a bowl. Pull the head from the tail. Keep the head and shells for the consommé.

3. To remove the tail flesh, turn the tail over and insert a strong pair of fish scissors at the head of the tail, cutting either side of its flesh. Pull out the tail and with a knife make a shallow incision cutting along the middle to expose a black entrail line. Remove this and discard.

4. Slice one of the lobster tails lengthways into six equal pieces. Reserve aside in a bowl: this will be used to marble the ravioli. In another bowl place the flesh from the four claws and the remaining tail. This will be used to make the mousse.

Preparing the lobster mousse

5. Blanch the tarragon, and then chop it.

6. Add the blanched tarragon to the lobster consommé in a small saucepan. Boil and reduce the consommé until it thickens to a syrup. Take great care not to let it burn. Remove from the stove and with a spatula scrape it on to a plate to cool.

7. Add the lobster flesh – the four claws and one whole tail (total weight approximately 240 g/8 oz) – to a processor bowl (or similar machine). Cut to a smooth paste.

8. When smooth, add 1 teaspoon salt and continue to mix. Stop the machine, remove the bowl and refrigerate it. This is important. Whilst cutting the lobster meat the blade tends to get hot and in turn warms the meat. If this happens the lobster meat will start to cook and when the cream is added, the mousse might split.

9. Place the cold lobster meat back on the machine. Cut the mixture for a further 30 seconds. Add 1 teaspoon lemon juice and scrape in the reduced lobster consommé or *glace*. When thoroughly mixed in, add the egg and egg yolk. Stop the machine and with a spatula clean around the edge of the bowl. Make sure no flesh is trapped (unmixed) under the blades of the machine.

10. Start the machine again and gradually pour in the cream. When this is completely incorporated stop the machine again. Taste the mousse and add a little cayenne, and more salt and lemon juice if necessary.

11. Beat for a further 30 seconds. Remove the bowl and with the aid of a plastic scraper pass the mousse through a fine sieve into a bowl. Reserve aside in the fridge.

Preparing the lemon and garlic butter

12. In a small saucepan gently melt the butter. Peel the garlic and slice into three. Blanch and chop the tarragon. Add the garlic and tarragon to the butter and season with a little salt, a pinch of cayenne and the lemon juice. Keep warm above the stove.

Preparing the ravioli

13. Prepare the pasta paste, then cut it in two. On a pasta machine roll out the paste through the numbers, starting with the thickest (no. 1), gradually working down to the finest (no. 6) on the sliding scale. (Or roll out by hand if you have the patience.)

14. Dust the work top with plain flour and

carefully lay the rolled sheet of paste down. Roll the second half of the ravioli paste in the same fashion.

15. With a knife cut each piece of rolled paste into six equal pieces approximately 15 x 10 cm (6 x 4 in).

16. Remove the lobster mousse from the fridge and transfer to a piping bag with a plain 1.5 cm (¾ in) nozzle. Pipe half of the lobster mousse into the centre of six ravioli bases, leaving a border of paste about 3 cm (1½ in) wide.

17. With the warmed lemon and garlic butter brush the pieces of lobster tail and lay them down on top of the mousse. Pipe the remaining mousse over these.

18. Dip a small brush into cold water and moisten the paste around the edges of the mousse. Carefully lay the remaining pieces of pasta paste on top of the mousse. Shape the ravioli and press around the edge to completely seal. Be careful while doing this not to trap any air in the ravioli pillows or they will burst open on cooking.

19. Cut six butter papers to the required size and shape. Using a fish slice lift the ravioli and lay them down on the papers. Reserve in the fridge to relax for about 15 minutes.

Preparing the sauce

20. Skin, seed and dice the tomatoes and reserve aside in a bowl.

21. Trim and peel the fennel and cut it into small dice. Add the fennel dice to a small pan of boiling water, and cook for 3 minutes. Strain and refresh under cold running water. Strain again, turn the dice out on to a clean kitchen cloth and squeeze dry. Reserve aside in a bowl.

22. In a pan bring the fish stock to the boil and reduce down to a third of its original volume. Remove from the stove.

23. With a whisk, beat the prepared vinaigrette into the reduced fish stock, then add the diced blanched fennel and the raw tomato dice. Check the seasoning, adding salt and pepper to taste. Add a little lemon juice for extra acidity. Keep the sauce warm on the side of the stove but do not re-boil.

Cooking the ravioli

24. Bring a large saucepan, half filled with water, to the boil.

25. Remove the lobster ravioli from the fridge and very carefully turning them upside down, put them into the boiling water. Turn down the flame a little (between boiling and simmer) and cook for 5 minutes. With a fish slice turn them over and cook for a further 5 minutes.

To serve

26. Warm six 28–30 cm (11¼–12 in) plates, and in the centre of each, place the ravioli. Around these spoon 2 large tablespoons of the warm tomato and fennel sauce. Top each ravioli with a sprig of fresh chervil.

As an option I like to mask the ravioli with a dessertspoon of Butter Sauce for Fish (see p.231) and bead a few drops of lobster oil around the plates. This lobster oil is the clear oil which surfaces in the latter stages of the production of a shellfish consommé (see Consommé of Langoustine, p.56).

FILLET OF WELSH LAMB WITH A HERB AND PASTRY CRUST

SERVES 6

*T*his is quite a simple and inexpensive dish, and very tasty. It can look superb if presented and cooked correctly. Ask the butcher to remove the fillets if you do not fancy doing it yourself, but do keep the bones as they make a good sauce. You'll need to buy a whole best end, the first seven ribs on both sides.

1 x 2.5 kg (5½ lb) best end of lamb	*Sauce*
salt and pepper	150 g (5 oz) *Mirepoix* (see p.239)
120 ml (4 fl oz) cooking oil	2 tomatoes
Herb and pastry crust	6 garlic cloves
English or French mustard	30 g (1 oz) tomato paste
1 quantity Parslied Breadcrumbs (see p.240)	1 sprig fresh thyme
350 g (12 oz) Puff Pastry (see p.242)	1 bay leaf
1 egg	1.25 litres (2 pints) Chicken Stock (see p.225)
	a few drops of lemon juice

Preparing the lamb and crust

1. Remove the lamb fillets from the bones or ask the butcher to do it. Take out and discard the silver membrane from the fillets. Chop the bones and set aside for the sauce.
2. Season the fillets with salt and pepper and seal quickly all over in 60 ml (2 fl oz) of the hot oil. Cool and dry on kitchen paper.
3. Spread the fillets all over with a thin layer of mustard, then roll in the parslied breadcrumbs. Place to one side.
4. Roll the puff pastry out into two equal-sized rectangles, 28 x 20 cm (11¼ x 8 in).
5. Place a lamb fillet in the middle of each pastry rectangle, and neatly wrap, leaving the join on the bottom to stop it undoing itself.
6. Brush well with beaten egg and place in the refrigerator. It can only stay there for a short time – 2–3 hours maximum – or else the lamb starts to bleed and will ruin the pastry.

Making the sauce

7. Heat up the remaining cooking oil in a roasting tray. Add the lamb bones, and sauté until golden brown, about 10 minutes. Remove with a slotted spoon, and place in a large saucepan.

8. Add the *mirepoix* vegetables to the roasting pan and sauté to brown evenly. Add to the bones, again using a slotted spoon.
9. Squash the tomatoes, and peel and chop the garlic, then add, along with the tomato paste, thyme and bay leaf, to the bones. Cover with chicken stock, bring to the boil, skim, and simmer for 1 hour.
10. Strain through a fine strainer or muslin and then boil to reduce by half. (A few more cloves of chopped garlic and a little thyme may be added to enhance the flavour.) If the stock is passed through a muslin cloth it will trap all the tomato paste sediment, but the stock should remain clear and a lovely light red colour. Taste for seasoning and add salt, pepper and lemon juice to taste. Keep warm.

Cooking the lamb

11. Preheat the oven to 230°C (450°F) Gas 8.
12. Place the egg-washed, pastry-wrapped lamb fillets on a greased baking tray, and bake in the preheated oven, turning once for an even colour and checking that the pastry does not burn – approximately 8 minutes for rare, 10 minutes if you like the lamb pink, or longer if you like it well done. Be careful, though, to

turn the oven down if you are cooking it longer, as the pastry will not stand the high heat and will burn.

To serve

13. With a serrated knife, cut through the pastry and hot lamb into six large nuggets. Repeat with the other fillet.

14. Turning the slices uppermost so as to expose the pink lamb, green herbs and white pastry, arrange on warm plates, two per plate. Spoon over the sauce and serve at once.

WHITE CHOCOLATE MOUSSE WRAPPED IN DARK CHOCOLATE TOPPED WITH GLAZED RASPBERRIES

SERVES 8

This is a dish for those people who don't particularly care for milk or dark chocolate, but who adore white chocolate. The raspberries here add another flavour and texture, but also cut the richness of the mousse.

500 g (18 oz) raspberries
140 ml (4½ fl oz) Stock Syrup (see p.249)
Mousse
190 g (6¼ oz) white chocolate
360 ml (12 fl oz) whipping cream
1 egg yolk
20 g (⅔ oz) icing sugar

8 x 4 cm (1¾ in) round discs Biscuit Sponge (see p.245)
75 g (2½ oz) dark chocolate
To serve
510 ml (17 fl oz) Vanilla Egg Custard Sauce (see p.250)
8 sprigs fresh mint

Preparing the raspberries

1. Carefully wash the raspberries and drain them in a colander.

2. Place half the raspberries and 110 ml (3½ fl oz) of the stock syrup in a liquidiser and purée until smooth. Strain through a fine-mesh sieve into a bowl.

3. Measure out 30 ml (1 fl oz) of this raspberry purée and add the remaining stock syrup. Blend together and reserve separately.

Preparing the mousse

4. Chop the white chocolate finely and place into a bowl.

5. Bring 60 ml (2 fl oz) of the whipping cream to the boil in a saucepan and pour boiling over the chopped white chocolate. Stir until smooth.

6. Stir the egg yolk and icing sugar into this, then leave to cool.

7. Whisk the remaining cream to a stiff peak, then carefully fold into the white chocolate mixture. This is the mousse.

Assembling the dessert

8. Place eight 6 x 3 cm (2½ x 1¼ in) ring moulds on a tray lined with greaseproof paper. Place a dessertspoon of white chocolate mousse in the base of each mould.

9. Soak the biscuit sponge discs in the small quantity of raspberry purée and stock syrup. Place these discs into the centre of the moulds, gently pressing them level into the mousse.

10. Put 3 dessertspoons of raspberry purée in a bowl and add 40 of the whole raspberries. Glaze them by gently mixing with a spoon, then place five on top of each biscuit disc.

11. Fill the moulds with the remaining white chocolate mousse, then place into the freezer and freeze for 3 hours.

'Wrapping' the mousses

12. Chop the dark chocolate, place in a bowl, and melt over hot water.

13. Prepare eight plastic bands for wrapping the mousse in dark chocolate. Cut eight strips of clean, flexible plastic 26 cm (10½ in) in length, by 3.25 cm (1¼ in) high.

14. Remove the mousses from the freezer when frozen. To unmould, rub the outside of the ring moulds in your hands to free the edges and gently ease the mousses out on to a clean work surface.

15. Using a palette knife, spread some of the melted dark chocolate over one of the plastic bands. Carefully pick up the band and wrap it around a mousse, leaving a little overlap. Repeat this process for the other mousses, return them to a tray, and refrigerate for a further 2 hours.

To serve

16. Lay out eight plates, and place a tablespoon of raspberry purée into the centre of each. Pour the vanilla egg custard around the outside of the raspberry purée.

17. Add the remaining raspberries to the remaining purée and mix together, being careful to keep the raspberries whole.

18. Remove the mousses from the fridge and place the remaining glazed raspberries neatly on top.

19. Carefully peel away the plastic, leaving a chocolate band around the outside of the mousses. Using a palette knife carefully lift and place the mousses into the centre of the plates.

20. Using the point of a knife, feather the raspberry purée into the vanilla egg custard. Place a sprig of mint on to each mousse, and serve.

If desired, *langue de chat* handkerchief tuiles dusted with icing sugar can be served with this dessert (see p.246).

Summer Menu 6

AVOCADO PEAR SALAD WITH CRAB AND PINK GRAPEFRUIT

ROAST SQUAB PIGEON WITH PUY LENTILS AND A HONEY SAUCE

L'ORTOLAN'S STRAWBERRY CREAM CHEESECAKE

AVOCADO PEAR SALAD WITH CRAB AND PINK GRAPEFRUIT

SERVES 6

This is an excellent light dish for the summer, and served in this fashion is very refreshing. Although very simple, it is composed of several stages, each of which must be carried out properly. The best avocado pears come from Africa, the West Indies, America and Israel, but many other countries are now producing and exporting a number of different varieties. The most important thing to remember when purchasing is that the pears are ripe and unblemished. Gently press a thumb just below the top of the pear; if it feels slightly soft, it is ripe.

1 x 1.4 kg (3¼ lb) crab (a cock or male has the most meat)

2 litres (3½ pints) *Court Bouillon* or *Nage* (see p.224)

3 x 130 g (4¼ oz) ripe avocado pears

1 pink grapefruit

Salad

60 g (2 oz) prepared lettuce leaves

1 shallot

a small handful of chives

240 ml (8 fl oz) Tarragon Vinaigrette (see p.234)

Tomato mayonnaise

about ¼ cucumber

60 ml (2 fl oz) Mayonnaise (see p.234)

1 tablespoon tomato ketchup

1 teaspoon Cognac

salt and pepper

lemon juice and cayenne pepper to taste

1 small eating apple

Cooking the crab

1. Cook the crab in the boiling *court bouillon* for approximately 15 minutes. Remove to a tray and leave to cool.

Preparing the salad

2. While the crab is cooling prepare the salads. Use four different types of lettuce: for colour and flavour I like to use yellow frisée, radicchio, and corn salad and, for its peppery flavour, rocket. Wash and thoroughly dry, and reserve aside in a bowl.

3. Peel and finely chop the shallot. Chop the chives. These are added to the salad just before serving.

Making the tomato mayonnaise

4. Peel the cucumber and slice in two. Discard the seeds and sprinkle the cucumber with a teaspoon of salt. Leave for about 10 minutes to draw out all the impurities from the cucumber.

5. Spoon the mayonnaise into a bowl and add the tomato ketchup and Cognac. Whisk together until fully mixed. Check the seasoning and finish with a little lemon juice and a pinch of cayenne.

6. Peel and core the apple, then chop about 30 g (1 oz) of it into small dice. Add to the tomato mayonnaise.

7. Wash the cucumber, dry and dice as for the apple. Again stir this into the sauce.

To finish

8. The crab should now be cold. Pull off its claws and with a meat bat crack them open and remove the white meat. Do not allow any shell splinters to fall into the meat. Repeat this process for the legs. Place all the crab meat in a bowl and mix with the tomato mayonnaise. Check the seasoning, then refrigerate.

CHEF'S TIP

The box or inner shell of the crab contains a little more white meat but in the main is mostly dark or lung meat, thus for this particular dish it will not be necessary to break the main shell. Freeze this, as it can be used when making a crab soup or bisque.

9. Cut the avocados in two, remove the stones and discard. Peel and lay the six halves down on a tray. With a filleting knife, slice each half about five or six times, from bottom to top, leaving about 1 cm (½ in) from the top intact. The narrower end should remain uncut. Then gently press the cut plump ends open to form a fan shape. To stop any discoloration I brush them with a little lemon juice or vinaigrette.

10. Peel and segment the pink grapefruit and reserve aside.

11. Add the chopped shallot and chives to the salad, and bind the leaves with the tarragon vinaigrette.

To serve

12. Lay out six large plates and into the centre of each spoon a large mound of crab mayonnaise. Cut two segments of grapefruit in two lengthways, and lay these around the base of the crab meat.

13. Place the fanned avocado on top of the mound of crab, and carefully arrange the salad leaves around the outer border. Serve.

As an option sprinkle a little tomato dice around the plates for added colour and acidity.

ROAST SQUAB PIGEON WITH PUY LENTILS AND A HONEY SAUCE

SERVES 6

*T*he pigeons we use in the restaurant are bred for us in Kent. The breeding pair was bought from France and the pigeons produced are some of the finest. The skin is buttery with small pockets of fat on the breast. They are pale in colour and have a delicate flavour all of their own, as opposed to wild or wood pigeons that are dark fleshed and stronger in flavour. Squab are about four or five times the price of wood pigeons and are therefore more difficult to buy but should be available from a quality butcher.

6 squab pigeons
vegetable oil
salt and pepper
Sauce
240 g (8 oz) chicken bones
30 ml (1 fl oz) sherry vinegar
60 g (2 oz) honey
60 g (2 oz) shallots
2 garlic cloves
½ celery stalk
½ leek
1 sprig fresh thyme
1 bay leaf
1 litre (1¾ pints) Chicken Stock (see p.225)

Lentils
90 g (3 oz) Puy lentils
1 bacon bone (optional)
1 garlic clove
a few thyme leaves
½ bay leaf
510 ml (17 fl oz) Chicken Stock (see p.225) or water
Garnishes
2 large potatoes
30 g (1 oz) unsalted butter
60 g (2 oz) baby spinach leaves
60 g (2 oz) *foie gras* (optional)

Preparing the pigeons and sauce

1. Remove the wing tips and wishbones from the pigeons. Chop these and the chicken bones coarsely.

2. Heat 60 ml (2 fl oz) of the vegetable oil in a large heavy pan. When smoking, add the bones to the pan, being careful not to splash the hot oil. Cook until brown, stirring often to obtain an even colour.

3. Meanwhile, in another large saucepan bring the vinegar and honey to the boil. Reduce to a syrup.

4. When the bones are brown, remove with a slotted spoon, and add to the vinegar and honey pan. Stir until coated with the syrupy glaze.

5. Peel and quarter the shallots. Peel the garlic. Coarsely chop the celery and leek. Add all of these to the bones, along with the thyme and bay leaf. Cover with the stock, bring to the boil and skim. Simmer for an hour.

Preparing the lentils and potato galettes

6. Place the lentils in a large pan with the bacon bone, garlic, thyme and bay leaf. Cover with the stock or water, bring to the boil, cover and simmer until the lentils are tender, about 40 minutes. When cooked remove from the heat and keep warm.

7. Peel the potatoes, then shred them on a mandoline.

8. Brush a film of oil over a small skillet pan, and when smoking add a sixth of the shredded potato, spreading a thin layer over the bottom of the pan. Fry until golden brown, then carefully turn over with a palette knife. Continue to cook until an even colour is obtained on either side. Make five more potato galettes in the same way, one per person. Keep warm.

Cooking the pigeon

9. Preheat the oven to 220°C (425°F) Gas 7.

10. Season each pigeon with salt and pepper and then place them into a hot pan or roasting tray with 1 tablespoon oil. Seal the breasts first, then turn the birds over until an even colour is achieved all over.

11. Place the birds on their backs and roast in the preheated oven for 10 minutes if a pink breast is required. Cook for longer if you like the meat well done. When cooked to the desired degree, remove from the oven and allow to relax.

To finish and serve

12. Strain the stock and place into a reducing pan. Skim off all surfacing fat and reduce over a high flame to half its original volume.

13. Bring 150 ml (5 fl oz) of water to the boil in a smallish pan, and add some salt, pepper and the butter. Whisk until emulsified and then plunge in the baby spinach leaves. Remove from the heat.

14. If using *foie gras*, dice it into 1 cm (½ in) squares and season. Keep cool.

15. Remove the legs from the pigeon, and remove the breasts whole. Carefully remove the thigh bones from each leg. Keep warm.

16. Season the sauce to taste; warm the potato galettes through; reheat the lentils.

17. If using *foie gras*, heat up a large skillet pan, and quickly fry the *foie gras* cubes for about 10 seconds only. Drain on kitchen paper.

18. Scatter the lentils and hot foie gras cubes around each plate. In the centre of each plate place first the pigeon legs and then the breast meat on top to create height.

19. Around the pigeon drop hot leaves of spinach, then spoon around the sauce and finally top with the hot potato galette. Serve at once.

L'ORTOLAN'S STRAWBERRY CREAM CHEESECAKE

SERVES 8

*T*his is a light strawberry dessert made with fromage blanc. It can be made as small individual puddings ideally, or as a large cake, when it can be used as a birthday cake.

8 x 6 cm (2½ in) discs Biscuit Sponge (see p.245)	**Mousse filling**
	150 g (5 oz) fromage blanc
30 g (1 oz) redcurrant or strawberry jam	120 ml (4 fl oz) whipping cream
40 small strawberries	70 ml (2½ fl oz) Stock Syrup (see p.249)
20 g (¾ oz) icing sugar	1 egg yolk
Sablé biscuits	1½ gelatine leaves, soaked in cold water to soften
120 g (4 oz) plain flour	**Strawberry sauce**
75 g (2½ oz) caster sugar	110 g (4 oz) very ripe strawberries
120 g (4 oz) unsalted butter	60 g (2 oz) icing sugar
1 egg yolk	*To finish*
	20 g (½ oz) shelled pistachio nuts
	75 g (2½ oz) white almond paste or white marzipan
	8 sprigs fresh mint

Baking the sablé biscuits

1. Place the plain flour and caster sugar into a bowl. Dice the butter into 1 cm (½ in) cubes and place in the bowl. Rub the ingredients together with your fingertips until resembling fine breadcrumbs. Mix in the egg yolk to bind the mixture. Place the mixture in a bowl, cover the surface with cling film and refrigerate for 1 hour.

2. Preheat the oven to 200°C (400°F) Gas 6, and line a baking tray with greaseproof paper.

3. Remove the sablé mixture from the refrigerator and roll out on a lightly floured surface to 5 mm (¼ in) thick. Cut eight rounds of sablé using a 6 cm (2½ in) plain cutter and place them on to the lined tray. Bake in the preheated oven for 15–20 minutes until they look dry, not coloured.

4. Remove from the oven and sprinkle each sablé with a little extra caster sugar. Leave to cool before attempting to pick them up, as they are very fragile at this stage. Reserve aside.

Lining the moulds

5. Using a palette knife, evenly spread the jam on to one side of each biscuit sponge disc. Place on top of the sablé biscuits, jam side down.

6. Place eight 6 cm (2½ in) ring moulds on a tray. Place the biscuit sponge and sablé 'sandwiches' into the base of each mould, sablé to the bottom.

7. Wash and hull 32 of the small strawberries (reserve the remainder for garnishing). Slice them in half lengthways and place in a bowl. Roll them in the sifted icing sugar.

CHEF'S TIP
Rolling the cut strawberries in icing sugar will improve their flavour, and when they are in the mousse will draw some of the water from them, which in turn will be absorbed into the biscuit sponge base.

8. Line each ring mould with the strawberries by gently pressing them, sliced face against the inside of the mould, leaving the centre empty for the cream filling. Reserve any strawberries and juice left over from this operation, as these can be used in the sauce.

Preparing the mousse filling

9. Whisk the fromage blanc in a bowl until smooth. Pour the cream into another bowl and whisk until it holds a peak. Reserve both aside.

10. Put the stock syrup in a saucepan and bring to the boil. Put the egg yolk in a bowl and whisk in the boiled syrup until the mixture is a white and thick sabayon.

11. Pour 20 ml (⅔ fl oz) of water into the saucepan and warm over the stove. Add the soaked gelatine and stir until it has completely dissolved. Fold this liquid, a little at a time, into the fromage blanc until fully incorporated. Then fold in the sabayon followed, lastly, by the whipped cream.

12. Spoon the finished mousse into the prepared ring moulds, level with a palette knife and refrigerate for 4 hours.

Making the strawberry sauce

13. Wash and hull the ripe strawberries, then slice in half and place in a liquidiser. Add any strawberries left over from the construction of the mousses. Add the icing sugar and liquidise for 1 minute until smooth. Strain the sauce through a fine-mesh sieve into a bowl. Reserve in the fridge.

Preparing the almond and pistachio tops

14. Scald the pistachios for about 1 minute in a saucepan of boiling water. Remove from the heat and refresh in cold water. Strain into a sieve and lay the pistachios on a clean tea towel. Rub in the cloth to remove their skins, then finely chop.

15. Knead the nuts into the almond paste or white marzipan. Roll this out thinly on a work surface sprinkled with a little icing sugar, to about 1 mm (¹⁄₁₆ in). Cut out circles using a 6 cm (2½ in) plain cutter. Lightly dust a tray with icing sugar and using a palette knife place the discs on to the tray. Leave them uncovered to dry a little for about 1 hour.

To serve

16. Lay out eight plates, and spoon a little strawberry sauce into the centre of each.

17. Remove the mousses from the fridge. Rub the outside of the ring moulds with a cloth dipped in hot water and remove the ring moulds. Carefully place a mousse into the centre of each plate. Place a pistachio and almond lid on top of each mousse.

18. Roll the 8 reserved strawberries in a little extra caster sugar, then cut them into half lengthways with the green stalk remaining. Place two halves on top of the centre of each almond and pistachio top. Push a sprig of mint into the side of the mousses and serve immediately.

Instead of rolling in the caster sugar, I often dip the halved garnish strawberries in caramel (see p.139 for a recipe), and decorate the top with a little edible gold leaf.

CHEF'S TIP
If you want to make a birthday cake using this recipe, proceed as instructed but using a 16 cm (6½ in) ring mould. Pipe a birthday message on to the almond and marzipan top.

Summer Menu 7

RATATOUILLE

RUMP STEAK WITH CAFÉ DE PARIS BUTTER

AN ICED HONEYED NOUGAT WITH DRIED APPLE AND RASPBERRIES

RATATOUILLE

SERVES 6

*T*his is a dish from the south of France, wonderful for a summer lunch in the garden. The word 'ratatouille' means a stew, an *étuvée* of vegetables, *sauté à la niçoise*. There are many different variations of this dish according to the locality or region.

You may add many extra ingredients when preparing ratatouille, such as artichoke bottoms, bacon or anchovies. Some people sprinkle grated Gruyère or Parmesan over it and glaze it under the grill as a hot hors-d'oeuvre. Others prefer it cold. It can be bound with rice and meat and used to stuff whole peppers, or used as a hot garnish for pork or beef. I prefer it cold with black olives and fillets of anchovies.

210 g (7 oz) onions
150 g (5 oz) red peppers
110 g (3½ oz) yellow peppers
1 medium fennel bulb
salt
300 g (10 oz) courgettes
a little plain flour
110 ml (3½ fl oz) olive oil
110 g (3½ oz) aubergine
1 beef tomato, or 3 small plum tomatoes
3 garlic cloves
60 g (2 oz) smoked bacon rashers

1 bay leaf
1 sprig fresh thyme
1 teaspoon white peppercorns, finely crushed
60 g (2 oz) tomato paste
110 ml (3½ fl oz) white wine
110 ml (3½ fl oz) Tomato Sauce (see p.232)
1 sprig fresh basil
Optional garnish
24 black olives
12 anchovy fillets, drained
garlic bread

Preparing the vegetables and bacon

1. Peel and dice the onions and reserve aside in a bowl.

2. Cut the red and yellow peppers into four. Remove the seeds and core, then peel and dice as for the onions. In a small saucepan of boiling water cook them for 2 minutes, then strain and refresh in a bowl of cold water. Strain again, and turn them out on to a kitchen towel to dry.

3. Top and tail the fennel bulb. Cut it in two, remove the core, and separate and trim the leaves. Dice as for the other vegetables. Cook for 4 minutes in boiling salted water, strain, refresh and place on a cloth to dry.

4. Wash and trim the courgettes. With a canelle knife, cut decorative channels lengthways around each courgette. Slice the courgettes into 5 mm (¼ in) circles and coat lightly with seasoned flour. In a frying pan, in 30 ml (1 fl oz) of the olive oil, fry to a golden brown colour, then turn out onto a tray to drain.

5. Dice the aubergine and, in a large frying pan, heat another 30 ml (1 fl oz) of the olive oil. When the pan is smoking, throw in the diced aubergine. Toss in the oil for 2 minutes until golden brown, then remove from the stove and turn out on to kitchen paper to drain.

6. Blanch, skin and seed the tomato(es). Dice the flesh, and reserve aside.

7. Peel and chop the garlic cloves. To chop to a fine paste, just add 10 g (⅓ oz) of salt to the garlic when chopping. Garlic is 90 per cent oil, and the salt helps to absorb this oil so that a smooth paste can be obtained.

8. Remove the bacon rind and slice the bacon into lardons or strips approximately 2 cm (¾ in) long and 5 mm (¼ in) thick. In a small pan cover the bacon with cold water and bring to the boil. Remove all the surfacing scum with a ladle and as the water boils take off the stove and strain. Reserve aside.

Cooking the ratatouille

9. Heat the remaining olive oil in a large thick-bottomed saucepan. Add the diced onions and fry, stirring all the time, until soft, about 3 minutes (do not colour).

10. Add the bacon, bay leaf, thyme, finely crushed peppercorns and tomato paste. Cook for about 5 minutes, but take care not to burn the paste on to the bottom of the pan.

11. Add the white wine and reduce the liquid until it has fully evaporated.

12. Stir in the garlic and prepared tomato sauce, and continue boiling and reducing the mixture to a paste.

13. Stir in the fennel and the red and yellow peppers and continue cooking for a further 5 minutes.

14. Add the courgettes and bring the ratatouille to the boil. Add the aubergines. Stir and check the seasoning. Quickly turn the ratatouille out on to a tray to cool.

15. Pick the fresh leaves of basil from the stalk. Roll them together and with some kitchen scissors snip over the mixture.

To serve

16. Spoon the ratatouille on to your hors-d'oeuvre plates. If using, garnish the top with black olives. I like the huge ones from Provence, which are marinated in olive oil and rosemary. Top the dish with anchovy fillets and serve toasted garlic bread as an accompaniment.

RUMP STEAK WITH CAFÉ DE PARIS BUTTER

SERVES 6

*I*n this recipe we are using a rump steak, but the delicious butter can be used with various other meats like chicken, fillet steak etc., and also grilled fish dishes. The butter is beaten until it is very light and egg yolks are included to help the finished butter glaze under a hot grill. I have included a recipe for red wine sauce here as well, which is optional.

6 x 225 g (7½ oz) rump steaks	**Café de Paris butter**
salt and pepper	240 g (8 oz) unsalted butter
Red wine sauce (optional)	2 shallots
60 g (2 oz) shallots	1 garlic clove
3 garlic cloves	1 small sprig fresh thyme
240 g (8 oz) mushrooms	½ bay leaf
15 g (½ oz) fresh tarragon	30 g (1 oz) parsley
120 g (4 oz) butter	1 teaspoon capers
1 sprig fresh thyme	3 gherkins
½ bay leaf	2 anchovy fillets
30 ml (1 fl oz) port	6 tarragon leaves
300 ml (10 fl oz) red wine	30 ml (1 fl oz) white wine
300 ml (10 fl oz) Chicken Stock (see p.225)	1 teaspoon curry paste
30 ml (1 fl oz) Meat Glaze (see p.226)	2 egg yolks
	a pinch of cayenne pepper
	juice of ½ lemon

Making the red wine sauce (optional)

1. Peel and slice the shallots and garlic. Wash and slice the mushrooms. Blanch the tarragon.
2. Melt half the butter in a large shallow pan and add the shallots, garlic, tarragon, thyme and bay leaf. Cook over a gentle heat without colouring until the onions are opaque.
3. Add the mushrooms and cook more rapidly until all the moisture has been driven off.
4. Add the port, bring to the boil, then add the red wine. Bring to the boil again rapidly, and reduce by half.
5. Add the stock and the meat glaze, bring to the boil, then skim and simmer for 20 minutes.
6. Pass through a fine sieve, pressing the mushrooms to extract all the stock. Discard the mushrooms. Re-boil the stock, skim, then reduce by half and taste for seasoning.
7. Over the heat, whisk in the remaining butter, diced, until emulsified. When satisfied, remove from the heat and keep warm.

Making the Café de Paris butter

8. Chop the butter into cubes. Peel and chop the shallots and garlic. Pick the leaves of the thyme from the stalks, and finely chop the bay leaf. Separately, chop the parsley, capers, gherkins and anchovy. Blanch and chop the tarragon.
9. Place the chopped butter in a liquidiser and beat quickly until it turns white and fluffy. This may take about 10 minutes, but is necessary for perfection. (If the butter tends to stick to the side of the bowl, heat a little water and dip the bowl in it to warm the edges, or scrape the sides with a spatula.)
10. Meanwhile, place the shallots and garlic in a pan with a small quantity of the butter and cook gently until opaque, but with no colour.
11. Add the white wine and reduce by half, then add the curry paste and cook for 2 minutes.
12. Add the thyme leaves and finely chopped bay leaf, and continue cooking for 2 more minutes, then remove from the heat. Allow to cool.

13. If the butter is now white, add to it the chopped parsley, capers, gherkins, anchovy, tarragon, the egg yolks, cayenne pepper and finally the lemon juice.

14. Season with salt and pepper and add the shallot mixture. Mix well and taste for final completion. Place a small spoonful under a hot grill to see if it glazes as it should. If it does not, another yolk may be required, but if the recipe has been followed and the butter is beaten white, then it will glaze perfectly.

15. Place a piece of greaseproof paper on a table top and place the butter along the middle. Roll up the paper, turning the butter into a roll. Twist the edges and refrigerate. (The butter can be frozen at this stage and used at a later date.)

To cook and serve

16. Season the rump steaks with salt and pepper and seal on both sides in a hot pan. Cook to the required degree – 2 minutes each side for rare, 3 for medium.

17. Re-heat the sauce.

18. When the steaks are cooked, cut 1 cm (½ in) circles from the butter and place two pieces on each steak. Put under a hot grill and glaze. This should take only a minute. The butter should be golden brown and coating the top of the steak.

19. Place the steaks down on hot plates, spoon round a little of the red wine sauce, and serve.

We like to garnish the steaks with watercress and crisp potatoes, but this is optional.

An Iced Honeyed Nougat with Dried Apple and Raspberries

SERVES 8

*T*his recipe may seem complicated but all the different stages can be prepared in advance and brought together at the last moment.

Melrose apples are an American eating variety – large, red and perfumed. They keep their shape beautifully during cooking.

Apple slices and purée	**3 egg whites**
4 Melrose apples	**270 ml (9 fl oz) whipping cream**
110 ml (3½ fl oz) Stock Syrup (see p.249)	**60 g (2 oz) Nougatine (see p.248)**
juice of ½ lemon	***Raspberry purée and garnish***
Nougat parfait	**350 g (12 oz) raspberries**
30 g (1 oz) caster sugar	**20 g (⅔ oz) icing sugar**
60 g (2 oz) honey (choose a good quality one)	**8 sprigs fresh mint**
2 teaspoons liquid glucose	

Preparing and drying the apple slices

1. Wash the apples, and cut three of them into halves horizontally. Remove the cores, using a parisian scoop or cutter, then slice across the apple halves as thin as paper, using a razor-sharp knife.

2. Place the stock syrup and lemon juice into a bowl. Soak the apple slices in the syrup, just to coat them.

3. Preheat the oven to 120°C (250°F) Gas ½ , and line a couple of large baking trays with silicone paper.

4. Take the apple slices out of the syrup and piece by piece place them on to the baking trays. Arrange the slices, slightly overlapping each other, into 9 cm (3½ in) diameter circles.

You will need 24 circles in all. Reserve the syrup and any leftover slices of apple for the purée.

5. Place the tray into the preheated oven and bake for approximately 1 hour. The circles of slices will lift cleanly off the paper and will harden when cool. Reserve.

Preparing and cooking the apple purée

6. Peel, core and chop the remaining apple into 1 cm (½ in) cubes.

7. In a stainless-steel saucepan mix the reserved syrup, remaining apple slices and the cubed apple. Bring to the boil, reduce the heat and simmer for 5 minutes. Remove from the heat.

8. In a liquidiser liquidise to a smooth pulp, then pass through a stainless-steel sieve into a bowl. Reserve and leave to get cold.

Preparing the nougat parfait

9. Place the sugar, honey and liquid glucose in a saucepan, bring to the boil, then reduce the heat and boil slowly for 2 minutes. Remove from the heat.

10. In an electric mixer bowl whisk the egg whites to a stiff peak. Pour in the boiled sugar and honey mixture, and whisk this honey-flavoured meringue until cold. Reserve aside.

11. In a bowl, whisk the cream to a soft peak consistency. Crush the nougatine. Using a spatula gently fold the honey meringue mixture into the cream, then gently fold in the crushed nougatine.

12. Line a tray with greaseproof paper, and on it place eight ring moulds 6 cm (2½ in) in diameter, 3 cm (1¼ in) high. Fill them with the finished nougat parfait mixture. Freeze for 3 hours before using.

Preparing the raspberry purée

13. Carefully wash and drain the raspberries, then place a quarter of them in a liquidiser. Add the icing sugar, and liquidise until smooth. Pass the purée through a fine-mesh sieve into a bowl, and discard the trapped pips. Place the remaining raspberries into a separate bowl, and reserve in the refrigerator.

To serve

14. Lay out eight plates and spoon three pools of apple purée, at equal distances from each other, around the edges. Place a dried apple circle in the centre of the plates.

15. Remove the frozen parfaits from the freezer and gently push them out of the ring moulds on top of the apple circles. Place another dried apple circle on top of this.

16. Gently mix the reserved raspberries into the raspberry purée. Place one coated raspberry between each pool of apple purée, then place the remaining raspberries on top of the apple circles. Finally place another apple circle on top. Place a mint leaf beside the raspberries and serve immediately.

CHEF'S TIP

If the apple slices become soft (due to humidity) place them back into a hot oven for 1 minute. This will bring the crispness back.

Summer Menu 8

BREAST OF GUINEA FOWL
WITH A LIME GLAZE

PAN-FRIED VEAL KIDNEYS IN A PORT,
TARRAGON AND MUSTARD SAUCE

CHARLOTTE OF BLUEBERRIES

BREAST OF GUINEA FOWL WITH A LIME GLAZE

SERVES 6

In the hot summer months, what nicer way to start a meal than with a cold light salad of guinea fowl sharpened with a little lime. Like a chaudfroid, this is quite a simple dish, and should excite the appetite in preparation for the main course. Guinea fowl are readily available in all good supermarkets, usually reared in France or Belgium. They are not too expensive, and taste like a gamey chicken.

6 guinea fowl breasts	**3 gelatine leaves (optional)**
4 garlic cloves	*Salad*
120 g (4 oz) white button mushrooms	**180 g (6 oz) mixed salad leaves (to include**
600 ml (1 pint) strong Chicken Stock (see p.225)	**chicory, oakleaf, frisée, lamb's lettuce)**
30 g (1 oz) fresh tarragon	**2 shallots**
150 ml (5 fl oz) whipping cream	**6 tomatoes**
salt and pepper	**90 ml (3 fl oz) Tarragon Vinaigrette (see p.234)**
2 limes	

Preparing the guinea fowl and glaze

1. Remove the bones from the guinea fowl breasts, if there are any, and at an angle cut the breasts into three.
2. Peel and slice the garlic. Wash and finely slice the mushrooms.

3. Bring the chicken stock to the boil and skim if necessary, then add the garlic and the guinea fowl pieces. Poach gently for 5 minutes until just cooked. Remove with a slotted spoon and place on a wire rack to cool.
4. Add the sliced mushrooms and tarragon to

the boiling stock, and boil to reduce rapidly by two-thirds, skimming off any scum.

5. Add the cream, bring to the boil, then allow to simmer for a few minutes before passing through a fine sieve. Season with salt and pepper.

6. Squeeze one of the limes into the stock and taste.

7. If the stock is good and strong, no gelatine should be necessary as it will set on its own. Place a small quantity in the refrigerator to test how firmly, if at all, it will set. If it doesn't, soak the gelatine leaves in cold water until soft, and then mix thoroughly into the warm stock. If the stock still will not set, add more gelatine but 3 leaves should be more than enough. Set the stock to cool, stirring every now and again to prevent a skin forming.

To garnish and serve

8. When the guinea fowl is cool, place the wire rack on a tray. Spoon the now cold stock over the breasts, coating them evenly. The first coat may not adhere very well, but do not dismay! Retrieve the stock from the tray underneath, and once a layer of stock on the breasts has set, repeat the process until each piece is completely covered with the creamy

stock. Place in the refrigerator to set.

9. Meanwhile, carefully peel the zest from the remaining lime and very finely shred it, making sure the bitter pith is removed first. Plunge the lime zest into a pan of boiling salted water and cook rapidly until tender, about 5 minutes. The salt helps to keep its colour. Refresh under cold water and drain.

10. Wash and dry the salad leaves. Separate the chicory leaves, and chop the centre, leaving about six of the larger leaves whole. Peel and finely chop the shallots. Blanch, skin and seed the tomatoes, then dice the flesh.

11. Place the clean salad leaves in a large bowl, then add the chopped shallots and toss with most of the vinaigrette.

12. Decoratively arrange the salad leaves in the centre of six large plates, placing the chopped chicory heart on the bottom and the larger leaves around.

13. Sprinkle the tomato dice with the remaining vinaigrette and place three piles on each plate, spaced equally.

14. In between the tomatoes, position the guinea fowl breast pieces, and carefully drape over each a cross of the cooked lime zest. The dish is now ready to eat.

PAN-FRIED VEAL KIDNEYS IN A PORT, TARRAGON AND MUSTARD SAUCE

SERVES 6

*T*here are numerous ways of cooking kidneys, but this is the most direct and the quickest. All the lovely juices are trapped inside, and the kidneys are most succulent.

When buying kidneys, try to buy them enclosed in their fat. The kidney itself should be a milky colour, not dark like an ox kidney. There should be very little smell when breaking open the fat and on no account buy one that has been frozen.

3 milk-fed veal kidneys, in their fat	60 ml (2 fl oz) ruby port
30 ml (1 fl oz) clarified butter	450 ml (15 fl oz) Chicken Stock (see p.225)
(see Chef's Tip, p.15) or oil	30 ml (1 fl oz) Meat Glaze (optional, see p.226)
salt and pepper	60 ml (2 fl oz) whipping cream
Sauce	30 g (1 oz) Dijon mustard
120 g (4 oz) shallots	1 teaspoon tinned soft green peppercorns,
4 garlic cloves	drained
60 g (2 oz) fresh tarragon	lemon juice
450 g (1 lb) white mushrooms	*Garnishes*
45 g (1½ oz) butter	275 g (9 oz) basmati rice
1 sprig fresh thyme	500 g (18 oz) raw spinach leaves
1 bay leaf	½ garlic clove
120 ml (4 fl oz) dry white wine	15 g (½ oz) butter

Preparing the kidneys

1. Carefully trim the kidneys, leaving a thin layer of fat around each one. Slice each kidney into about 16 slices.
2. If necessary remove the central core or hard fat from the middle pieces with a small sharp knife. Reserve in the refrigerator.

Preparing the sauce

3. Peel and slice the shallots and garlic. Blanch, then roughly chop the tarragon. Wash and slice the mushrooms.
4. Melt 30 g (1 oz) of the butter and add the shallots, garlic, most of the tarragon, the thyme and bay leaf. Cook gently without colouring, until the shallots are opaque.
5. Add the mushrooms to the shallot mixture, and stir over a gentle heat until a liquid is released. Increase the heat and evaporate until virtually dry.
6. Add the white wine and boil to reduce by half. Add the port, bring to the boil once, then

cover with the chicken stock. Bring to the boil, skim and simmer for 20 minutes, adding the meat glaze at this stage if desired.

Preparing the garnishes

7. Meanwhile, cook the rice in boiling salted water, for about 20 minutes. When cooked, season and keep warm.
8. Wash and trim the spinach leaves. Bring 300 ml (10 fl oz) water to the boil and whisk in some salt, pepper, the ½ clove of garlic and the butter. Keep hot. This is for the last-minute cooking of the spinach.

Finishing the sauce and kidneys

9. Strain the sauce, pressing all the liquid out of the mushrooms against the side of the sieve. Boil to reduce by half.
10. Add the cream and whisk in the remaining butter. Taste for seasoning and adjust if necessary. Keep hot.
11. Heat two skillet pans until very hot and the

clarified butter or oil is smoking. Season the sliced kidneys and carefully divide them between the pans. Turning once only, the kidneys should be browned on each side but still pink in the middle. The whole operation should take only 2 minutes. Remove from the pans and keep hot.

To serve

12. Plunge the spinach into the boiling water to scald it, then drain well and place around the hot plates, using a fork.
13. Press the rice mixture into six dariole moulds and invert on to the centre of each plate.
14. Tip the juices from the kidneys into the sauce and whisk before it coagulates.
15. Place the kidneys around each dariole, working as quickly as you can.
16. Add the mustard to the sauce, strain through a fine sieve and add the remaining chopped tarragon and the peppercorns. Taste for seasoning and add a few drops of lemon juice if required. Spoon quickly over the kidneys, remove the dariole moulds and serve at once.

CHEF'S TIP
To add interest to the rice, you could mix wild and basmati. Wild rice needs soaking in cold water for about 1½ hours, and then takes about 40 minutes to cook. Mix with cooked basmati and proceed as in the recipe.

CHARLOTTE OF BLUEBERRIES

SERVES 8

*B*lueberries are more popular in America than they are in Great Britain. Although they lack the strength of flavour that perhaps blackcurrants have, treated properly they can make an excellent summer dessert.

Sponge base
1 sheet baked Biscuit Sponge 35 x 25 cm (14 x 10 in) (see p.245)
60 g (2 oz) blueberry jam
Blueberry purée and mousse
270 g (9 oz) blueberries
60 g (2 oz) caster sugar
2 gelatine leaves, soaked in cold water to soften
1 tablespoon Crème de Myrtilles (wild bilberry liqueur)
120 ml (4 fl oz) whipping cream
juice of ½ lemon
Italian meringue
60 g (2 oz) caster sugar
30 g (1 oz) egg whites

Vanilla mousse
110 g (3½ oz) Pastry Cream (see p.249)
½ vanilla pod
1 gelatine leaf, soaked in cold water to soften
120 ml (4 fl oz) whipping cream
Blueberry jelly
60 ml (2 fl oz) Stock Syrup (see p.249)
1 gelatine leaf, soaked in cold water to soften
30 ml (1 fl oz) blueberry purée (see Step 6)
1 tablespoon Crème de Myrtilles
To serve
1 quantity Lemon Egg Custard Sauce (see p.250)
60 g (2 oz) blueberries
caster sugar
8 sprigs fresh mint

Lining the moulds

1. Cut the sheet of biscuit sponge into two. Spread one half with some of the blueberry jam and sandwich it to the other half. Cut in two again and sandwich together with a little more jam. Repeat this process for a third time.

2. Wrap the layered sponge in greaseproof paper, place it between two trays and weigh down to flatten. Place the sponge in the freezer for an hour to harden.

3. Line another tray with greaseproof paper and place on it eight ring moulds, 6 cm (2½ in) across and 4 cm (1½ in) deep. Remove the sandwiched biscuit sponge from the freezer and cut it into strips 3 cm (1¼ in) wide. Cut these into rectangles 3 mm (⅛ in) wide. Line the inside of the moulds ensuring that the jam lines on the sponge are vertical, and stop 1 cm (½ in) from the top of the ring mould.

Preparing the blueberry purée

4. Place the blueberries, caster sugar and 60 ml (2 fl oz) water in a saucepan. Bring to the boil, reduce the heat, and simmer for 8 minutes.

5. Pour into a liquidiser and liquidise until smooth. Pass the blueberry purée through a fine-mesh sieve into a measuring jug. Discard the trapped seeds and skin.

6. Pour off 30 ml (1 fl oz) of the finished purée into a separate bowl and reserve aside for the jelly. Pour the remaining purée (you need 120 ml/4 fl oz) into another pan and bring it back to a simmer. Stir in the softened gelatine, then remove from the stove and add the Crème de Myrtilles. Reserve aside to cool.

Preparing the Italian meringue

7. In a pan, bring the sugar to the boil with 20 ml (⅔ fl oz) water. Remove the pan from the heat.

8. Whisk the egg whites to a peak, and gradually add the hot sugar syrup. Continue whisking the meringue until it is firm and cold. Reserve aside. (See also the basic recipe on p.247.)

Finishing the blueberry mousse

9. Lightly whisk the whipping cream to a soft peak.

10. Fold the meringue into the reserved 120 ml (4 fl oz) of blueberry purée. Stir in the lemon juice and, finally, fold in the whipped cream.

11. Fill the sponge-lined moulds three-quarters full with the blueberry mousse, and refrigerate to set.

Preparing the vanilla mousse

12. Place the pastry cream in a bowl and whisk until smooth. Scrape in the seeds of the split vanilla pod.

13. Warm through a tablespoon of water in a saucepan and stir in the soaked gelatine until dissolved. Whisk this into the pastry cream.

14. Whisk the whipping cream to a firm peak, and fold this into the pastry cream.

15. Remove the blueberry mousses from the fridge and top them with the vanilla mousse. Level with a palette knife and place into the freezer to set.

Making the blueberry jelly

16. Warm the stock syrup in a pan, add the gelatine and stir until dissolved. To this add the 30 ml (1 fl oz) reserved blueberry purée (see Step 6) and the Crème de Myrtilles. Cool the mixture by adding 20 ml (⅔ fl oz) cold water, then strain through a fine-mesh sieve into a bowl.

17. Remove the mousses from the freezer and spoon their surfaces with jelly. Leave to set and then repeat the procedure twice to ensure a deep glaze. Return the mousses to the fridge each time to set the jelly.

To serve

18. Lay out eight plates, and divide the lemon egg custard sauce between them.

19. Warm a thin-bladed knife and run it along the inside of the ring moulds, then place each mousse into the centre of the sauce on the plates.

20. Roll the washed blueberries in a little caster sugar in a bowl, then sprinkle them into the sauce.

21. Place a sprig of mint into the side of each mousse, and serve immediately.

Autumn Recipes

Menu 1

ROASTED QUAIL AND CHOUCROÛTE WITH A
WHITE WINE AND SHALLOT SAUCE

GRILLED BRILL SERVED WITH A BÉARNAISE SAUCE

LEMON MOUSSE CROUSTILLANT

Menu 2

SALAD OF HOT CALF'S TONGUE WITH CAPERS AND GHERKINS

ROYAL SEA BREAM WITH A SHALLOT CREAM AND A
RICH RED WINE SAUCE

JELLIED TERRINE OF RASPBERRIES AND QUINCES

Menu 3

CURRIED LAMB SAMOSAS

FILLETS OF RED MULLET STEAMED AND SERVED WITH
A WARM VINAIGRETTE AND TOMATO SAUCE

TOFFEED PEACHES ON BUTTER GALETTE WITH
A RASPBERRY SAUCE

Menu 4

TERRINE OF RABBIT AND BACON AND CRISP BABY VEGETABLES

ZANDER WITH CHOUCROÛTE AND CHICKEN JUICE

HOT APPLE FRITTERS AND PLUM SAUCE

Menu 5

HOT OYSTER FLAN WITH A HERB BUTTER SAUCE

GRILLED BREAST OF WILD PIGEON, FRESH PASTA AND
RED WINE SAUCE

CHARLOTTE OF CHOCOLATE AND VANILLA

Menu 6

SMOKED SALMON AND OYSTERS IN ENGLISH WINE JELLY

ROASTED GROUSE

BURNT ENGLISH CUSTARD MOUSSE

Menu 7

SOUP OF MUSSELS SCENTED WITH CURRY

SADDLE OF VENISON, RED CABBAGE AND A BRANDY
AND PORT SAUCE

GRATIN OF PEAR, CHOCOLATE AND NUTS

Menu 8

ESCALOPES OF TUNA STEAMED WITH CRUNCHY
VEGETABLES IN A WARM VINAIGRETTE

SAUTÉ OF CALF'S LIVER, CARROTS AND ORANGE

CHOCOLATE SOUFFLÉ WITH A WARM
FROTHY VANILLA CUSTARD

Autumn Menu 1

ROASTED QUAIL AND CHOUCROÛTE WITH A WHITE WINE AND SHALLOT SAUCE

GRILLED BRILL SERVED WITH A BÉARNAISE SAUCE

LEMON MOUSSE CROUSTILLANT

ROASTED QUAIL AND CHOUCROÛTE WITH A WHITE WINE AND SHALLOT SAUCE

SERVES 6

I have included *choucroûte* several times in this book, which demonstrates its versatility. *Choucroûte* can be served either as a vegetable garnish, or as a main course by itself with the addition of ham and French regional sausage.

6 quail
salt and pepper
30 ml (1 fl oz) vegetable oil
1 quantity *Choucroûte* (see p.237)
Sauce
450 g (1 lb) shallots
1 onion
½ carrot
6 garlic cloves
1 celery stalk

1 medium leek
450 g (1 lb) chicken bones
60 ml (2 fl oz) vegetable oil
60 ml (2 fl oz) white wine vinegar
½ bottle white wine
1.2 litres (2 pints) Chicken Stock (see p.225)
1 sprig fresh thyme
½ bay leaf
60 g (2 oz) unsalted butter

Preparing and cooking the sauce
1. Peel and chop the shallots, onion, carrot and garlic. Keep them separate. Prepare and chop the celery and leek.
2. Chop the chicken bones into small pieces,

place in a roasting tray, and sauté in hot oil on top of the stove until golden brown, about 5 minutes.
3. Transfer the bones with a slotted spoon to a casserole pan. Tip out and retain all the

remaining oil. Put the roasting tray back on the heat, deglaze with the white wine vinegar and evaporate until a syrup. Add the white wine and boil to reduce by half. Add to the bones.

4. Cover with the stock and bring to the boil, skimming all the while. Add the thyme, bay leaf and garlic, and reduce the flame to a simmer.

5. Meanwhile, brown the onion, carrot, celery and leek in the retained hot oil, and add to the stock, discarding the oil.

6. Melt the butter in a separate pan, slowly over a low heat. Add the shallots, cover with a butter paper and lid, and cook until very tender, about 7 minutes. Make sure the shallots do not stick or burn in any way as this will impair the flavour of the finished sauce. When soft, purée in a liquidiser, and add to the simmering sauce. Skim.

7. After an hour strain off the stock. At this stage I like to pass it through muslin to trap all the shallot purée as this is more difficult when the sauce has reduced.

8. Place the stock on a high heat to reduce by half, skimming all the while.

Cooking the quail

9. Preheat the oven to 200°C (400°F) Gas 6.

10. Season the quail with salt and pepper and seal in hot oil, breasts first, then transfer to the preheated oven, for 3 minutes on one side, 3 minutes on the other and 4 minutes on the back. Remove from the oven and allow to rest.

To serve

11. Heat up the *choucroûte* gently.

12. Carefully remove the quail legs, leaving them whole, and remove the breast meat, leaving that whole also.

13. Place the warm cabbage in the centre of each plate, and push the legs vertically into the mound, giving the dish more height. Put the breasts on each side of the *choucroûte*. Taste the sauce and alter the seasoning if necessary with a little salt and pepper, then finally spoon over the quail and serve immediately.

GRILLED BRILL SERVED WITH A BÉARNAISE SAUCE

SERVES 6

This dish is simplicity itself. If brill is not available, and money is no object, substitute turbot for it. As for the red mullet dish on p.15 the fish must be marinated the night before. The only extra ingredient to be added to the marinade is fennel sticks: these can be purchased at most health-food shops or delicatessens.

6 x 500–550 g (18–20 oz) brill, or 3 larger fish, approx. 900 g (2 lb) each	15 g (½ oz) white peppercorns
	60 g (2 oz) unsalted butter
1 quantity Basic Fish Marinade (see p.224), with the addition of 6–7 dried fennel sticks	1 sprig fresh thyme
	½ bay leaf
a bunch of crisp watercress	45 ml (1½ fl oz) white wine vinegar
Béarnaise sauce	45 ml (1½ fl oz) dry white wine
2 sprigs fresh tarragon	2 egg yolks
60 g (2 oz) fresh chervil	270 g (9 oz) unsalted butter, clarified (see Chef's Tip, p.15)
1 bunch fresh parsley	
½ bunch fresh chives	salt to taste
3 shallots	2 teaspoons lemon juice, to taste
1 garlic clove	

Preparing the brill

1. Snip off the tails with sharp scissors, then snip off the fins on the two sides. Cut the gills out and remove any entrails. Wash under cold running water and dry well.
2. Place whole in a dish and cover with the marinade. Marinate overnight in the fridge.

Preparing and cooking the Béarnaise sauce

3. The next day, pick the tarragon leaves from their stalks and blanch in boiling water. Refresh in cold water, strain, dry and chop. Repeat the process for the chervil. Pick the parsley leaves from their stalks, then wash, dry and finely chop. Wash and chop the chives.
4. Peel and chop the shallots; peel and chop the garlic to a smooth paste. Crush the peppercorns.
5. In a shallow pan melt the 60 g (2 oz) butter, and add the shallots, thyme, bay leaf and peppercorns. Cook for about 3 minutes over a gentle flame without colouring.
6. Add the white wine vinegar and reduce until a syrup. Add the white wine and again reduce the liquid until a syrup. This is important: if you do not fully reduce the alcohol and vinegar, the finished sauce will be too acidic.
7. Add the garlic paste to the pan, stir and keep warm.

8. Put the egg yolks in a stainless-steel or copper bowl and add 1 tablespoon water. Place over a saucepan of boiling water and beat the yolks vigorously with a whisk until they thicken and peak. That is, and this is important (see Chef's Tip), cook them to 80°C (176°F).

CHEF'S TIP

Cooking the egg yolks to the correct temperature is the most important part of the sauce. Cook the egg yolks insufficiently and the sauce, at best, will be like a mousse or, at worst, will be thin and split. To test you have the right consistency, put the whisk in the mixture and, on lifting it out, the sauce should look like a ribbon and have the density of cold treacle.

9. At this stage, and very gradually, beat in all the warm clarified butter, whisking all the time until a smooth sauce is attained. Check the seasoning, adding salt and lemon juice to taste.
10. Finally add the shallot base and the chopped and prepared herbs to the sauce. Stir thoroughly and keep warm until needed.

Cooking and serving the fish

11. Take the fish out of the marinade and grill or char-grill. Allow approximately 6 minutes on each side for a 500 g (18 oz) fish.
12. Present the fish on a board or tray decorated with watercress. Serve the Béarnaise sauce separately in a sauceboat.

Steamed or buttered potatoes and French beans are a good accompaniment.

LEMON MOUSSE CROUSTILLANT

SERVES 6

This is a light, sharp lemon mousse layered between thin, crisp biscuit and served with a lemon cream sauce.

Lemon mousse
180 ml (6 fl oz) whipping cream
225 ml (7½ fl oz) lemon juice
120 g (4 oz) egg yolks (approx. 4 yolks)
210 g (7 oz) caster sugar
20 g (⅔ oz) cornflour
3 gelatine leaves, soaked in cold water
to soften
180 ml (6 fl oz) egg whites

To finish and serve
2 lemons
60 g (2 oz) caster sugar
18 x 8 cm (3¼ in) Langue de Chat biscuit discs
(see p.246)
icing sugar for dusting
1 quantity Lemon Egg Custard Sauce
(see p.250)
18 mint leaves, washed

Preparing the lemon rind and biscuits

1. Remove the rind of the lemons with a zester – this will give you very thin, long julienne – and cook for 2 minutes in a pan of boiling water. Strain and refresh in cold water. Repeat the process again to remove *all* the bitterness in the rind. In another saucepan bring to the boil the 60 g (2 oz) sugar with 30 ml (1 fl oz) cold water and add the lemon rind. Reduce the heat and simmer until the rind is tender. Transfer to a clean bowl and reserve.

2. Lay out six of the biscuit discs on an upturned metal tray. Dust them liberally with icing sugar. Heat a metal skewer over a fierce naked flame until it is glowing red and scorch the sugared discs, giving a criss-cross effect. Reserve to top the dessert.

Preparing the mousse

3. In a large saucepan bring the whipping cream to the boil. Immediately add the lemon juice, and remove the pan from the stove.

CHEF'S TIP
You must *boil the cream before you add the lemon juice, or the cream will curdle.*

4. In a stainless-steel bowl whisk together the egg yolks and half the caster sugar until pale and thick, then whisk in the cornflour.

5. Bring the cream and lemon juice back to

the boil. When boiling pour one-third of it over the whisked egg yolks and sugar, stir them together then return to the bulk of the cream and lemon juice, stirring all the time. Bring back to the boil and stir until thick, then remove from the heat. Stir in the gelatine and turn the mixture out into a stainless-steel bowl.

6. Put the egg whites into an electric mixer bowl and whisk to a peak. Slowly add the remaining caster sugar. The egg whites must be firm and have a smooth texture.

CHEF'S TIP
Over-whipping the whites would give them a granular texture, and in turn ruin the mousse.

7. With a plastic spatula fold half of the egg whites into the warm lemon cream. When incorporated, fold in the other half and refrigerate to set.

To serve

8. Lay out six dinner plates and pour the lemon sauce into the middle, leaving a 2.5 cm (1 in) gap around the outside of the plates.

9. Take a piping bag fitted with a large plain nozzle and fill it with the lemon mousse.

10. Place a plain biscuit disc on to the centre of each plate on top of the sauce. Pipe on to it a 2.5 cm (1 in) rosette of lemon mousse, leaving

a border of biscuit showing around each disc. 11. Gently place another disc on top of the mousse and pipe the same amount of mousse on it. To finish, top each dessert with the scorched discs.

12. With a fork, place three piles of lemon zest, at equal distance from each other, around the outside of the sauce. Then finally place a mint leaf between each pile of lemon zest. Serve immediately.

Autumn Menu 2

SALAD OF HOT CALF'S TONGUE WITH CAPERS AND GHERKINS

ROYAL SEA BREAM WITH A SHALLOT CREAM AND A RICH RED WINE SAUCE

JELLIED TERRINE OF RASPBERRIES AND QUINCES

SALAD OF HOT CALF'S TONGUE WITH CAPERS AND GHERKINS

SERVES 6

This salad is full of flavours. It isn't too heavy, or too expensive, and it's quite simple to prepare. The capers and gherkins give the slightly bland tongue a necessary lift in flavour and the salad leaves a texture. Calf's tongue is available throughout the year.

1 calf's tongue
salt and pepper
For cooking the tongue
1 onion
4 garlic cloves
½ carrot
1 leek
½ celery stalk
10 black peppercorns
1 sprig fresh thyme
1 bay leaf
Sauce
2 garlic cloves
1 sprig fresh tarragon
60 g (2 oz) capers

6 gherkins
1 bunch fresh parsley
150 ml (5 fl oz) White Veal Stock (see p.226)
600 ml (1 pint) Chicken Stock (see p.225)
2 hard-boiled eggs
To serve
180–240 g (6–8 oz) salad leaves (including endive, frisée and oakleaf)
3 tomatoes
120 ml (4 fl oz) Tarragon Vinaigrette (see p.234)
a handful of tiny croûtons (see p.138)
about 90 ml (3 fl oz) Rémoulade Sauce (see p.235)
juice of 1 lemon

Preparing and cooking the tongue

1. Soak the tongue in cold water for 2-3 hours.
2. Peel the onion and garlic. Chop the onion, garlic, carrot, leek and celery coarsely. Crush the peppercorns.
3. Transfer the tongue to a casserole. Cover with fresh cold water and bring to the boil. Skim.
4. Add the coarsely chopped vegetables, the thyme, bay leaf, garlic and peppercorns. Cover and simmer for 2-3 hours. Test with a needle and if the juices run clear the tongue is cooked.
5. Remove and, carefully so as not to tear the tongue, peel off the skin. This is much easier while the tongue is still warm. Place back into the strained stock.

Making the sauce

6. Peel and halve the garlic. Blanch the tarragon. Chop the capers, gherkins and parsley.
7. Place the veal stock, chicken stock, garlic and tarragon into a saucepan and boil to reduce by half.
8. Shell the hard-boiled eggs and separate the yolks from the whites. Press them separately through a fine-mesh sieve.
9. Combine in a pan the sieved egg yolk, egg white, chopped parsley, gherkins, capers and salt and pepper to taste. Strain in the stock reduction. Keep warm.

To serve

10. Slice the tongue into eighteen pieces, place into a shallow pan and cover with the tongue stock. Bring to the boil and keep hot.
11. Wash and pick over the salad leaves. Blanch, skin, seed and dice the tomatoes. Add the tarragon vinaigrette to the leaves, and dress in the centre of six plates starting with the endive and frisée, building up a tall mound.
12. Season the diced tomato with salt, pepper and some lemon juice and place at equal distances around the plate in three piles. Sprinkle with croûton dice.
13. In between each pile of tomato carefully spoon a little dollop of *rémoulade* sauce. Lay the pieces of tongue on top of these. *The tongue should be hot.*
14. Season the sauce with salt, pepper and a little lemon juice if required and spoon over the tongue. Serve at once.

ROYAL SEA BREAM WITH A SHALLOT CREAM AND A RICH RED WINE SAUCE

SERVES 6

*T*his fish is excellent and not to be confused with its second-rate, much cheaper relation, the black bream, which is more common at the local fishmonger's. The best way to buy sea bream, as with most fish, is to get one large one rather than several smaller ones. Large fish seem to travel better from the sea ports and reach the shops in a fresher condition.

CHEF'S TIP
Points to check to make sure you are buying the freshest possible fish.
1. The eyes should be bright.
2. Sometimes called `red bream', it should have a clear pink to red colour on its back fading to orange, and then silver on its stomach.
3. The gills should be a bright red colour.
4. The scales should be intact.
5. Check for any marks or dents on the fish. The flesh is delicate, and you do not want any bruising.

1 large royal sea bream, approx. 1.8 kg (4 lb)
salt and pepper
Poaching liquor
4 shallots

2 garlic cloves
60 g (2 oz) unsalted butter
120 ml (4 fl oz) dry white wine
1 sprig fresh basil
300 ml (10 fl oz) Fish Stock (see p.223)

Sauces
300 ml (10 fl oz) Shallot Purée (see p.235)
300 ml (10 fl oz) Red Wine Sauce for Fish
(see p.238)
60 g (2 oz) unsalted butter
1 teaspoon lemon juice

Preparing the fish

1. With a pair of fish scissors cut all the fins off the bream. With the back of a filleting knife, from tail to head, scrape off all the fish scales. Open its stomach with the scissors and discard all the entrails. Cut out the gills. Wash the fish thoroughly and dry it with kitchen paper.
2. Lay the fish on its side on a board. To remove the fillets, with a very sharp knife make a cut just behind the head following the angle of its skull. Cut along the back of the fish, head to tail, the knife angled towards its backbone, and carefully remove the first fillet. Turn the fish over and repeat the process. (Keep the carcass and bones, freeze and use at a later date to make a fish stock.)
3. With fish pliers (or tweezers), remove all the exposed bones running down the middle of the fillets. Cut each fillet into three equal pieces. Season with salt and pepper and reserve aside.

Cooking the fish

4. Preheat the oven to 180°C (350°F) Gas 4.
5. Peel and slice the shallots; peel and crush the garlic.
6. Melt half the butter in a large, shallow ovenproof pan over a moderate flame. Before it colours, add the shallots and, stirring with a spoon, cook for approximately 3 minutes. *Do not* colour.
7. Add the white wine, garlic and basil, turn up the flame and reduce the wine until a syrup. Take care not to let the shallots colour or burn.
8. Add the fish stock, bring to the boil and with a ladle remove all the surfacing fat and scum.
9. Turn down to a gentle simmer and carefully, skin-side down, place in the pieces of sea bream. Cover the fish with a butter paper and a lid. Cook in the preheated oven for approximately 7 minutes.
10. When cooked, take the sea bream out of the oven, remove the lid and discard the butter paper. Take out the pieces of fish with a fish slice or palette knife and, turning them over, place them on to a plate. Cover with another butter paper and keep warm.

Finishing the sauces

11. In one pan heat the shallot purée through gently and in another the red wine sauce. Keep warm on the side of the stove.
12. Pass the fish poaching liquor through a fine-mesh conical strainer into another pan and boil to reduce by half its volume. Piece by piece gradually add the butter. Whisk until fully dissolved. Check the seasoning and add the lemon juice to bring out the flavour.

To serve

13. Lay out your hot plates. At the centre of each, spoon 2 dessertspoons of the shallot purée.
14. With a small knife, carefully peel off the skins from the pieces of fish and lay each immediately down on top of the shallot purée.
15. Spoon the hot red wine sauce around the outer rim of each plate. Finally, with a spoon, mask the fish with the butter sauce.

As an optional accompaniment I like to eat creamed leeks and steamed potatoes with this dish.

Fillets of Red Mullet Steamed and Served with a Warm Vinaigrette and Tomato Sauce

Terrine of Rabbit and Bacon and Crisp Baby Vegetables

Hot Oyster Flan with a Herb Butter Sauce

Smoked Salmon and Oysters in English Wine Jelly

JELLIED TERRINE OF RASPBERRIES AND QUINCES

SERVES 10

$\mathscr{M}$ost people know that quinces make a delicious jam or preserve. Here the raspberries and quinces, married together, give not only an excellent colour to the terrine, but a delicious flavour.

2 kg (4½ lb) raw quinces	*Quince syrup*
400 g (14 oz) raspberries	500 g (18 oz) caster sugar
10 gelatine leaves, soaked in cold water to soften	1 vanilla pod, split in half lengthways
10 small sprigs fresh mint	juice of 1 lemon

Preparing and cooking the quinces

1. To prepare the syrup, place the sugar, vanilla and lemon juice in a stainless-steel pan. Add 1 litre (1¾ pints) water and bring to the boil. Remove from the heat and reserve aside.

2. Peel the quinces and place in a bowl under running cold water. Remove from the water and cut them in half, then each half into four (all lengthways). Remove the woody core with a small knife and discard. Place the fruit into the saucepan of syrup.

3. Cover the syrup and quinces with greaseproof paper and place a small saucepan lid on top to keep the fruit totally submerged. Return the pan to the stove and poach gently until tender, about 5 minutes, depending on ripeness. Do not boil as they will simply break up. Remove from the heat when cooked. The texture will resemble a ripe pear. Leave to cool, submerged in the syrup.

Preparing the jelly

4. Carefully wash and drain all the raspberries. Keep 50 aside for garnishing. Place the bulk of the raspberries in a liquidiser. Add 100 ml (3½ fl oz) of the quince syrup to the liquidiser and liquidise until smooth. Strain through a fine strainer. Remove 120 ml (4 fl oz) of purée for the jelly, and keep the rest for the sauce.

5. In a saucepan bring to the boil 240 ml (8 fl oz) of quince syrup and 120 ml (4 fl oz) of water. Remove from the heat and whisk in

the gelatine. Pour the liquid over the reserved 120 ml (4 fl oz) of raspberry purée, then pass it all through a fine sieve into a bowl. Reserve aside to cool.

Assembling the terrine

6. Remove the poached quinces from the syrup and lay on a clean towel. Thinly slice twelve of the pieces lengthways.

7. Line a 2 litre (3½ pint) terrine mould with cling film. Lay the quince slices slightly overlapping each other along the bottom of the mould and up the sides of the terrine. With a pair of scissors, cut any of the fruit overlapping the edges of the mould and keep them for the sauce.

8. Pour 1 cm (½ in) of raspberry jelly into the bottom of the mould. Lay down a layer of quince segments and cover with the raspberry jelly. Repeat this process until the terrine is full. (Use the quince *segments*, saving the slices for the top.)

CHEF'S TIP

The idea is to pack as many quinces into the terrine as possible and set it with as little jelly as possible.

---

9. Top the terrine with more finely sliced quince and brush over with a little more jelly. Now seal with cling film. Place an empty terrine mould on top to press and weight the completed terrine. Refrigerate for at least 4 hours to set.

Making the sauce

10. Liquidise all the remaining quince segments, slices and trimmings to a smooth paste. Remove the split vanilla pod from the syrup and scrape any remaining seeds into the liquidiser. Add approximately 100 ml (3½ fl oz) of syrup and again liquidise. Pass the quince sauce through a fine sieve into a clean bowl and refrigerate.

To serve

11. Remove the terrine from the fridge and turn it upside-down on to a wooden board. Dip a cloth into hot water and rub the outside of the terrine to ease the jelly out. Carefully remove the cling film.

12. Warm a sharp knife in hot water and cut the jelly into ten slices. Lay each slice carefully in the centre of each large dinner plate.

13. Place 5 teaspoons of quince sauce around the jelly on each of the plates, leaving room in between each for a teaspoon of the retained raspberry purée.

14. Place five raspberries on each plate, one between each sauce. At one corner of each slice of the terrine, place a small sprig of mint.

A nice accompaniment would be *langue de chat* biscuits (see p.246).

Autumn Menu 3

CURRIED LAMB SAMOSAS

FILLETS OF RED MULLET STEAMED AND SERVED WITH A WARM VINAIGRETTE AND TOMATO SAUCE

TOFFEED PEACHES ON BUTTER GALETTE WITH A RASPBERRY SAUCE

CURRIED LAMB SAMOSAS

SERVES 6

I serve miniature versions of these as part of the canapé plates for guests to nibble with their pre-dinner drinks. A plate of these or two larger ones per person is quite adequate as an hors-d'oeuvre substitute. I prefer to use lamb to make the mince because lamb always seems to be the sweetest, but beef or chicken are good as well.

12 sheets filo pastry
1 egg
vegetable oil for deep-frying
salt and pepper
Filling
500 g (18 oz) lean lamb (or beef or chicken), minced
4 garlic cloves
120 g (4 oz) *Mirepoix* (see p.239)
30 g (1 oz) Madras curry powder

30 g (1 oz) plain white flour
30 g (1 oz) tomato paste
270 ml (9 fl oz) Chicken Stock (see p.225)
1 sprig fresh thyme
1 bay leaf
1 dessertspoon redcurrant jelly
60 g (2 oz) Puy lentils, cooked until tender (see p.105)
30 g (1 oz) fresh grated or desiccated coconut

Preparing and cooking the filling

1. Peel the garlic. Mince the garlic and *mirepoix* vegetables.
2. In a large, shallow, heavy-bottomed pan, heat up a little of the deep-frying oil until it smokes. Put in the lamb, minced vegetables and garlic, and stir, breaking up the mince into fine pieces. (Large lumps of meat will spoil the end result.) Continue cooking over a high heat until the meat is cooked and the moisture

given off has evaporated, about 10 minutes.

3. Add the curry powder, reduce the heat, and cook for a few more minutes. Add the flour and continue to cook gently, stirring all the time. After a further 4 minutes' cooking, add the tomato paste. Mix well in and cook for a few moments.

4. Slowly, a little at a time, add the chicken stock, stirring in each measure or ladleful thoroughly before adding the next. Increase the heat and bring to the boil, stirring and taking care not to let it stick.

5. Add the thyme, bay leaf and redcurrant jelly. The mixture should already be quite thick but keep on a gentle heat to cook for approximately 15 minutes. The finished mince should not be too runny. If it is, turn up the heat and boil rapidly so as to reduce some of the moisture. Do *not* leave the pan if you are doing this, as it will stick and burn very easily and will ruin the flavour. Stir.

6. Finally, add the lentils and coconut, taste for seasoning and pour on to a clean tray to cool. Cover with a sheet of cling film or butter paper to stop a skin forming.

Making the samosas

7. Beat the egg to make an egg wash. Carefully bring out one sheet of filo and lay it down on a clean table. Brush with the beaten egg and lay another sheet on top. Cut each double sheet in half for two even-sized strips. Paint the top edge with egg wash down about 4 cm (1½ in).

8. At the near end of the filo strip (the non-egg-washed end), place a dessertspoon of the cooled mince, 4–5 cm (1½–2 in) from the end.

9. Take the left-hand corner of filo and fold over the mince, moving to the right to create a triangle. Next fold the semi-covered mince over from the right to the left, and continue thus, working up the strip. Finish with the egg-washed end which should stick the whole thing together. Repeat this, doing only two samosas at a time, or else the filo will dry and crack.

Cooking the samosas

10. Heat the oil in a tall pan, one-third full, to 182–193°C (360–380°F). When it is at the correct temperature, test by lowering a samosa into it. It should bubble but not brown too quickly. If nothing happens, the oil is too cold; if the samosa turns brown too quickly, the mince inside will not be hot.

11. After 3 minutes' frying, the samosas should be hot and golden brown and the filo crisp. Drain on kitchen paper and season with salt. Only cook two at a time, keeping the others hot in the oven. The whole process takes about 15 minutes.

FILLETS OF RED MULLET STEAMED AND SERVED WITH A WARM VINAIGRETTE AND TOMATO SAUCE

SERVES 6

*S*ome chefs say that the best red mullet come from the Mediterranean. I have found that the freshest are caught off the Cornish coast and, although larger, are of good quality. The best way of buying mullet is whole. A general rule of thumb is the brighter in colour the fresher it is. The gills should be deep red-black, and the eyes bright.

This is a dish which can be prepared the night or day before serving and, although its preparation is quite complex and in several stages, the actual cooking and serving of it is mere minutes. It also makes a good starter dish.

6 red mullet, approx. 225 g (7½ oz) each in weight
1 quantity Basic Fish Marinade (see p.224)
salt and pepper
Vegetable garnish
1 red and 1 yellow pepper
1 medium aubergine
2 large courgettes
1 fennel bulb

1 garlic clove
Vinaigrette sauce
110 ml (3½ fl oz) Fish Stock (see p.223)
60 ml (2 fl oz) Tarragon Vinaigrette (see p.234)
a little lemon juice
To serve
240 ml (8 fl oz) Tomato Sauce (see p.232)
6 garlic croûtons (see Chef's Tip)
6 sprigs fresh chervil

Preparing and marinating the fish

1. Scale and clean the red mullet as described on p.15. Discard all the entrails including the gills, but carefully remove the livers and keep them in a bowl for use when serving the dish. (I cover the livers with a little olive oil to prevent oxidisation.) Wash the fish and dry thoroughly on kitchen paper.
2. Fillet the fish as described on p.15, and remove all the fine bones. (Freeze the bones and trimmings for use in a sauce or soup at a later date.) Prepare all the fish in the same way. You will have twelve fillets.
3. Put the fillets into a dish, and cover with the marinade. Leave in the fridge overnight.

Preparing the vegetables

4. The vegetables can be prepared the day before as well. Skin and seed the peppers, and cut them into 1 cm (½ in) dice. Slice the aubergine and cut into dice the same size as the pepper dice. Do the same with the courgettes, and the fennel after trimming.

Keep the vegetables separate.
5. In two separate pans, blanch and cook the red and yellow peppers and the fennel until tender, about 2 minutes. Refresh in cold water. Strain and dry them in a cloth. Leave the courgettes in their raw state.
6. In a shallow frying pan, heat a little of the olive oil from the marinade and fry the aubergine dice to a golden colour. Turn out on to a kitchen-paper-lined tray to cool. Store all the vegetables in the fridge overnight.

CHEF'S TIP
I have a professional steamer. Portable steamers can be purchased but the cheapest and most efficient are the Chinese bamboo steamers which you can stack up one on top of another over a wok or a pan of boiling water.

Cooking the mullet fillets

7. After marination, and when ready to cook and serve, the red mullet fillets are steamed. Divide them between two separate plates that will fit into your steamer baskets. Season with

salt and pepper.

8. Sprinkle the fish with the prepared vegetables. Peel and cut the garlic clove in two and place one half on each plate along with a basil leaf taken from the marinade. Spoon on a tablespoon of olive oil, again from the marinade, and cover the plates with cling film. Steam in your Chinese steamer for approximately 6 minutes, ensuring that the film is tight over the plates and that the water below the steamer is constantly boiling.

Preparing the sauces and croûtons

9. Meanwhile, boil and reduce the fish stock by half its volume. Keep warm.

CHEF'S TIP

To make croûtons, cut slices from a French stick loaf or baguette, and in a shallow pan heat a little oil. Fry the croûtons until golden. Remove and turn them out on to kitchen paper to drain. To flavour with garlic, take a garlic clove, peel it and with a knife prick it several times to help extract the oil. Rub the garlic clove over both sides of the croûtons.

Use the same process to make different sized croûtons: cutting them to a particular shape, or into tiny dice. You can also oven-bake croûtons (see p.15).

---

10. Heat the prepared tomato sauce in another pan, and warm through the garlic croûtons.

To serve

11. When ready, take the mullet fillets out of the steamer and remove the cling film. To test if they are sufficiently cooked, carefully turn one of the fillets over: the pink flesh should now be white. Retain the vegetables.

12. In the centre of each plate put 2 tablespoons of tomato sauce. With a fish slice or large palette knife place the red mullet fillets on top, skin-side up.

13. Mix the reserved vegetables and any remaining cooking juices thoroughly into the fish stock. Add the vinaigrette and lemon juice, stir and spoon around the outer rim of the plates.

14. Season the red mullet livers and fry them quickly, in a little oil from the marinade, to a golden brown colour. Place on top of the prepared garlic croûtons and then on top of your mullet. Garnish with chervil and serve immediately.

I garnish this dish with fresh basil tagliatelle or noodles (see p.240), warmed through in a little butter and fish stock.

TOFFEED PEACHES ON BUTTER GALETTE WITH A RASPBERRY SAUCE

SERVES 6

*T*his dessert is dead simple! It has three wonderful textures - the crackle of the toffee, the softness of the peach flesh, and the crumbly, buttery and melting texture of the galettes.

6 ripe peaches
110 g (3½ oz) quite runny fromage frais or natural yoghurt
12 large mint leaves
Galettes
225 g (7½ oz) finest unsalted butter, at room temperature
110 g (3½ oz) icing sugar

350 g (12 oz) plain flour
Raspberry sauce
300 g (10 oz) raspberries
100 ml (3½ fl oz) Stock Syrup (see p.249)
Caramel
210 g (7 oz) caster sugar
60 ml (2 fl oz) liquid glucose

Preparing and cooking the peaches

1. Wash the peaches in cold water, being careful not to bruise them.
2. Half fill a saucepan with water and bring it to the boil. Remove from the heat and scald the peaches. Leave them in for 20 seconds, then remove with a slotted spoon and plunge into iced water.
3. With a sharp knife, carefully remove the skins; they should peel away easily. Cut the peaches in half with a sharp knife, through the flesh to the stone, and gently twist the peach halves in opposite directions to remove the stone. Keep the peaches in iced water.

Making the galettes

4. Preheat the oven to 190°C (375°F) Gas 5.
5. Dice the butter and, in an electric mixer bowl, gradually beat together with the icing sugar until it becomes white in colour. Switch off the machine.
6. Sieve the flour and add to the bowl. Switch the machine back on and, gradually increasing the speed, beat the mixture rapidly for at least 5 minutes or until it appears white and fluffy. This is very important: if you under-beat the mixture, it will be impossible to pipe and the galettes will be heavy and dense.
7. Fill a piping bag fitted with a large star nozzle with the mixture. Pipe it into a bun

tray (you will need twelve, two galettes per person).
8. Bake the galettes in the preheated oven for 20 minutes. Leave them to cool in the tray before turning them out.

Making the raspberry sauce and caramel

9. Wash the raspberries, strain in a colander, then place in the liquidiser. Pour in the stock syrup, and liquidise for 1 minute to a smooth pulp. Strain the pulp through a fine-mesh conical strainer into a bowl. Refrigerate.
10. In a small saucepan boil the caster sugar, glucose and 60 ml (2 fl oz) water until the mixture starts to caramelise. Remove from the heat. We want a very 'blond' caramel for this dish.

To finish and serve

11. Preheat the oven to very low – 110°C (225°F) Gas ½ – and warm the galettes through slightly.
12. Remove the peach halves from the water and, with a clean towel, gently pat them dry. Place them on a cooling rack, flat-side down. Gently bring the caramel back to the boil. With a tablespoon coat the tops of the peaches, as thinly and evenly as possible, with the hot caramel. This will set almost immediately.
13. Pour some raspberry sauce into the centre

of each plate. Put a tablespoon of fromage frais in the middle of this and, with the point of a knife, swirl it into the raspberry sauce. Any pattern of your choice will do!

14. Place the warmed butter galettes opposite each other on the plate and, on top of these, the toffeed peach halves. Finally, place a large mint leaf on to each peach half. Serve immediately.

CHEF'S TIP

All the stages of this recipe can be prepared in advance of serving, with the exception of the actual coating of the peaches with caramel. Do not attempt to do this too long beforehand because after as little as 10 minutes, the caramel will disintegrate and dissolve.

Autumn Menu 4

TERRINE OF RABBIT AND BACON AND CRISP BABY VEGETABLES

ZANDER WITH CHOUCROÛTE AND CHICKEN JUICE

HOT APPLE FRITTERS AND PLUM SAUCE

TERRINE OF RABBIT AND BACON AND CRISP BABY VEGETABLES

SERVES 6

This is a good-flavoured terrine, which is best made at least seven days in advance in order for the terrine to mature and reach the fullest flavour. It makes enough for six, but it keeps well in the fridge, and is nice on a piece of toast for supper.

2 rabbits
1 kg (2½ lb) smoked streaky bacon in the piece
cooking oil
salt and pepper
Marinade
120 g (4 oz) shallots
6 garlic cloves
10 peppercorns
1 sprig fresh thyme
2 bay leaves
15 g (½ oz) fresh basil
300 ml (10 fl oz) dry white wine
Jelly
rabbit bones
1 quantity *Mirepoix* (see p.239)
1 sprig fresh thyme
1 bay leaf

4 garlic cloves
1 litre (1¾ pints) Chicken Stock (see p.225)
Clarification
1 onion
1 leek
½ carrot
1 celery stalk
4 egg whites
90 ml (3 fl oz) very dry Madeira
1 sprig fresh thyme
1 bay leaf
Garnish
6 each of baby leeks, baby carrots, baby turnips and green beans
6 each of button mushrooms, shallots and asparagus tips
6 cherry tomatoes
150 ml (5 fl oz) Tarragon Vinaigrette (see p.234)

Preparing and marinating the rabbit

1. Remove all the rabbit flesh from the bones in as large pieces as possible, at the same time removing the silvery tough membrane surrounding the flesh. Place in a bowl or plastic container. Reserve the bones for the sauce.
2. Remove the rind from the bacon, cut the bacon in half, and cut one half into 2 cm (¾ in) length strips.
3. Peel the shallots and garlic and cut into quarters. Crush the peppercorns.
4. Combine the bacon strips, shallots, garlic, peppercorns, thyme, bay leaves and basil with the rabbit and pour over the wine. Mix thoroughly. Cover with cling film and leave to marinate for 12 hours in the fridge.

Lining the terrine

5. Cut the remainder of the bacon into thin rashers. Carefully line a 30 x 10 cm (12 x 4 in) terrine mould or similar dish of about 10 cm (4 in) deep, overlapping the rashers as the dish is turned. Be careful to leave some bacon hanging over the edge, so it can be placed over the top after the rabbit has been added.

Making the jelly stock

6. Meanwhile chop the rabbit bones finely. Heat a little oil in a roasting tray and sauté the bones until golden brown, about 5-10 minutes. Remove using a slotted spoon, and place in a large saucepan.
7. Add the *mirepoix* to the oil in the tray, brown for about 5 minutes, then add to the bones.
8. Add the thyme, bay leaf and garlic, cover with the chicken stock, bring to the boil and simmer for 1 hour.

Clarifying the jelly

9. Peel the onion. Dice the onion, leek, carrot and celery.
10. Combine the diced raw vegetables in a tall pan with the egg whites, the Madeira and herbs.
11. Strain off the rabbit stock and carefully, adding a little at a time, add to the egg white mixture. Return to the stove and bring to the boil, stirring every 2 minutes. When the egg

whites coagulate and float to the top, reduce the heat right away and simmer for 15 minutes.
12. With a ladle, carefully strain through a muslin cloth and taste for salt. Do not add pepper as this will show in the jelly. Cool down, and then chill and freeze (it will not be used until the terrine has matured).

Assembling and cooking the terrine

13. Preheat the oven to 110°C (225°F) Gas ¼.
14. Drain off the rabbit pieces. Pick out all the shallots, garlic, basil, thyme and bay leaf, and discard. Taste for seasoning, not by eating raw rabbit, but by passing a spoon through the flesh and tasting the residue on the spoon. Adjust the seasoning if necessary.
15. Carefully pack the rabbit pieces into the lined terrine mould. Press well down, then bring over the overlapping bacon to cover the rabbit. The rabbit should be completely covered.
16. Place a roasting tray of boiling water – a bain-marie – at least 10 cm (4 in) high on the stove, and put the terrine mould into it. Bring back to the boil and place into the preheated cool oven. Cook for 2½–3 hours.
17. Pierce with a needle and after 4 seconds remove and test the needle for hotness on the lips. If it is very warm the terrine is cooked. Remove and allow to cool, then chill. The terrine is better after seven days' maturation.

To serve

18. Defrost the jelly until liquid again. Bring to the boil, skim off any surfacing scum, then allow to cool. Prepare and cook the baby garnish vegetables as appropriate, then cool. Do not cook the tomatoes (but you could skin them if you like).
19. Chill six plates thoroughly and flood them with the cool rabbit jelly. Allow to set.
20. In a bowl toss the cooked vegetables and the tomatoes in most of the vinaigrette. Arrange around the plate.
21. Slice the terrine and place in the centre of each plate. Brush with the vinaigrette, and serve at once with brown toast or sourdough bread.

ZANDER WITH CHOUCROÛTE AND CHICKEN JUICE

SERVES 4

Zander or pike-perch, known in French as *sandre*, is little known in this country. On the rare occasion when you see it at fishmongers, grab it - it's delicious! In France, because it is so highly prized by gourmands and chefs alike, it is becoming quite rare. In this country, where stocks were introduced to the Norfolk Broads from Holland about fifteen years ago, they are becoming more and more commonplace. This is mainly due to the fact that these waters always contain a healthy supply of young trout which zander like to feed off and, unlike other species, have little trouble from our anglers. Many rivers in the southern part of this country also contain zander.

If zander is not available, perch or salmon trout (when in season) are good alternatives. As for pike and perch and many other freshwater fish, it is better to purchase several small fish than one big one. The big fish always taste muddy to me.

2 small zanders, weighing 700–900 g (1½–2 lb) in total
salt and pepper
juice of 1 lemon
60 ml (2 fl oz) clarified butter (see Chef's Tip, p.15)

1 quantity *Choucroûte* (see p.237)
Chicken juice
1 garlic clove
1 sprig fresh tarragon
2 shallots
420 ml (14 fl oz) Chicken Stock (see p.225)

Preparing the fish

1. With fish scissors cut off all the fins. Be careful when cutting away the dorsal fins because, like those on perch and bass, these are as sharp as needles and can give you a nasty cut. Where at all possible, do not attempt to de-scale a zander. The skin and scales are like armour plating. It is an exercise which could well take half an hour and many a blunt knife!
2. Turn the fish on its side and with scissors open its stomach and discard the entrails. Wash the fish thoroughly under running water and dry on a clean kitchen cloth.
3. With a chopping knife, at the back of the skull, chop off its head and discard. With a strong filleting knife, remove the fillets: insert the knife at the top of the fish and, at an angle towards its backbone, carefully cut down towards its tail. Turn the fish over and repeat the process.
4. To skin the fish, insert a filleting knife at the tail end of the fillet, clearing enough skin for your thumb and forefinger to take a hold. Ease your knife tail to head, angled towards the skin (your left hand moving left to right to aid the process).
5. With fish pliers remove all exposed bones. Season the fillets.

Making the chicken juice

6. Peel the garlic and cut in half. Blanch the tarragon. Peel and finely chop the shallots. They want to be cut into *very* fine dice.
7. Pour the chicken stock into a saucepan, and add the garlic and tarragon. Bring to the boil, removing all surfacing fats with a ladle. Turn down the flame and simmer to reduce the liquid by half (as it does so, it will begin to thicken, turn darker in colour and take on an extra depth of flavour.) Once reduced to the required consistency, pass through a fine-mesh conical strainer into another pan. Add the shallots and some of the lemon juice to taste.

Cooking the fish

8. Place two frying pans on the stove, get them red hot, and very quickly put in the clarified butter. As they begin to smoke, put the fillets of zander in, skinned-side down first.
9. Fry the fillets for 2 minutes or until golden in colour and crisp, then turn over and cook for a further 2 minutes. With a fish slice or a large palette knife, remove the fillets and sprinkle with a little lemon juice.

To serve

10. Meanwhile, warm the *choucroûte* through gently in a stainless-steel pan, covered with a butter paper.

11. At the centre of each plate, place a mound of *choucroûte*. On top of it, carefully place your zander fillets. Spoon the chicken juice and raw shallots around the outer edge of the plate, and serve immediately.

HOT APPLE FRITTERS AND PLUM SAUCE

SERVES 4

*F*or this dessert I use small, crisp table apples. Cox's are best, because they are sweet in flavour but not full of water. As a contrast, the plum sauce is rather sharp, which creates a sweet and sour effect.

4 Cox's apples	150 g (5 oz) cornflour
60 g (2 oz) ground almonds	1 level tablespoon baking powder
110 g (3½ oz) plain flour	10 g (⅓ oz) caster sugar
vegetable oil for deep-frying	*Plum sauce*
caster sugar for serving	8 ripe red plums
Fritter batter	110 g (3½ oz) granulated sugar
150 g (5 oz) plain flour	

Preparing and cooking the sauce

1. Wash the plums in cold water, cut them in half and remove the stones. Place them in a saucepan and add 270 ml (9 fl oz) water and the sugar.

2. Over a gentle heat bring them to the boil. Boil for 2 minutes, then remove from the heat and leave them to cool.

3. Liquidise the plums, then strain through a sieve into a clean bowl. Reserve aside.

Preparing the batter and apples

4. To make the batter, sieve the flour, cornflour and baking powder into a bowl. Slowly beat in 375 ml (12½ fl oz) cold water until smooth. Add the sugar. If the batter appears lumpy, strain it through a sieve.

5. Peel the apples and cut them in halves, then quarters. Remove the core and cut each quarter lengthways into three. You want twelve pieces of apple per apple and person.

6. On a plate mix together the ground almonds and flour. Roll the apple slices in this, dusting them on both sides, then dip them into the batter.

Cooking the fritters

7. Meanwhile, in a deep pan, have the vegetable oil heated to 195°C (390°F) for deep-frying.

8. Piece by piece carefully drop the battered apple slices into the hot oil and fry until golden in colour, about 4 minutes. Remove from the hot oil and drain on kitchen paper. Keep warm in a low oven whilst you quickly cook the remaining apple fritters.

To serve

9. Lay out four plates, and cover each one with a layer of the prepared plum sauce.

10. Take the apple fritters from the oven and dip them immediately into a saucer of caster sugar. Sugar-side up, place on top of the plum sauce. Serve immediately.

As an option, I like to serve a fresh almond ice cream at the centre of the plate.

Autumn Menu 5

HOT OYSTER FLAN WITH A HERB BUTTER SAUCE

GRILLED BREAST OF WILD PIGEON, FRESH PASTA AND RED WINE SAUCE

CHARLOTTE OF CHOCOLATE AND VANILLA

HOT OYSTER FLAN WITH A HERB BUTTER SAUCE

SERVES 7

*O*ur native oysters, Colchester or Whitstable, are probably best eaten raw. These, however, I find too rich, and I prefer the Portuguese type for this cooked dish. The best French oysters are from Marennes (*fines de claires* and Belons).

All oysters must be purchased as fresh as possible and their shells must be tightly closed.

CHEF'S TIP

To open oysters, you must use an oyster knife, as using any other could be dangerous.

1. Place the oyster in a thick cloth, in the palm of your hand, and carefully insert the tip of the knife at the hinge of the shell.

2. Cut through the ligament which attaches the mollusc to the flat part of its shell or top.

3. Ease off the top shell and discard.

4. Again, using the knife, ease under the oyster and cut the muscle which attaches it to the bottom half of its shell.

5. When released, pour the oyster and juice into a clean bowl.

37 medium oysters
60 ml (2 fl oz) clarified butter
(see Chef's Tip, p.15)
Oyster flan
⅓ large garlic clove
1 sprig fresh tarragon
3 eggs
3 egg yolks
270 ml (9 fl oz) whipping cream
2 teaspoons lemon juice
salt
a pinch of cayenne pepper
Sauce and garnish
1 quantity Butter Sauce for Fish (see p.231)

30 g (1 oz) fresh parsley

30 g (1 oz) fresh chervil

30 g (1 oz) fresh chives

2 beef tomatoes

Preparing the oysters and ramekins

1. Open the oysters (see Chef's Tip).
2. Have ready seven ramekin moulds, 6.5 cm (2½ in) in diameter and 3.5 cm (1¼ in) deep, and a sheet of waxed or greaseproof paper. Using the bottom of one of the ramekins as a stencil, cut out seven discs from the sheet of greaseproof paper.
3. Melt the clarified butter and with a brush generously line the ramekins. Turn upside-down on a tray and refrigerate for 5 minutes or until the butter has set. Remove from the fridge and line each ramekin base with the prepared paper discs.

Preparing and cooking the oyster flans

4. Preheat the oven to 160°C (325°F) Gas 3.
5. Peel and crush the garlic. Blanch the tarragon.
6. Place the eggs, egg yolks, cream, garlic, lemon juice and tarragon into a liquidiser bowl. With a fork take sixteen oysters (no juice) and add to the bowl. Liquidise all the ingredients for 2 minutes until smooth.
7. Taste the mixture, and season with salt and cayenne pepper. Add more lemon juice if necessary, and liquidise for a further 30 seconds.
8. Strain through a fine-mesh conical strainer into a clean bowl and leave to rest for 5 minutes. With a ladle, skim off all the surfacing froth. This is important because if you do not do it properly, air bubbles will form in the flan during cooking.
9. Pour the liquid into a measuring jug and carefully fill the ramekins. Be sure you fill them to the top: during cooking a slight skin will form on the flans which will have to be removed before serving, therefore reducing its volume. Cover the ramekins with ovenproof cling film.

10. Three-quarters fill a deep roasting tray with water and bring to the boil. Carefully place the ramekins in the water, ensuring that the level of the water is just below the lip of the dishes. Cover the tray with butter paper for added protection, and cook for 10 minutes in the preheated oven.

Making the sauce and garnish

11. While the flans are cooking, prepare the butter sauce or *beurre blanc*.
12. Wash the parsley, pick off the leaves, re-wash, dry and chop. Chop the chervil and chives (keep a few sprigs of the former for garnish). Add the chopped herbs to the butter sauce and keep warm.
13. Blanch, skin, seed and dice the tomatoes. Warm through very gently.

To serve

14. Warm the oyster juice in a pan but *do not boil*. Add the remaining oysters, and warm only until the beards of the oysters begin to crinkle - no more than 1½ minutes. If you boil the oysters, they will become tough.
15. When cooked and set, remove the flans from the oven. Take off the butter paper and cling film and, with a knife, gently peel off the surface skins. Then run the knife along the inner edge of each ramekin and turn out on to the centre of each plate. Remove the greaseproof paper discs.
16. Garnish each plate with three oysters. Mask the dish with the prepared butter and herb sauce, and garnish the outer edge of the plates with a little of the warmed tomato dice topped with chervil sprigs.

As an extravagant option, I top each flan with a little Beluga caviare.

GRILLED BREAST OF WILD PIGEON, FRESH PASTA AND RED WINE SAUCE

SERVES 6

*W*ild pigeons are readily available and have a superb taste. In this recipe they are marinated and grilled in cream which seems to give them an extra succulence. We use only the breast meat as the legs tend to be tough and there is little meat to be had. If need be, the legs can be removed and kept for a game casserole or the like, but I usually put them in the sauce as pigeons are quite cheap.

6 wild or wood pigeons
salt and pepper
Marinade
4 garlic cloves
6 juniper berries
90 ml (3 fl oz) double cream
1 sprig fresh thyme
1 bay leaf
Red wine sauce
pigeon carcasses and legs
90 ml (3 fl oz) cooking oil
60 ml (2 fl oz) red wine vinegar
30 g (1 oz) redcurrant jelly
4 garlic cloves
6 juniper berries

1 sprig fresh thyme
1 bay leaf
300 ml (10 fl oz) red wine
1.5 litres (2¾ pints) Chicken Stock (see p.225)
1 quantity *Mirepoix* (see p.239)
Watercress and parsley coulis
90 g (3 oz) each of parsley and watercress leaves, washed
90 ml (3 fl oz) double cream
To serve
1 quantity Fresh Pasta for Ravioli (see p.241), cut into tagliatelle
12 small carrots
12 small turnips
game chips (optional, see Chef's Tip)

Preparing and marinating the pigeon

1. Remove the breast meat from the pigeon and pull the skin off. Reserve the legs if not using, otherwise chop them up with the carcass for the sauce.

2. Peel and chop the garlic, and crush the juniper berries.

3. In a heatproof dish large enough to hold the pigeon in one layer, place the cream, with the thyme, bay leaf, garlic and crushed juniper berries. Put in the pigeon breasts, mix well and cover with cling film. Leave to marinate for 12 hours in the fridge.

Making the sauce

4. Heat the cooking oil in a roasting tray and sauté the pigeon bones on top of the stove until golden brown, about 5 minutes.

5. Heat a casserole pan and add the red wine vinegar with the redcurrant jelly. Reduce until sticky but not burnt.

6. Peel and chop the garlic and crush the juniper berries. Add, along with the thyme and bay leaf to the casserole. When the bones are browned, add those too, lifting them in with a slotted spoon. Mix well.

7. Tip the cooking oil out of the roasting tray and retain. Pour in the red wine, and bring to the boil. Reduce by half, scraping off the sediments with a wooden spoon. Add to the bones.

8. Cover with the chicken stock (reserve a little for the cooking of the breasts), bring to the boil and skim. Brown the *mirepoix* vegetables in the retained hot oil, and add to the stock. Simmer for 1 hour.

9. When cooked, strain the stock and place back on the stove to reduce by half. Skim often. Taste for seasoning, adding salt and pepper if necessary. Pass through clean muslin

to trap all the coagulated blood particles.
Keep hot.

Cooking the pigeon

10. Preheat the grill.
11. Season the marinated pigeon breasts, and
add a little chicken stock to the dish: this will
help prevent the cream burning. Place the dish
under the hot grill, and leave for 4–5 minutes.
12. Turn the pigeon breasts and continue
grilling until the breasts feel firmish but giving
slightly in the middle. The whole grilling
should take only 8 or so minutes.

Making the watercress and parsley coulis

13. Bring a small pan of water to the boil, add
a little salt, and toss in the parsley. Boil for
about 3 minutes, then add the watercress. Boil
for a further minute. Strain through a fine
strainer and refresh in cold water.
14. Turn on to a clean kitchen cloth and
squeeze dry. Then cut into a fine paste in the
liquidiser. Add the cream.

To serve

15. Meanwhile reheat or cook the pasta, and
season. Heat the parsley through gently. Trim
and cook the carrots and turnips. Warm
through the game chips if using.
16. In the middle of each plate place a spoon
of parsley coulis: at the top a swirl of hot
pasta, to the left two turnips, to the right two
carrots, and at the base, if using, a pile of
warm game chips. Carve the breasts in half
and lie on top of the warm parsley coulis.
17. Quickly pour the hot pigeon sauce around
and serve immediately.

CHEF'S TIP
*Game chips - basically home-made potato crisps - are
traditionally served with feathered game. Peel some
medium potatoes then wash them. Slice them finely on a
mandoline then wash again to remove the starch. Drain
and dry the slices thoroughly, then deep-fry as for chips
until golden and crisp. You can make them in advance
as they will remain crisp.*

Roasted Grouse

Burnt English Custard Mousse

Soup of Mussels Scented with Curry

Escalopes of Tuna Steamed with Crunchy Vegetables in a Warm Vinaigrette

CHARLOTTE OF CHOCOLATE AND VANILLA

SERVES 8

*T*his dessert can be made as one large charlotte or as individual ones. Everyone must recognise the beauty of fruit charlottes. This is just an adaptation of a classic theme using a vanilla sabayon cream and a chocolate mousse. The vanilla cream takes away a little of the richness of the dessert.

Sponge fingers
3 eggs
90 g (3 oz) caster sugar
30 g (1 oz) plain flour
30 g (1 oz) cornflour
caster sugar for sprinkling
Chocolate mousse
120 g (4 oz) dark chocolate
2 egg yolks
60 ml (2 fl oz) Stock Syrup (see p.249)
270 ml (9 fl oz) whipping cream

Vanilla mousse
210 g (7 oz) Pastry Cream (see p.249)
1 vanilla pod
300 ml (10 fl oz) whipping cream
20 ml (⅔ fl oz) Crème de Cacao Blanc (white chocolate liqueur)
3 gelatine leaves, soaked in cold water to soften
Chocolate curls
60 g (2 oz) dark chocolate
60 g (2 oz) white chocolate
icing sugar for dusting

Preparing and cooking the sponge fingers

1. Preheat the oven to 230°C (450°F) Gas 8, and line a baking tray with greaseproof paper.
2. Separate the eggs. Whisk together the egg yolks and 60 g (2 oz) of the caster sugar in a bowl until pale and thick.
3. In an electric mixer bowl whisk the egg whites until they come to firm peaks, and add the remaining caster sugar.
4. Fold the egg whites into the egg yolks, and then sieve in the flour and cornflour, gently folding until mixed in.
5. Fill a piping bag fitted with a plain nozzle with the sponge mixture, and pipe into fingers about 1 cm (½ in) wide by 5 cm (2 in) long on the lined tray. This quantity will make about 48 fingers.
6. Sprinkle with extra caster sugar and bake in the preheated oven for 5–6 minutes until golden and firm to the touch. Remove from the oven when cooked and cool on a wire rack.
7. Place a 20 cm (8 in) round cake ring on a large plate. Use the sponge fingers to line the sides of the ring.

Preparing the chocolate mousse

8. Chop the chocolate, place in a bowl and melt over a pan of simmering water until smooth.
9. Whisk together the egg yolks and stock syrup in a bowl, then place the bowl over simmering water and whisk until thick and white in colour, to make a sabayon.
10. Whisk the cream until firm but not stiff.
11. Fold the warm melted chocolate into the sabayon and then fold in the whipping cream, being very careful not to *over*-mix at this stage. With the aid of a plastic spatula pour the mixture into the sponge-finger-lined cake ring. Place in the refrigerator to set for 1 hour.

Preparing the vanilla mousse

12. In a bowl whisk the pastry cream until smooth. Split the vanilla pod and whisk the seeds into the pastry cream.
13. In another bowl whisk the cream to firm peaks.
14. Warm the Crème de Cacao Blanc in a small saucepan, then add and dissolve the pre-soaked gelatine. Whisk this into the pastry cream.
15. Fold together the whipped cream and pastry cream. Place this on top of the chocolate mousse, and, using a palette knife, draw the

edges up towards the centre giving a dome shape. Refrigerate the charlotte.

Making the chocolate curls

16. Chop the dark chocolate and place in a bowl. Over a pan of simmering water stir the chocolate until melted and smooth. Remove and leave until almost set, then melt again and leave to cool to almost set.

CHEF'S TIP

To achieve a glaze or sheen to the chocolate, it will be necessary to repeat the melting and setting process twice – melt and set, melt and set.

---

17. Chop the white chocolate, place in a bowl and proceed as for the dark chocolate.
18. When both chocolates are on the point of setting for the second time, put them, separately, on a clean surface and, using a palette knife, spread them out in a thin layer to set.
19. As soon as they have set, drag the palette knife across the surface to form the chocolate curls, both dark and white. Put the finished chocolate curls on to a plate and refrigerate to chill.

To serve

20. Stud the vanilla mousse top with the white and dark chocolate curls, and lightly dust the charlotte with icing sugar.
21. Carefully remove the cake ring from the charlotte. Cut into the required portions and serve chilled.

I recommend a dark chocolate sauce with this and *langue de chat* biscuits rolled into cigarettes with both ends dipped into milk chocolate (see pp.250 and 246).

Autumn Menu 6

SMOKED SALMON AND OYSTERS IN ENGLISH WINE JELLY

ROASTED GROUSE

BURNT ENGLISH CUSTARD MOUSSE

SMOKED SALMON AND OYSTERS IN ENGLISH WINE JELLY

SERVES 6

This menu is the one I created when I represented Great Britain at the first International Meeting of Gastronomy in Madrid in 1992. I received two gold medals, and came joint first with France and Spain.

The following oyster dish was the one about which the judges were most divided, and which won me a silver medal: they thought it 'untypical' of British cooking, but I think it was its unexpected sophistication that perplexed them. However, it uses some of the glorious ingredients that Britain can be so proud of, and it is perfectly feasible to achieve at home. Its essence is a clear, intensely flavoured jelly.

18 oysters
350 g (12 oz) Scottish smoked salmon
1 bunch watercress (it should be good and strong and peppery)
6 sprigs seaweed (optional)
Wine jelly
420 (14 fl oz) Fish Stock (see p.223)
1½ gelatine leaves, soaked in cold water to soften
150 ml (5 fl oz) English dry white wine (or a Sancerre)
Clarification
2 garlic cloves

4–5 parsley stalks
1 sprig fresh tarragon
¼ bay leaf
1 sprig fresh thyme
1 small onion
1 small carrot
¼ fennel bulb
1 celery stalk
1 leek
salt, pepper and cayenne
a pinch of saffron strands
3 egg whites

Preparing the oysters and shells

1. First open the oysters (see p.145). Pour the oysters with their juices into a bowl. Scrub the bottom shells clean and lay them on a kitchen towel to dry.

2. Carefully slice the smoked salmon as thin as possible. Using an upturned shell as a stencil, cut out the salmon and line the shell. With your thumb press the salmon flat into the shell. With some scissors trim off any overlapping excess.

3. Pick the watercress leaves from their stalks. Submerge the leaves in a small pan of boiling water for 20 seconds, then strain through a fine-mesh conical strainer. Refresh the leaves under cold running water. Turn the leaves out on to a plate and, one by one, open them up. Lay them flat around the upper edges of the lined oyster shells. Line all the shells in similar fashion.

4. With a cocktail stick carefully pick the oysters out from their juices and put them into the pre-lined shells. Put the shells on a tray and refrigerate.

5. Strain the oyster juices through a fine-mesh conical strainer into another bowl and reserve aside for the jelly.

Preparing the clarification

6. Peel and crush the garlic. Wash the parsley stalks and finely chop them. Blanch the tarragon. Place into a large bowl along with the bay leaf and thyme.

7. Peel and chop the onion and carrot. Chop the fennel and celery: it is not necessary to peel these. Wash and finely chop the leek. Add these to the bowl. Season with a little salt, pepper, a pinch of cayenne and the saffron.

8. Add the egg whites to the bowl and with a whisk beat the mixture until the whites are fully incorporated into the vegetables. This is the clarification.

Preparing the jelly

9. Pour the fish stock and strained oyster juices into a saucepan. Bring to the boil and with a ladle remove and discard any surfacing scum or froth.

10. Stir in the gelatine and, as soon as the stock has reboiled, all at once throw in the clarification from the bowl. Whisk the jelly back up to the boil. As soon as the clarification 'crust' has set and begins to crack, turn the heat down to a gentle simmer and cook for 15 minutes.

11. When cooked, remove the consommé from the stove. Strain the liquid into a bowl lined with a muslin cloth. Gently lift the cloth with both hands and discard the trapped sediment. (Wash out the muslin - it can be used again.)

12. Pour the white wine into the consommé in the bowl. In most cooking it is essential to boil and reduce the alcohol, but in this dish we leave the wine in its raw state to retain all of its flavour and acidity.

CHEF'S TIP

Be careful not to allow the muslin cloth to fall into the jelly during the clarification. You might find it easier to support the cloth over a fine-mesh conical strainer.

13. Put the clarified jelly over a bowl of crushed ice to cool. When cool, refrigerate to start to set the jelly, about 20 minutes.

To finish and serve

14. As the jelly begins to set remove the oysters from the fridge and with a small ladle or spoon carefully, and as quickly as possible, mask over the oysters. Repeat this process twice to achieve the best results. It is important not to allow the jelly to become too thick or set. If this happens just re-melt the jelly, cool it, and try again. Once covered with jelly put the oysters back on a tray in the refrigerator until ready to serve.

15. Fill six soup plates with crushed ice. If available top each plate with a sprig of washed seaweed.

16. Carefully place three oyster shells at equal distance from each other, on top of the seaweed, and serve immediately.

If money is no object, top each oyster with a little Beluga caviare for added effect. A slice of toasted brioche is a good accompaniment to this dish, or brown toast.

ROASTED GROUSE

SERVES 6

*G*rouse is one of those birds of which the British can be justifiably proud, as it is unique to our shores (apart from the snow grouse from Sweden). The season is short – from 12th August until mid-October – the better birds being in the earlier part of the season. In this recipe the grouse is dressed and simply roasted, therefore it is recommended that only young fresh birds be used.

6 young grouse	30 g (1 oz) redcurrant jelly
60 g (2 oz) butter, softened	60 ml (2 fl oz) port
salt and pepper	450 ml (15 fl oz) full-bodied red wine
12 smoked streaky bacon rashers	1.75 litres (3 pints) Chicken Stock (see p.225)
60 ml (2 fl oz) cooking oil	30 ml (1 fl oz) cooking oil
Sauce	1 quantity *Mirepoix* (see p.239), using 6 shallots
4 garlic cloves	instead of the onion
8 juniper berries	1 sprig fresh thyme
60 ml (2 fl oz) red wine vinegar	1 bay leaf

Preparing the grouse

1. Remove the wishbones and feet. Singe the birds to remove all feathers and remaining quills.
2. Rub each bird well with the softened butter. Season with salt and pepper.
3. Rind the bacon. With a meat bat or the flat of a large knife, flatten the rashers out. Lay a rasher either side of each breast and tie on with kitchen string.

Cooking the grouse

4. Preheat the oven to 230°C (450°F) Gas 8.
5. Heat the cooking oil in a roasting tray and carefully place each grouse in on its left thigh. Allow to brown well, and then turn over to the right side.
6. Place the grouse in the preheated oven and roast for 5 minutes on their right thighs, and then return to their left for a further 5 minutes. Finally place the birds on their backs to finish off cooking for a further 4 minutes. The time can vary according to the size of the bird but the nicest way to eat it is to leave it pink in the breast with the legs more cooked.
7. Remove from the oven, snip the string and take off the bacon. Still in the roasting tray, place the birds on their breasts to brown the skin where the bacon has been. This operation takes place on top of the stove, and only takes 30 seconds or so per bird.
8. Remove the birds from the tray and allow to rest. Keep the tray and the oil.
9. Remove the legs and breast meat in four whole joints per bird. Carefully, with a knife, remove the thigh bones. Place the meat on a plate or tray and keep warm, covered with foil or butter paper.

Preparing and cooking the sauce

10. Chop the carcasses coarsely. Peel and chop the garlic. Crush the juniper berries.
11. Add the coarsely chopped carcasses to the roasting tray and oil. Turning often, sauté on top of the stove until golden brown – about 5 minutes – and remove with a slotted spoon to a tall saucepan.
12. Tip off the oil and pour the red wine vinegar into the hot tray. Allow to boil and reduce, scraping off any sediment stuck on the tray bottom with a wooden spoon. Add the jelly and allow the liquid to become syrupy, then pour over the bones in the saucepan and mix well. Add the port.
13. Add the red wine to the roasting tray, bring to the boil and reduce by half. Pour into the saucepan. Cover with chicken stock and bring to the boil.

14. Meanwhile, in a clean pan, heat the fresh oil and colour the *mirepoix* vegetables all over until golden brown, then add to the stock. Add the juniper berries, garlic, thyme and bay leaf. Skim and simmer for only 10 minutes then strain through a fine strainer or muslin.

15. In a clean saucepan, reduce the stock by half, skimming any surfacing scum. The sauce can get very bitter if cooked for too long so be careful not to simmer it for more than 15 minutes.

To serve

16. Place the grouse back in a hot oven to reheat if necessary. Be careful not to lose the pink colour.

17. Put the legs on six hot plates, creating a foundation, and on top carefully balance the breast meat, giving the dish height. Spoon the sauce around without flooding the plates.

A nice garnish is a pile of hot game chips (see Chef's Tip, p.148) at the crown, left and right a little salsify or Brussels sprouts and, at the base, a small spoonful of cranberries.

BURNT ENGLISH CUSTARD MOUSSE

SERVES 8

*T*his dish is made up of three recipes carefully assembled together.

Caramel mousse
170 g (5½ oz) caster sugar
150 ml (5 fl oz) double cream
150 ml (5 fl oz) milk
4 egg yolks
3 gelatine leaves, soaked in cold water to soften
225 ml (7½ fl oz) whipping cream
Toffee squares and tops
210 g (7 oz) caster sugar
60 ml (2 fl oz) liquid glucose
60 g (2 oz) unsalted butter

a little cooking oil
Vanilla cream
150 g (5 oz) Pastry Cream (see p.249)
1 vanilla pod
270 ml (9 fl oz) whipping cream
To serve
icing sugar for dusting
8 x 4 cm (1¾ in) discs Biscuit Sponge (see p.245)
30 ml (1 fl oz) Tia Maria
8 sprigs fresh mint
A little edible gold leaf (optional)

Preparing the caramel mousse

1. Gently melt 110 g (3½ oz) of the caster sugar on the stove until an 'amber' caramel is attained. Immediately add the double cream, stirring all the time. Remove from the heat and stir in the milk.

2. In a stainless-steel bowl whisk the egg yolks and remaining sugar together until pale and thick.

3. Return the saucepan with the cream, milk and caramel to the stove and bring back to the boil. When boiling pour half the liquid over the yolks and sugar and whisk together. Pour

all of this back into the pan. Cook over a gentle heat until the liquid thickens, stirring all the time. The liquid should coat the back of the spoon.

4. Add the gelatine and stir until dissolved. Pass the liquid through a fine-mesh conical strainer into a bowl and leave to cool. Stir the liquid from time to time.

5. In a bowl, whisk the whipping cream until it forms a soft peak. Fold half the cream into the caramel cream and when smooth fold in the remainder.

6. On a tray lined with greaseproof paper,

place eight moulds of approximately 5.5 cm
(2¼ in) in diameter, and 3 cm (1¼ in) high.
Fill them with your caramel mousse and
refrigerate for at least 4 hours. (In Madrid I
used hexagonal ring moulds, but any moulds
will do, so long as they are approximately the
same size and volume.)

Preparing the toffee squares and tops

7. Preheat the oven to 220°C (425°F) Gas 7.
8. Line two thin baking trays with greaseproof
paper and gently brush them with a little extra
melted butter. If using silicone paper, the
butter will not be necessary.
9. In a saucepan, mix the sugar, glucose and
60 ml (2 fl oz) water together with a spoon.
Bring to the boil and reduce until caramelised.
Remove from the heat and immediately stir in
the butter until fully incorporated. Spoon eight
puddles of toffee (the size of a 50p coin) on to
one of the lined trays. It is important to leave
plenty of space between the puddles. Pour the
remaining toffee on to the other tray. Take a
palette knife and spread the toffee thinly,
covering all the tray. Whilst this sheet of toffee
is still warm, cut it into 3 cm (1¼ in) squares.
You will need six squares per mousse, 48 in
all. Reserve aside.

CHEF'S TIP
*If the toffee sets before you have time to spread it, place it
in a warm oven for a few minutes, just to melt.*

10. Place the tray with the puddles of toffee
into the preheated oven for 2 minutes. Take it
out and with a palette knife spread each one
into a circle approximately 7 cm (2¾ in) in
diameter. Lightly oil the inside of a 60 ml
(2 fl oz) ladle and carefully push a toffee circle

inside it, moulding it into the shape of the
ladle. Remember you can only achieve this if
the toffee is still warm. Trim off any
overlapping excess with a pair of scissors,
remove the toffee dome from the ladle and
reserve aside. Repeat this process until you
have eight dome tops.

Preparing the vanilla cream

11. In a stainless-steel bowl whisk the pastry
cream until smooth. Cut the vanilla pod
lengthways in half and with the point of a
knife scrape out the seeds. Whisk these into
the pastry cream.
12. In another bowl whisk the cream to a firm
peak. Fold half into the pastry cream and
when smooth fold the other half. Refrigerate.

To serve

13. Lay out eight soup plates and dust them
with icing sugar.
14. Dip the biscuit sponge discs into the Tia
Maria and place one in the centre of each
plate.
15. Remove the caramel mousses from the
fridge and place on top of the soaked biscuit
base. With a warm knife cut around the inner
edge of the ring moulds and remove them.
16. Place six toffee squares around the sides of
each mousse. With a spoon, carefully fill each
toffee dome with the vanilla cream and place
them, rounded side up, on top of the mousses.
Garnish each plate with a sprig of mint and a
little gold leaf if liked, and serve immediately.

CHEF'S TIP
*Take particular care not to break the dome tops whilst
filling them with the vanilla cream. They are extremely
fragile.*

Autumn Menu 7

SOUP OF MUSSELS SCENTED WITH CURRY

SADDLE OF VENISON, RED CABBAGE AND A BRANDY AND PORT SAUCE

GRATIN OF PEAR, CHOCOLATE AND NUTS

SOUP OF MUSSELS SCENTED WITH CURRY

SERVES 6

*T*his is an unusual dish, and very nourishing. I use a little curry in its making to give it an extra sharpness.

2.25 kg (5 lb) mussels, shell weight	**a pinch of cayenne pepper**
salt and pepper	**15 g (½ oz) saffron strands**
Soup	**120 ml (4 fl oz) Noilly Prat**
4 shallots	**375 ml (12½ fl oz) dry white wine**
1 leek	**900 ml (1½ pints) Fish Stock (see p.223)**
1 celery stalk	**120 ml (4 fl oz) double cream**
3 garlic cloves	**30 ml (1 fl oz) lemon juice**
15 g (½ oz) white peppercorns	*Garnish* (optional)
60 ml (2 fl oz) olive oil	**1 red and 1 yellow pepper**
120 g (4 oz) butter	**2 large courgettes**
1 sprig fresh thyme	**some fine pasta noodles, cooked**
1 bay leaf	**some fresh coriander leaves**
30 g (1 oz) curry paste	

Preparing the garnish

The garnish, as with most dishes, is purely optional. I like to do the following and it must be prepared in advance of making the soup.

1. Peel and cut the red and yellow peppers

into fine strips (*julienne*) and blanch in boiling salted water for 2 minutes. Remove and refresh in cold water. Strain off the water and keep the strips warm in a small saucepan with a little of the recipe fish stock.

2. Slice the courgettes lengthways and cut into fine strips. Do not cook them. In this form, they are always best added raw to keep their taste and texture.

Preparing the mussels and soup ingredients

3. Very carefully clean and scrape all the mussels, removing any barnacles and beards which show on the outside of the shells. Wash thoroughly in cold water.

CHEF'S TIP

The best way to determine mussel freshness is to make sure they are closed tight. Any mussel open before cooking is probably dead, and should immediately be discarded. Any that remain closed after cooking should be discarded too.

4. Peel and finely chop the shallots. Wash the leek and celery and trim. Cut into small dice. Peel and crush the garlic. Crush the peppercorns.

Preparing the soup base

5. Put the olive oil and half the butter into a deep saucepan. Heat until the butter has melted but not coloured.

6. First add your shallots and gently cook, but do not colour. Add the celery and the diced leek, then the thyme and bay leaf.

7. Add the curry paste and cayenne pepper, stirring continuously, and allow the mixture to cook for approximately 5 minutes over a moderate flame. Then put in the saffron and crushed white peppercorns, and moisten with the Noilly Prat.

8. Turn up the flame and, again stirring continuously, reduce the liquid until syrupy. Do not allow the soup base to catch on the bottom of the pan or burn in any way, because this would give the soup a bitter aftertaste.

9. Add the white wine, bring to the boil and reduce by half. Add the crushed garlic.

10. Add the fish stock and bring to the boil. With a ladle, remove all surfacing fat and scum.

Cooking the mussels

11. At this stage, and all at once, throw in the mussels. Stir them thoroughly, turning bottom to top, bottom to top. Repeat the process two or three times. Place a lid on the saucepan and, over a fierce flame, cook the mussels for 8 minutes.

12. Remove the lid. When the mussels are cooked they will open; if not, continue cooking until they do.

13. When cooked, immediately tip the mussels into a colander, making sure you have a saucepan underneath to trap the cooking juices. Shake off all the liquid from the mussels and turn on to a tray. This will help them to cool down quickly and evenly. Take the mussels out of their shells and arrange them in the individual soup dishes. Keep warm. Discard all but a few of the shells, which can be arranged around the dishes on serving.

14. Pass the liquid in the saucepan (the mussel soup) firstly through a conical strainer, then very carefully through a muslin cloth into a bowl.

CHEF'S TIP

Sieving the soup twice is important because any sand or sediment that might come out of the mussels during cooking will be trapped in the cloth. (The cloth can be washed and re-used.)

To finish and serve

15. Pour the strained soup into another saucepan, boil and, with a ladle, remove all the surfacing scum. Add the cream and reduce down to the required consistency. Check the seasoning and add the lemon juice to bring out the flavours.

16. Finally, cut the remaining butter into dice and, a piece at a time, whisk it into the soup until fully dissolved. This will bring a beautiful shine to the soup and round off the raw edges of its taste.

17. Arrange the strips of peppers and courgettes over the mussels in the soup plates. If using, with a meat fork place the fine noodles at the centre of each plate. Pour over the prepared mussel soup and sprinkle the plates with the fresh coriander.

SADDLE OF VENISON, RED CABBAGE AND A BRANDY AND PORT SAUCE

SERVES 6

*T*echnically, venison is available all the year round due to farming, but I find the nicest venison is that available in the cooler months, in autumn, winter and spring. There are various joints to be had but the most tender cut and the one I've used in this recipe is the saddle or fillet. The meat is marinated for 24 hours, as is the red cabbage but as alcohol would disguise the venison flavour none is used. Instead an oil and herb marinade enhances the meat.

1 kg (2¼ lb) saddle of venison, boned (keep the bones for the sauce)

salt and pepper

240 ml (8 fl oz) vegetable oil

Marinade

3 garlic cloves

5 black peppercorns

1 quantity *Mirepoix* (see p.239)

zest of 1 orange

1 sprig fresh thyme

1 bay leaf

Braised red cabbage

1 small red cabbage

5 juniper berries

1 onion

1 cooking apple

lemon juice

1 garlic clove

30 g (1 oz) brown sugar

Sauce

5 juniper berries

5 black peppercorns

120 ml (4 fl oz) red wine vinegar

60 g (2 oz) redcurrant jelly

1 sprig fresh thyme

1 bay leaf

60 ml (2 fl oz) cooking port

60 ml (2 fl oz) cooking brandy

60 ml (2 fl oz) red wine

1.5 litres (2¾ pints) Chicken Stock (see p.225)

60 ml (2 fl oz) whipping cream

30 g (1 oz) butter

Marinating the venison

1. Peel and slice the garlic. Crush the peppercorns.
2. Place the venison fillets into a shallow tray with the *mirepoix*, 60 ml (2 fl oz) of the oil, the orange zest, thyme, bay leaf, the crushed peppercorns and the sliced garlic. Mix well together, cover and leave for 24 hours. Retain the *mirepoix* vegetables to use in the sauce.

Preparing the braised red cabbage

3. Cut the cabbage in quarters, remove the root and slice crossways. Crush the juniper berries. Peel and slice the onion and apple. Toss the apple in lemon juice. Peel and crush the garlic.
4. Place the cabbage in a stainless-steel bowl. Add the sugar, the crushed juniper berries, garlic, sliced onion and apple. Cover and leave for 24 hours.

Preparing and cooking the sauce

5. Crush the juniper berries and peppercorns separately.
6. Heat a little of the oil and sauté the venison bones until brown in a roasting pan on top of the stove.
7. Meanwhile put the red wine vinegar and redcurrant jelly in a casserole and boil until a syrup is obtained. Add the crushed juniper berries, thyme and bay leaf.
8. Lift the bones from the roasting pan, using a slotted spoon, and add them to the syrup. Mix well.
9. Heat the port and brandy together, set alight, and add to the bones.
10. Drain the *mirepoix* vegetables from the marinade and brown in the oil remaining in the roasting pan. Add to the bones, using a slotted spoon. Tip the oil out of the pan.
11. Pour the red wine into the roasting pan

and boil, scraping off the sediment. Add to the bones with the crushed peppercorns. Cover with the chicken stock and bring to the boil. Skim and simmer for 1½–2 hours.

Cooking the cabbage
12. Preheat the oven to 150°C (300°F) Gas 2.
13. Place the marinated cabbage and all the other cabbage ingredients into a thick-bottomed casserole. Bake in the preheated oven for 1–2 hours, turning often until the cabbage is tender and all the liquid has evaporated. It should become a dark mauve colour when cooked. Check the seasoning and add salt and pepper if necessary.

Cooking the venison
14. Preheat the oven to 220°C (425°F) Gas 7.
15. Remove the fillets from the marinade, season with salt and pepper, and seal on all

sides in some hot oil.
16. Roast the fillets in the preheated hot oven for 4–5 minutes. The nicest way to eat venison is medium rare, still moist in the middle. When firm but slightly giving to the touch, remove and allow to relax.

To finish and serve
17. Strain the stock and reduce rapidly by half. Add the cream and continue boiling. Whisk in the cold butter in pieces, allow to thicken and taste for seasoning.
18. Reheat the red cabbage and the venison.
19. Place a large mound of hot red cabbage in the middle of each plate. Around the cabbage place the sliced venison fillet. Strain over the finished sauce and serve at once.

A nice accompaniment is some baby sprouts which you can sprinkle around the perimeter of the plate.

GRATIN OF PEAR, CHOCOLATE AND NUTS

SERVES 6

This excellent hot dessert shows the contrasts between the crispness of the nuts, the soft melting chocolate and the delicate flavour and texture of the pear.

I first encountered this idea whilst working for my friend and mentor, Raymond Blanc, at his restaurant Les Quat' Saisons in Summertown, Oxford.

3 large ripe pears	**30 g (1 oz) flaked almonds**
120 g (4 oz) caster sugar	**30 g (1 oz) whole shelled hazelnuts**
juice of 1 lemon	***Sabayon***
icing sugar to dust	**6 egg yolks**
Chocolate base	**150 ml (5 fl oz) syrup from cooking the pears**
110 g (3½ oz) dark chocolate	**60 g (2 oz) caster sugar**
10 g (⅓ oz) unsalted butter	**1 tablespoon pear liqueur**
75 ml (2½ fl oz) whipping cream	**(Poire William *eau-de-vie*)**
30 g (1 oz) walnut halves	

Poaching the pears
1. Bring to the boil in a saucepan the sugar, lemon juice and 270 ml (9 fl oz) water. Remove from the heat and reserve aside.
2. Peel and halve the pears and place them into the prepared syrup. Cover with

greaseproof paper. Poach over a gentle heat until tender, about 5 minutes, depending on size and ripeness. Remove the pan from the stove and leave to cool.

Preparing the chocolate base

3. Preheat the oven to 230°C (450°F) Gas 8.

4. Chop the chocolate and place in a bowl. Dice the butter.

5. In a saucepan, bring the cream to the boil, pour it over the chocolate and stir well until the chocolate has completely melted. Piece by piece, stir in the butter.

6. In a small saucepan of boiling water, cook the walnuts for 1 minute. Remove from the heat and, whilst still warm, peel the skins off with the point of a small knife. (If you leave the walnuts to get cold, it will be impossible to peel them.)

7. Place the almonds and walnuts on a tray and roast in the preheated oven until golden brown, about 7 minutes. On a separate tray roast the hazelnuts. When brown remove them all from the oven and place the hazelnuts on a clean kitchen cloth. Rub the cloth together to remove the dry skins.

8. Stir all the prepared nuts into the chocolate base.

Preparing the sabayon

9. Place the egg yolks in a stainless-steel bowl. Whisk in the measured pear syrup, caster sugar and pear liqueur. Pass the mixture through a sieve into another stainless-steel bowl and reserve aside.

To finish and serve

10. Preheat your grill, and lay out six serving plates.

11. Remove the pears from the syrup and drain them on kitchen paper. Remove the core and slice the pears (bottom to top), leaving 2 cm (¾ in) at the stalk end intact. Gently press them open to form a fan shape.

12. In the centre of each plate, place 2 dessert-spoons of the chocolate base. Place an 8 cm (3¼ in) pastry cutter around this and, using a palette knife, spread out to form an even circle. Remove the cutter and top with a fanned pear.

13. Half fill a large saucepan with water and bring it to simmering on the stove. Place the bowl containing the sabayon over the hot water and whisk rapidly until the sabayon thickens and becomes white in colour. To check if the sabayon is ready, lift your whisk out and it should show a peak. This should take about 3–4 minutes.

14. Spoon the sabayon over the pears. Dust the tops with icing sugar and place each plate in turn under the grill to brown and glaze. Serve immediately.

Autumn Menu 8

ESCALOPES OF TUNA STEAMED WITH CRUNCHY VEGETABLES IN A WARM VINAIGRETTE

SAUTÉ OF CALF'S LIVER, CARROTS AND ORANGE

CHOCOLATE SOUFFLÉ WITH A WARM FROTHY VANILLA CUSTARD

ESCALOPES OF TUNA STEAMED WITH CRUNCHY VEGETABLES IN A WARM VINAIGRETTE

SERVES 6

*T*una is the largest member of the mackerel family. The flesh is somewhat coarse and rather oily but, when treated in this fashion, it is quite delicious and makes a welcome change at the beginning of the autumn.

The fresh tuna you can buy in England usually comes from the Mediterranean and, because large fish keep longer, they are invariably huge. Ask your fishmonger for a piece from the thicker part of the fish, nearest the head, for this is the best meat.

6 x 120 g (4 oz) tuna steaks (skinned weight)	1 garlic clove
salt and pepper	300 ml (10 fl oz) Fish Stock (see p.223)
Vegetables	*Potato garnish*
½ red cabbage	450 g (1 lb) potatoes
½ bunch fresh chives	corn oil for deep-frying
1 sprig fresh tarragon	*Garlic and lemon butter*
1 carrot	1 sprig fresh tarragon
2 courgettes	2 garlic cloves
1 fennel bulb	120 g (4 oz) unsalted butter
2 celery stalks	juice of ½ lemon

a pinch of cayenne pepper
Sauce
60 ml (2 fl oz) each of Groundnut Vinaigrette

and Walnut Vinaigrette (see p.233)
½ bunch fresh chives

Preparing the vegetables
1. Cut the red cabbage into two, and remove and discard the outside leaves and stalk. Wash in a sink of cold water, drain in a colander and dry on a cloth. Shred into long thin strips.
2. Wash the chives, shake off the excess water, and dry. Cut in half. Blanch the tarragon.
3. Wash, peel and slice the carrot and courgettes. Cut to the same approximate thickness as the chives, and about 10 cm (4 in) in length.
4. Cut off the top of the fennel and slice in two. Separate the leaves, peel and slice. Peel the celery and, as near as possible, cut both vegetables into long *julienne* strips as for the carrots. Peel the garlic.

Preparing and cooking the potato garnish
5. Wash, peel and re-wash the potatoes. With the aid of a processor or a hand grater shred the potatoes as finely as possible. In French, this is called *'cheveux d'ange'* (angel hair), and is twice as thin as a matchstick. Wash the shredded potatoes to remove all the excess starch. This is important or they will all stick together in frying. Drain in a colander and dry thoroughly on a clean kitchen cloth.
6. In a fryer or thick-bottomed pan start to heat the corn oil to 182–193°C (360–380°F).
7. When the oil is up to temperature, fry the potatoes in two batches until golden then remove and drain on kitchen paper. When drained, season with a little salt and transfer to a clean plate. Keep them warm above the stove.

CHEF'S TIP
When deep-frying, it is important to choose the correct size pan. A general rule of thumb is to make sure that the oil never exceeds one-third of the total volume of the pan. This will prevent the oil from boiling over on initial contact with the food being cooked.

Preparing the garlic and lemon butter
8. Blanch and dry the tarragon, and peel and crush the garlic.
9. In a small pan gently melt the butter with the lemon juice, tarragon, the crushed garlic, some salt and a pinch of cayenne pepper. Stir from time to time. Reserve aside.

Cooking the vegetables
10. In a large pan, boil the fish stock over a fierce flame and add the garlic, tarragon and salt and pepper to taste.
11. In order of cooking times, first add the fennel, carrot and lastly the celery to the boiling fish stock. Cook for approximately 2 minutes. Leave the red cabbage, chives and courgettes raw. Over another pan strain the vegetables through a fine-mesh conical strainer and quickly turn these out on to a tray to cool. Remove and discard the garlic and tarragon.
12. When cool, mix all the vegetables together in a bowl, and add 2 dessertspoons of the strained garlic and lemon butter. Season with salt and pepper and mix thoroughly again.

Cooking the tuna
13. Brush the tuna steaks with the remaining garlic and lemon butter, and season them.
14. Cover the base of two plates with the prepared vegetables and halved chives and on top of each place three tuna steaks. Cover with cling film and place in a steamer to cook. (If a steamer is not available, you can use the bamboo steamer baskets which stack one on top of another over a wok or pan of boiling water.) The cooking time is just 10 minutes.

To finish and serve
15. Boil the stock used for the vegetables to reduce it by half.
16. Mix together this reduced fish stock and the prepared vinaigrettes. Whisk together and keep warm.

17. Wash and dry the chives. Chop them finely, but do not add to the sauce until the last moment or they will lose their colour.

18. When the tuna is cooked remove from the steamer, and lift off the film. With a fish slice remove each piece of tuna. In the centre of each serving plate, place the vegetables and lay a piece of tuna on top. Top with the warm and crisp fried potatoes.

19. Any excess juices left behind from the cooking of the fish, pour into the sauce. Whisk and finally add the chopped chives just before serving, and spoon around the mound of vegetables.

For added colour and flavour, warm some skinned and diced tomatoes in a little seasoned fish stock and use, along with some chervil sprigs, to decorate the edge of each plate.

SAUTÉ OF CALF'S LIVER, CARROTS AND ORANGE

SERVES 6

This is best done with calf's liver and not lamb's liver. Calf's liver is sweeter and a lot less bitter. It should always be bought fresh and never frozen, as freezing alters the texture. It should also be skinned, which is quite easy. Push an index finger in between the liver and the silvery skin and gently ease off the skin, moving from left to right.

6 x 120 g (4 oz) slices of fresh calf's liver	**1 litre (1¾ pints) Chicken Stock (see p.225)**
salt and pepper	**1 sprig fresh thyme**
60 g (2 oz) clarified butter	**½ bay leaf**
(see Chef's Tip, p.15)	**60 ml (2 fl oz) Meat Glaze (see p.226)**
Sauce	***Glazed carrots***
6 shallots	**3 large carrots**
1 large onion	**1 garlic clove**
3 garlic cloves	**1 sprig fresh tarragon**
2 oranges	**30 ml (1 fl oz) white wine vinegar**
90 g (3 oz) butter	**1 teaspoon caster sugar**
30 ml (1 fl oz) sherry vinegar	**15 g (½ oz) butter**
30 g (1 oz) caster sugar	

Preparing and cooking the sauce

1. Peel and chop the shallots, onion and garlic. Squeeze the juice of the oranges into a small pan.

2. Melt half the butter in a pan and add the shallots, onion and garlic. Cook without colouring until soft. Add the sherry vinegar and reduce until dry. Add the sugar and continue gently cooking and stirring to caramelise the onion.

3. Bring the orange juice to the boil. Lift off the surfacing bubbles and strain the juice on to the caramelised onion. Add the chicken stock, thyme and bay leaf, and bring to the boil. Skim and simmer for 20 minutes.

4. Remove the thyme and bay leaf. Pour the orange sauce into a liquidiser and liquidise until smooth. Strain through a fine sieve and place on the stove to boil. Skim and continue boiling to reduce by half.

5. Add the meat glaze and skim again. Whisk in the remaining butter and season to taste. Reserve.

Preparing and cooking the carrots

6. Peel the carrots and garlic. Cut the carrots into even-sized batons, 3.75 cm x 5 mm (1½ x ¼ in). Halve the garlic. Blanch the tarragon.

7. Cook the carrot batons in boiling salted water for 10 minutes only, then drain and allow to cool naturally.

8. Put the white wine vinegar and sugar in a small pan. Boil and reduce to a caramel. Before it gets too dark add 30 ml (1 fl oz) water, the garlic and tarragon. Boil and reduce, whisking in the butter. When syrupy remove from the heat, and season with salt and pepper. Keep warm.

9. Place the carrot batons in this tarragon glaze and coat the carrots while heating them up. The carrots must be glistening and hot when the liver is cooked.

Cooking the liver

10. Season the liver with salt and pepper, and heat the clarified butter in a large skillet pan until it is smoking.

11. Carefully place in the slices of liver and cook rapidly until little beads of blood show on the top. Turn over and repeat on the other side. Lift out of the pan and keep hot.

To serve

12. Criss-cross the hot glazed carrot batons decoratively around the outsides of six large plates.

13. Strain into the centre of each plate a splash of the finished orange sauce. Place the cooked liver on top, and serve at once.

The liver can be garnished with caramelised orange segments and a good vegetable could be a timbale of leaf spinach.

CHOCOLATE SOUFFLÉ WITH A WARM FROTHY VANILLA CUSTARD

SERVES 6

This is a chocolate dessert that will impress even the most experienced gourmet. The idea is that when you put the spoon through the soufflé, the hot liquid chocolate centre pours out into the vanilla custard sauce.

90 g (3 oz) bitter chocolate
45 g (1½ oz) unsalted butter
90 g (3 oz) Pastry Cream (see p.249)
15 g (½ oz) cocoa powder
2 egg yolks
5 egg whites

90 g (3 oz) caster sugar
To serve
150 ml (5 fl oz) Vanilla Egg Custard Sauce (see p.250)
110 ml (3½ fl oz) whipping cream
icing sugar for dusting

Preparing the soufflés

1. Chop 60 g (2 oz) of the bitter chocolate, and grate the rest.
2. Melt the chopped chocolate in a bowl over hot water, and use to fill six cubes of an ice-cube tray. Place in the freezer to set.
3. Melt the butter and brush the insides of six non-stick metal dariole moulds, 7.5 cm (3 in) in diameter and 5 cm (2 in) high. Dust with the grated chocolate, completely covering the insides of the moulds and gently tap out any excess. Put the moulds on a tray and refrigerate to set.
4. In a stainless-steel bowl, whisk the pastry cream until smooth, then beat in the cocoa powder. When smooth again, add the egg yolks and whisk in. Reserve aside.
5. Remove the chocolate cubes from the freezer and tap them out of their moulds.
6. In an electric mixer bowl whisk the egg whites on maximum speed to soft peaks or until they have trebled in volume. As the whites peak, whisk in the caster sugar.
7. With a spatula gently fold the whisked egg whites into the chocolate pastry cream base. Be careful at this stage not to *over*-mix.
8. Remove the prepared dariole moulds from the fridge and two-thirds fill them with the soufflé mixture. In the centre of the soufflé, place a frozen chocolate cube and cover with

the soufflé mixture. Do not *over*-fill the moulds and ensure that no soufflé mixture is overlapping the edge of the mould or it will stick and prevent the soufflé from rising.

Cooking the soufflés

9. Preheat the oven well to the highest it will go – 250°C – with a baking tray inside.
10. Place the soufflés into the preheated oven on the hot baking tray and cook for approximately 6 minutes.

To serve

11. While the soufflés are cooking, warm the vanilla egg custard sauce on a low heat, then whisk in the cream. Continue whisking until the custard becomes frothy, but *do not boil*. Spoon into six warm soup plates.
12. Remove the soufflés from the oven and quickly, cloth in hand, pick them up one by one and, squeezing slightly to release the sides, turn them upside-down gently into the custard. Repeat for each soufflé. Dust with icing sugar, and serve immediately.

CHEF'S TIP
When the soufflés are cooked they will feel firm to the touch. They should rise 2.5 cm (1 in) above the rim of the moulds and show very little colour.

Winter Recipes

Menu 1
CARPACCIO OF SALMON
SALTED COD WITH LENTILS AND SHALLOT CREAM
MANDARIN SORBET WITH MELON

Menu 2
BAKED BLACK PUDDING WITH CIDER AND APPLES
ESCALOPE OF HALIBUT WITH COCKLES IN A
TOMATO AND PARSLEY SAUCE
CLEMENTINES FILLED WITH A HONEY AND ALMOND NOUGAT

Menu 3
PIGEON SALAD WITH PINE KERNELS IN A RED WINE SAUCE
SEA BASS IN OYSTER AND CHAMPAGNE SAUCE
HOT GRAND MARNIER SOUFFLÉ

Menu 4
SCALLOPS IN PUFF PASTRY WITH CHIVE BUTTER SAUCE
GLAZED FILLETS OF SOLE IN A MUSHROOM
AND PARSLEY SAUCE
ICED MOUSSE NOUGATINE WITH A CARAMEL SAUCE

Menu 5

ONION TART

LAMB CASSEROLE

A LIGHT CHOCOLATE TRUFFLE CAKE TOPPED
WITH A COFFEE SABAYON MOUSSE

Menu 6

NEW POTATOES FILLED WITH SNAILS,
MARROW, SHALLOT AND BACON, SERVED WITH
A RED WINE SAUCE

BARON OF RABBIT COOKED IN VINEGAR,
TOMATOES AND FRESH HERBS

GÂTEAU ST HONORÉ

Menu 7

HOT MOUSSE OF JERUSALEM ARTICHOKE
WITH A WATERCRESS COULIS

DUCK LEGS BRAISED IN RED WINE AND SERVED
ON A SHALLOT CREAM

APPLES IN A WALNUT CARAMEL

Menu 8

MULLIGATAWNY SOUP

BREAST OF PHEASANT COOKED IN SHALLOTS AND
WINE, WITH CHICORY AND GAME CHIPS

CARAMELISED BANANAS AND
ICED PISTACHIO PARFAIT

Winter Menu 1

CARPACCIO OF SALMON

SALTED COD WITH LENTILS AND SHALLOT CREAM

MANDARIN SORBET WITH MELON

CARPACCIO OF SALMON

SERVES 6

*T*he best time for English and Scottish salmon is from February to August, but salmon fishing on the River Tay opens on 15 January for rod fishing. Because of its long season and because of its popularity in this country, I have included several recipes for salmon, spanning three seasons.

For this particular dish, ask your fishmonger for a piece nearest the tail (but not the actual pointed tail piece), with skin attached. I find that it takes less time to marinate and there are no bones to remove in preparation. Wild salmon is quite expensive at the start of the season but, as we require such a small amount, it makes it quite affordable.

500g (18 oz) wild salmon, off the bone, skin on	1 large carrot
1 large lemon	1 red and 1 yellow pepper
20 g (½ oz) coarse sea salt	1 fennel bulb
15 g (⅔ oz) caster sugar	2 celery stalks
1 garlic clove	30 g (1 oz) French beans (about 12)
1 teaspoon fennel flowers (the feathery leaves at the top of the bulb)	1 shallot
½ teaspoon black peppercorns	½ garlic clove
1 star anise	salt and pepper
extra virgin olive oil	40 ml (1½ fl oz) Tarragon Vinaigrette (see p.234)
Garnishes	30 ml (1 fl oz) marinade
1 large courgette	(liquid from the marination of the salmon)
	2 tomatoes

Marinating the fish

1. Squeeze the juice of the lemon (you need 60 ml/2 fl oz) into a bowl, add the salt and sugar, and stir with a whisk until dissolved.

2. Peel and finely slice the garlic. With kitchen scissors, snip the fennel flowers. Crush the peppercorns.

3. Add these, along with the star anise and 30 ml (1 fl oz) of the oil, to the lemon juice, and whisk for 2 minutes until fully emulsified. This is your marinade.

4. Pour the marinade on to a flat stainless-steel or plastic tray. *Do not* use an aluminium one, or it will taint the fish. Place the salmon, flesh-side down, on to the tray. Cover with cling film and refrigerate. The marinating time is approximately 10 hours. Half-way through this time, turn the fish over to complete the process. When using a large piece of fish or a thicker cut, allow a longer period of time to complete the marination.

5. Once the fish is ready, remove it from the liquid. Lay it on a clean chopping board and with the back of a knife gently scrape off all the peppercorns, fennel flowers and garlic. Brush it with a little olive oil. Reserve aside while you prepare the garnishes.

Preparing the garnishes

6. Slice and finely dice the courgette (3 mm/⅛ in square). This is left raw, and can be put in a large bowl.

7. Trim, peel and dice to the same size the carrot, peppers, fennel and celery. Cut the beans to the same size as well. Keep them all separate.

8. In a large saucepan of boiling, salted water blanch in order of their cooking times: cook the carrot for 1 minute; then add the fennel; 30 seconds later add the celery; 30 seconds later the beans and lastly the peppers. Strain immediately through a fine-mesh conical strainer. Refresh in cold water and, again, strain the vegetables. Turn them out on to a clean kitchen cloth and dry thoroughly. When dry add to the bowl containing the courgettes.

9. Peel and finely chop the shallot and garlic, and add to the bowl. Season with salt and pepper and finally add 30 ml (1 fl oz) of the tarragon vinaigrette and the measured marinade. Stir.

10. Skin, seed and dice the tomatoes (see Chef's Tip, p.25), and reserve aside in a small bowl seasoned and sprinkled with a little of the vinaigrette.

To serve

11. Spoon the crunchy vegetable dice on to six plates and, with the back of the spoon, flatten the mixture to form an even base for the salmon.

12. Lay out the salmon on a chopping board and, with a very sharp filleting knife, slice, the thinner the better. Lay the sliced salmon on top of the vegetables.

CHEF'S TIP

When slicing the salmon, it is important to cut out all the blood along the spine, or any discoloured flesh. This flesh lies beside the skin; it is bitter and spoils the appearance of the dish.

---

13. Using a small brush, carefully brush the salmon with the remaining vinaigrette, then, on the outer borders of each plate, place the tomato dice. Serve.

As an option, I like a little more milled black pepper over the salmon and a teaspoon of caviare.

SALTED COD WITH LENTILS AND SHALLOT CREAM

SERVES 6

This makes an excellent winter fish dish. I find that most of the salted or preserved cod and haddock that you buy in fishmongers' shops nowadays is of poor quality, so here is a recipe that tells you how to prepare your own!

900 g (2 lb) cod (a choice cut from just behind the head is best)
3 lemons
30 g (1 oz) granulated sea salt
15 g (½ oz) caster sugar
1 teaspoon fennel flowers (the feathery leaves at the top of the bulb)
1 teaspoon black peppercorns
3 garlic cloves
a pinch of saffron strands
extra virgin olive oil
Cooking liquor
500 ml (17 fl oz) milk
freshly grated nutmeg

1 sprig fresh thyme
¼ bay leaf
Sauce
1 garlic clove
60 g (2 oz) white mushrooms
3 bacon rashers, cut into lardons (optional, see Chef's Tip, p.196)
210 ml (7 fl oz) Chicken Stock (see p.225)
210 ml (7 fl oz) Fish Stock (see p.223)
1 sprig fresh tarragon
90 g (3 oz) cooked Puy lentils (see p.105)
To serve
1 quantity Shallot Purée (see p.235)

Curing the cod

1. Place the cod skin-side down on a tray. Use a plastic or stainless-steel tray (if you use an aluminium one you will taint the fish). Make sure that all the bones have been removed.
2. Squeeze the lemon juice into a bowl. Add the sea salt and sugar.
3. Chop the fennel flowers, crush the peppercorns, and peel and slice the garlic. Add to the lemon juice along with the saffron, but keep a few garlic slices back for later.

CHEF'S TIP
I prefer to use the pistil or strand variety of saffron. Powdered saffron is invariably stale or goes stale very quickly, and can be adulterated.

4. Mix all these ingredients together well and carefully pour over the cod. Cover with cling film and leave to 'cure' for 3 hours; then turn the cod over and leave for a further 3 hours on the other side. During this time, and when the cod is ready, you will find that the fish gives out a lot of water. This is quite normal: during the curing process the salt draws the liquid from the fish. When the fish is ready it will feel slightly firm to the touch and the outer skin will be rough and dehydrated.
5. Remove the fish from the marinade and thoroughly wash under cold water. This is important because if you leave any salt liquid on the fish it will continue the process of pulling the juices from it.
6. Dry the cod thoroughly on clean kitchen paper, and brush with a little olive oil. Sprinkle with the remaining sliced garlic. Cover with cling film and refrigerate. The cod can keep like this for up to a week without deterioration, which I find most useful as it can be used if and when I need it.

Cooking the cod

7. Preheat the oven to 190°C (375°F) Gas 5.
8. Heat in a large pan the listed cooking liquor ingredients.
9. Skin the cod and carefully cut into six equal

portions.

10. Place the cod into the milk, bring to the boil, cover with butter paper and poach in the preheated oven for approximately 10 minutes. When cooked remove the pan and leave the fish to keep warm in the milk until ready to serve.

Making the sauce

11. Peel and slice the garlic. Slice the mushrooms. If using, blanch the lardons and fry in a little oil until golden.
12. Bring the chicken and fish stocks to the boil with the mushrooms, garlic and tarragon. Reduce the liquid by half to achieve a consistency which will coat the back of a spoon. Pass through a sieve. A little squeeze of lemon juice helps to bring up the flavours at the very end.

13. To finish the sauce, and to give it a little extra texture, add the lentils and, if you like, the lardons.

To serve

14. In a small pan bring the shallot purée to the boil. Turn down the flame and simmer. Keep warm to one side.
15. Lay out six hot plates. On each, in the middle, spoon 2 dessertspoons of the shallot purée. Gently remove a piece of cod from the milk and place this on top of the shallot. Around the outer rim of the plate spoon the finished mushroom and lentil sauce.

I like to finish this dish by decorating the top of the cod with deep-fried vegetable strips (*julienne*) – leek, carrot and potato are the best for this. It gives more colour and texture, and adds another dimension to the finished dish.

MANDARIN SORBET WITH MELON

SERVES 6

*W*hen choosing a ripe melon it will be slightly soft at the stalk and have a delicious smell. A good melon will seem heavy for its size, so pick up two or three before buying one. Galia has a green to brownish-yellow skin and green flesh. Charentais has a green skin and gives off a good fragrance. The flesh is deep orange in colour.

2 small ripe melons (Galia or Charentais)	***Mandarin sorbet***
18 fresh mint leaves	**375 g (13 oz) caster sugar**
juice of 2 oranges	**900 ml (1½ pints) mandarin orange juice**
***Langue de Chat* Biscuits (see p.246)**	

Making the sorbet

1. Boil the sugar together with 150 ml (5 fl oz) water until the sugar has melted, then remove from the heat.
2. Add the mandarin juice and leave to cool.
3. Churn in an ice-cream machine until frozen. Or place in a suitable container and freeze, mixing several times until frozen.

To serve

4. Remove the skin from the melons, then cut them in half lengthways and remove the

seeds. Cut each half again lengthways.
5. Slice each melon quarter thinly lengthways, then divide these slices and fan around each chilled plate.
6. Cut the mint leaves very finely into shreds with a sharp knife. Sprinkle over the fanned melon.
7. Divide the orange juice, pouring over each melon in the centre.
8. Place a large ball or quenelle of mandarin sorbet in the centre of each circle of melon slices, and serve immediately, accompanied by *langue de chat* biscuits.

Winter Menu 2

BAKED BLACK PUDDING WITH CIDER AND APPLES

ESCALOPE OF HALIBUT WITH COCKLES IN A TOMATO AND PARSLEY SAUCE

CLEMENTINES FILLED WITH A HONEY AND ALMOND NOUGAT

BAKED BLACK PUDDING WITH CIDER AND APPLES

SERVES 6

In my experience the best black pudding comes from France - they are known as *boudin noir*. If not available, try to get some from the north of England, the home of the best of British black puddings!

6 fresh French black puddings, about 120 g (4 oz) each, or 700 g (1½ lb) length of good black pudding	½ bay leaf
	30 ml (1 fl oz) cider vinegar
	300 ml (10 fl oz) dry cider
90 g (3 oz) plain flour	300 ml (10 fl oz) Chicken Stock (see p.225)
60 ml (2 fl oz) clarified butter (see Chef's Tip, p.15)	90 ml (3 fl oz) whipping cream
Sauce	salt and pepper
1 onion	juice of 1 lemon
2 garlic cloves	30 ml (1 fl oz) Calvados
60 g (2 oz) butter	*Apple purée*
1 sprig fresh thyme	2 large cooking apples
	caster sugar to taste

Preparing the sauce

1. Peel and finely chop the onion and garlic.

2. Melt half the butter in a pan and add the onion. Cook slowly without colouring, adding

176

the garlic, thyme and bay leaf after a few minutes. When the onion is opaque, add the cider vinegar and reduce until virtually dry.

3. Add the cider, bring to the boil and reduce rapidly by two-thirds. Add the chicken stock and bring to the boil. Skim and reduce by half.

4. Strain through a fine sieve into another pan, and add the cream. Bring to the boil and whisk in the remaining butter. Season with salt and pepper and a little lemon juice. Keep hot.

Making the apple purée

5. Peel the apples, and cut into quarters. Do not bother coring. Place in a pan and add 120 ml (4 fl oz) water. Cover with a lid and bring to the boil. Simmer until the apple is soft.

6. Pour into a fine sieve and press through with a wooden spoon. You should sieve out all the pips and be left with a fine apple purée. If it is thin and watery, return it to the heat in order to evaporate some of the water and

thicken the purée. When the desired thickness is achieved, add some sugar to taste and keep warm.

Cooking the black pudding

7. Preheat the oven to 200°C (400°F) Gas 6.

8. Skin the fresh black puddings. Or cut the length of black pudding into six equal pieces, and skin. Roll in a little flour, tapping off the excess.

9. Heat the clarified butter in an ovenproof pan and seal the black puddings or slices on both sides. Bake in the preheated oven for 10 minutes.

To serve

10. Put a spoonful of hot apple purée on each plate. Place a hot black pudding or black pudding slice in the centre of the purée.

11. Add the Calvados to the sauce as a final seasoning, and spoon around the plates. Serve immediately.

Escalope of Halibut with Cockles in a Tomato and Parsley Sauce

SERVES 6

In most top-class restaurants halibut is usually regarded as some way behind fish such as turbot and sea bass. This is also said of cockles, but the two together in this dish create a formidable fish main course. Cockles, unlike clams or other shellfish, are readily available at fishmonger's shops, especially those near the seaside.

**800 g (1¾ lb) skinned halibut fillet,
cut into 6 pieces**
salt and pepper
Halibut poaching liquor and sauce
4 shallots
2 garlic cloves
1 sprig fresh tarragon
110 g (3½ oz) unsalted butter
90 ml (3 fl oz) Noilly Prat
90 ml (3 fl oz) dry white wine
420 ml (14 fl oz) Fish Stock (see p.223)
110 ml (3½ fl oz) whipping cream
30 ml (1 fl oz) lemon juice

Cockles
1.75 kg (3¾ lb) cockles (shell weight)
2 garlic cloves
1 large onion
15 g (½ oz) black peppercorns
1 bay leaf
1 large sprig fresh thyme
60 g (2 oz) parsley stalks
120 ml (4 fl oz) white wine or white wine vinegar
To serve
a large bunch of parsley
2 ripe plum tomatoes

Preparing the cockles

1. Peel the garlic and onion. Slice the onion, and crush the peppercorns.
2. To a saucepan of boiling salted water add the bay leaf, thyme, parsley stalks, garlic, onion, peppercorns and vinegar. Put the cockles in, place a lid on the saucepan and cook for approximately 5 minutes. During the cooking, stir the cockles once or twice with a spoon, bringing the cockles from the bottom to the top.
3. When cooked, turn them out into a colander with another saucepan underneath to trap the cooking liquor. (This can then be strained through muslin, saved and used again at a later date.) Take the cockles out of the shells. Clean them by removing the muscle and the grit sac. Reserve the cleaned cockles (and the shells if you like) to use in the finishing of the sauce.

Poaching the fish

4. Preheat the oven to 180°C (350°F) Gas 4.
5. Peel the shallots and garlic; finely chop the former. Blanch the tarragon.
6. In a shallow ovenproof pan melt half the butter. Add the shallots, garlic and tarragon and cook over a gentle flame without colouring.
7. Pour in the Noilly Prat and reduce the liquid until a syrup. Pour in the dry white wine and reduce by half. Add the fish stock and bring to the boil. With a ladle, remove any surfacing fat or scum.
8. Carefully place the halibut in the stock and cover with a butter paper. Put a lid on the pan and poach in the preheated oven for 5 minutes.

9. Remove from the oven and, with a fish slice, take the pieces of fish out of the pan. At this stage you have to be very careful as cooked halibut is delicate and will break up easily. Place the fish on the individual hot serving plates, cover with butter paper and keep warm.

Making the sauce

10. Strain the poaching liquor through a conical strainer into another pan and, over a fierce flame, reduce the liquid by half. Add the cream and, piece by piece, feed the remaining butter into the sauce, whisking thoroughly until dissolved.
11. Throw in the cockles to enhance the flavour of the sauce and quickly remove them with a slotted spoon. Sprinkle them over the fish. (This is important because any remaining grit and sand will fall off the cockles into the sauce and not on to the fish.)

To finish and serve

12. Wash, pick off the leaves and dry the parsley. On a chopping board, finely chop it. Blanch, skin, seed and dice the tomatoes (see Chef's Tip, p.25).

13. Sprinkle the tomato dice and parsley over the fish.
14. Check the seasoning of the sauce. Mix in the lemon juice and pour the finished sauce through a strainer, trapping any grit or sand, on to the fish. Serve immediately.

To accompany the dish, I would suggest a few boiled or new potatoes or a coil of home-made noodles, and a few French beans or spinach.

CLEMENTINES FILLED WITH A HONEY AND ALMOND NOUGAT

SERVES 6

*W*hen buying clementines for this dish, try to pick the smallest with the green leaves on. They can be found on the market at the beginning of winter, and because they are readily available around Christmas, I would recommend this recipe as an alternative to our traditional puddings.

21 tiny clementines	**110 g (3½ oz) Nougatine (see p.248)**
Honey nougat	*Sorbet*
30 g (1 oz) granulated sugar	**140 g (4½ oz) caster sugar**
60 ml (2 fl oz) honey	**360 ml (12 fl oz) clementine juice (see method)**
2 teaspoons liquid glucose	*Sauce*
60 ml (2 fl oz) egg whites (approx. 2)	**150 ml (5 fl oz) clementine juice (see method)**
10 g (⅓ oz) caster sugar	**60 g (2 oz) caster sugar**
240 ml (8 fl oz) whipping cream	**1 teaspoon cornflour**

Preparing the clementines

1. Wash the clementines in cold water, and reserve three for garnishing. With a sharp knife, about a third of the way down the fruit, cut the tops off the remaining eighteen fruit. With a grapefruit spoon, scoop out all the inside from top and bottom, being careful not to break the skin.

2. Place the reserved pulp and juice into a fine-mesh conical strainer and, with the back of a ladle, push all the juice through into a bowl. This should yield 510 ml (17 fl oz) of strained juice, 150 ml (5 fl oz) for the sauce, the remainder for the sorbet.

3. Bring a large saucepan of water to the boil, and throw in the fruit shells and tops. Remove from the heat and place a tight-fitting lid or cling film on the pan. Leave for 10 minutes, then remove the shells and refresh under running cold water until completely cooled down. (This softens the skins and takes away the bitterness of the white pith.) Place the shells upside down on a clean tea towel to drain.

Making the nougat

4. In a small saucepan, warm together over a low heat the granulated sugar, honey and liquid glucose. Increase the heat and boil the syrup for approximately 4 minutes but *do not*

colour or caramelise.

5. Whilst waiting for your syrup, put the egg whites in an electric mixer bowl and whisk on maximum speed. When they have trebled in volume, add the caster sugar, turn down the speed and carefully pour in the boiled syrup. Increase the speed and whisk the mixture until cold (it takes about 8 minutes). This is now a meringue.

6. Meanwhile, in another bowl lightly whisk the cream *but not too stiff or firm.*

7. Crush the nougatine with a rolling pin. Fold it into the meringue using a spatula, then carefully fold in the cream. We now have a honey nougat.

8. Place the fruit shells on a tray and fill them to the top with the nougat. Top with the 'lids' and put them into the freezer for at least 3 hours before serving.

Making the sorbet

9. In a saucepan, over a fierce flame, boil together the caster sugar and 50 ml (2 fl oz) water. Remove from the stove when the sugar has dissolved, and add the fruit juice. Pour into a bowl, and allow to cool.

10. When cold, churn in an ice-cream machine, or freeze, stirring once or twice. When frozen, use to fill a piping bag fitted with

a large star nozzle. Pipe a rosette of sorbet on top of the nougat in each clementine and replace the lids. Quickly put them back in the freezer.

Making the sauce

11. In a saucepan bring to the boil the clementine juice, the caster sugar, and 50 ml (2 fl oz) water. Turn down the heat and remove any surfacing scum. Remove from the heat.

12. In a cup, moisten the cornflour with a little water to a smooth paste.

13. Bring the juice back to the boil, add the cornflour paste and stir until it re-boils. Pour the finished sauce into a bowl and cover with cling film.

To serve

14. Peel the remaining three clementines and, keeping them whole, slice each one across the segments into six equal slices.

15. Lay three slices down, slightly overlapping each other, in the centre of each serving plate and spoon the sauce over them.

16. Remove the clementines from the freezer and, for added effect, dip the bottom of the shells into some extra caster sugar. This gives them a frosted appearance.

17. Place three clementines on each plate equidistant from each other. Serve immediately.

Accompany with a lace tuile if you like.

Winter Menu 3

PIGEON SALAD WITH PINE KERNELS IN A RED WINE SAUCE

SEA BASS IN OYSTER AND CHAMPAGNE SAUCE

HOT GRAND MARNIER SOUFFLÉ

PIGEON SALAD WITH PINE KERNELS IN A RED WINE SAUCE

SERVES 4

I love wild pigeon. It is cheap, it has a delicious flavour, and in this country is always readily available. This is just one recipe from millions to demonstrate its plus points.

2 wild pigeon
salt and pepper
60 ml (2 fl oz) whipping cream
1 garlic clove
Red wine sauce
8 juniper berries
5 garlic cloves
1 onion
½ leek
½ carrot
½ celery stalk
1 tablespoon vegetable oil
60 ml (2 fl oz) red wine vinegar
15 g (½ oz) redcurrant jelly
½ bottle Cahors or similar red wine
1 litre (1¾ pints) Chicken Stock (see p.225)
1 sprig fresh thyme

1 bay leaf
1 tablespoon Meat Glaze (optional, see p.226)
Parsley purée
150 g (5 oz) flat parsley
150 g (5 oz) spinach
60 ml (2 fl oz) whipping cream
15 g (½ oz) Dijon mustard
Garnishes
about 120 g (4 oz) salad leaves (rocket, radicchio, endive, oakleaf, fordhook or very peppery watercress)
30 ml (1 fl oz) Walnut Vinaigrette (see p.233)
30 g (1 oz) pine kernels
60 g (2 oz) blanched lardons (see Chef's Tip, p.196)
12 garlic *croûtons* (see Chef's Tip, p.138)

Preparing the pigeon and sauce

1. Remove the breasts from the pigeons, and skin them. Chop the carcasses coarsely. Keep the breasts aside.

2. Crush the juniper berries. Peel the garlic and onion, and chop them and the leek, carrot and celery.

Cooking the sauce

3. Heat the oil in a large frying pan. When smoking hot, carefully add the chopped pigeon bones and roast evenly all over until golden brown, about 5–8 minutes. Do not allow them to get *too* brown or the sauce will taste bitter.

4. Meanwhile heat another saucepan until hot, and add the red wine vinegar which should sizzle right away. Immediately add the redcurrant jelly, the crushed juniper berries and three of the garlic cloves. Reduce until a syrup is obtained. Be careful at this stage not to burn the vinegar or the sauce will taste of burnt caramel.

5. Add the bones and off the heat turn over and over in the syrup until the bones are evenly coated and glazed.

6. Deglaze the pigeon roasting pan with the red wine and boil to reduce by half. Add to the bones and cover with the chicken stock. Add the thyme, bay leaf, remaining garlic and the chopped onion, leek, carrot and celery. Bring to the boil and simmer for 30 minutes, skimming often.

7. Strain the stock into another pan and reduce rapidly, adding the meat glaze (if used) when the stock is reduced by one-third.

Continue reducing until the flavours have concentrated. Season to taste and keep warm.

Making the parsley purée

8. Pick the parsley leaves off the stalks. Remove tough stalks from the spinach. In boiling salted water blanch the parsley and strain, but do not refresh. Blanch the spinach as well in the same way. Place both in the liquidiser and blend to a purée.

9. Add the cream to the parsley purée. Taste for seasoning and off the heat add the Dijon mustard but do not boil as this will make it bitter. Keep warm.

To finish and serve

10. Preheat the grill to very hot.

11. Season the pigeon breasts with salt and pepper and place in a heatproof dish. Cover with the cream. Peel and halve the garlic and add to the cream. Grill the breasts on each side for about 5 minutes until they are pink. Leave to rest.

12. Dress the salad leaves with vinaigrette, pine kernels and lardons, then arrange in the centre of six plates.

13. Place a spoon of the hot parsley purée in three points around the salad, at equal distances from each other. Slice each pigeon breast into two. Push each slice up against the salad. Drop the warmed garlic *croûtons* around the salad and in between each pool of parsley purée pour a little of the red wine sauce. Serve immediately.

SEA BASS IN OYSTER AND CHAMPAGNE SAUCE

SERVES 4

This dish must be the 'Rolls-Royce' of fish dishes, and yes, it is very expensive to combine three such ingredients. Do not be put off by this, though, as it is quite simple in its execution. It could be for one of those 'special occasion' dinner parties, Christmas perhaps.

You will note that the sauce has a fantastic and unusual texture, and although cream is used for the leeks, there is no cream in the sauce!

1 x 600 g (1¼ lb) sea bass, filleted but with the skin left on
12 oysters
salt and pepper
Poaching liquor and sauce
1 garlic clove
1 sprig fresh tarragon
240 ml (8 fl oz) Fish Stock (see p.223)
60 g (2 oz) unsalted butter

120 ml (4 fl oz) dry Champagne
Garnishes
3 leeks
1 garlic clove
30 g (1 oz) fresh chervil
2 large ripe tomatoes
60 g (2 oz) butter
60 ml (2 fl oz) double cream

Preparing the seafood

1. Cut the sea bass into four equal pieces and season with salt and pepper.
2. Wash and open the oysters (see Chef's Tip, p.145). Pour them into a bowl, being very careful not to break off any shell into their juices.

Preparing the garnishes

3. Wash and trim the leeks and dice them into 1 cm (½ in) pieces. Remember to remove the inner silver leaves as they are always tough and taste unpleasant. Blanch the leek pieces in salted boiling water, then strain and refresh in cold water. When cold, strain again and leave to one side.
4. Peel and halve the garlic. Wash, dry and pick the chervil leaves from their stalks and chop them.
5. Skin, seed and dice the tomatoes (see Chef's Tip). Place the dice in a small pan with a little of the oyster juices, a little of the butter, and some salt and pepper.

CHEF'S TIP

To prepare tomato dice, first skin and seed the tomatoes. To start, core them with a small knife. Make a small cross at the top of the tomatoes, just nicking the skin, and blanch them in boiling water for 10 seconds. From the top of the tomato (at the cross), peel them, then halve them. Remove and discard the seeds and pulp, and carefully dice the flesh into 5 mm (¼ in) pieces. These can be used in a variety of ways.

Poaching the fish

6. Preheat the oven to 180°C (350°F) Gas 4.
7. Peel and halve the garlic. Blanch the tarragon.
8. Pour all but a small ladleful of the fish stock into a shallow ovenproof pan. Add the halved garlic clove, and the blanched tarragon. Bring to the boil. Place the sea bass into the pan, flesh-side down, cover with a butter paper and then a lid. Cook for about 5 minutes in the preheated oven.
9. Remove the sea bass from the oven after its 5 minutes and, using a fish slice, place a piece of fish, skin-side up, in the centre of each serving plate. Carefully peel off the skin from each piece of fish. It is an easy task when the fish is warm and it comes off in one. Keep warm.

Heating the garnishes

10. Pour the remaining ladleful of fish stock into another shallow pan. Add the halved garlic and the remaining butter.
11. Throw in the diced leeks and, stirring with

a spoon, mix thoroughly. Add the chervil leaves and cream. When the leeks have taken up all the liquid they are ready.

12. Warm the tomato dice through in the small pan with the oyster juices and butter.

Finishing the sauce

13. Return the fish cooking juices to the stove and boil to reduce by half.

14. Remove the oysters from the bowl, quickly chop them to a paste and add them and any remaining juice to the reduced fish stock. Whisk thoroughly.

15. To thicken the sauce, dice the butter and, piece by piece, whisk it in until it has completely dissolved. Strain into another pan and keep warm. Discard the oyster 'paste'.

To serve

16. Top the bass on each plate with a heaped spoon of the hot leeks and chervil. Decorate the plates with the warm tomato dice.

17. Finally, pour the Champagne into the sauce. While it is still foaming, quickly and carefully spoon the sauce on to the plates. Serve immediately.

As a further garnish, I often line an oyster shell with blanched watercress leaves, a tiny coil of fine noodles, and an oyster, topped with a little caviare!

HOT GRAND MARNIER SOUFFLÉ

SERVES 4

*M*ost chefs portray the soufflé as being extremely difficult. Others keep their recipes secret! I believe, as for any dish, that you need a good foundation or basic recipe to work from – this is one such.

120 g (4 oz) Pastry Cream (see p.249)	icing sugar
60 g (2 oz) unsalted butter, melted	*Flavouring*
35 g (1¼ oz) caster sugar	**4 oranges**
1 egg yolk	**2 dessertspoons Grand Marnier**
6 egg whites	

Preparing the flavouring

1. Remove the zest from all the oranges, discarding the white pith. Blanch the zests in boiling water to remove all the bitterness, then refresh in cold water. Dry the zests in a clean cloth, then dice or very finely shred. Keep to one side.

2. Squeeze the juice from two of the oranges, and pour it into a small pan. Bring to the boil and skim off all surface scum. Pour into a bowl and allow to cool. This clarifies the juice. (Keep the two remaining oranges to make an optional accompanying salad, see below.)

Preparing the moulds

3. In a medium pan, gently melt the butter, then brush this over the insides of four moulds, 8 cm (3¼ in) in diameter and 8 cm (3¼ in) deep.

4. Coat the inside of each mould with some of the caster sugar (about 1 dessertspoon), tipping the moulds upside-down to get rid of any excess.

CHEF'S TIP
It is very important that the moulds are coated evenly with butter and sugar in order for the soufflés to rise evenly.

Preparing the soufflé base

5. Preheat the oven to 230°C (450°F) Gas 8.

6. Put the pastry cream in a stainless-steel

Chocolate Soufflé with a Warm Frothy Vanilla Custard

Salted Cod with Lentils and Shallot Cream

Escalope of Halibut with Cockles in a Tomato and Parsley Sauce

Clementines Filled with a Honey and Almond Nougat

bowl, and add the flavouring orange zest and clarified orange juice plus the Grand Marnier. Stir the mixture to a smooth paste and add the egg yolk. Stir.

7. Now pour the egg whites into the bowl of your electric mixer. Start to whisk, then, as they begin to stiffen and peak, add the remaining sugar. Whisk for a further 15 seconds. (If whipping by hand, or with an electric hand whisk, the whisking in of the sugar will take about 1 minute.) The meringue or egg whites should be smooth and not in any way granular, i.e. *over*-whipped.

8. Gently stir half of the meringue into the soufflé base until it is evenly mixed. Then very carefully fold in the remainder of the meringue.

CHEF'S TIP

Folding in the egg whites is a very crucial stage in soufflé construction, and the utmost care must be taken not to over-mix them. It is essential not to knock the air out of the mixture.

9. Fill the soufflé moulds to the top and level off with a palette knife. Clean around the edge of the dishes. Be careful not to let the mixture overlap the edges of the dishes as this will stick and prevent the mixture from rising evenly during cooking.

Cooking and serving the soufflés

10. Place the soufflés on a baking tray, put into the preheated hot oven, and cook for approximately 8–10 minutes. They will rise 2.5–3 cm (1–1½ in) above the rim of the soufflé dish, will be golden in colour and will wobble slightly when touched. Remove from the oven and dust the tops with icing sugar.

11. Serve immediately, either as they are, in the moulds, or with some orange sorbet and salad as below.

Orange Sorbet and Salad

This is an optional garnish for the soufflé. The sorbet should, of course, be prepared in advance.

120 g (4 oz) granulated sugar
juice of 6 oranges
1 tablespoon liquid glucose

Making the sorbet

1. Place the sugar and 150 ml (5 fl oz) water in a small pan and heat to melt the sugar. Leave to cool.

2. When cool, mix the syrup with all the remaining ingredients. Place in an ice-cream machine and freeze, or place in a suitable container and freeze in the freezer, mixing at least a couple of times during the process until frozen.

Making the salad

3. Segment the two oranges remaining from the making of the soufflés, and arrange decoratively – in a rosette shape, perhaps – on four plates. Top with a quenelle of sorbet. Add the hot soufflés in their dishes, and serve.

Winter Menu 4

Scallops in Puff Pastry with Chive Butter Sauce

Glazed Fillets of Sole in a Mushroom and Parsley Sauce

Iced Mousse Nougatine with a Caramel Sauce

Scallops in Puff Pastry with Chive Butter Sauce

SERVES 6

This dish may be used as an hors-d'oeuvre or as a main course, depending on the make-up of the other dishes in your menu.

Most good fishmongers have scallops which can be purchased live in their shells and this is essential for this dish. To check that the scallops are alive, the first rule is to check that they are closed: if open, when tapped they should close immediately. For further information on how to open scallops, see p.13.

18 large fresh scallops	2 celery stalks
salt and pepper	2 courgettes
1 tablespoon olive oil	1 fennel bulb
350 g (12 oz) Puff Pastry (see p.242)	1 large carrot
1 egg	60 g (2 oz) baby spinach leaves
30 ml (1 fl oz) milk	360 ml (12 fl oz) Fish Stock (see p.223)
Vegetable garnish	20 g (⅔ oz) chervil leaves
1 garlic clove	*Savoury butter*
10 tarragon leaves	1 garlic clove
2 leeks	60 g (2 oz) butter

1 sprig fresh thyme

½ bay leaf

a pinch of cayenne pepper

juice of ½ lemon

Sauce

3 shallots

1 garlic clove

60 g (2 oz) butter

90 ml (3 fl oz) Noilly Prat

90 ml (3 fl oz) dry white wine

juice of ½ lemon

Preparing the scallops

1. Prepare and clean the scallops as described on p.13. Season the corals and pierce them with the point of a knife. This is important as they have a tendency to burst on cooking. Wash and dry six of the deep scallop shells. Reserve aside.

2. In a frying pan heat the olive oil and fry the corals to a golden brown colour. Remove and drain on kitchen paper.

Preparing the vegetable garnish

3. Peel the garlic. Blanch all the tarragon leaves. You only need a few for the vegetables; the others are used in the sauce.

4. Wash and trim the leeks, celery, courgettes, fennel and carrot. Peel the celery and fennel to remove all the strings and sinews. Peel the carrot. Do not peel the courgettes. Cut into fine slices and then into long strips (*julienne*) all the same length and thickness.

5. Wash and blanch the spinach, and place on a clean kitchen towel to dry.

Preparing the pastry topping

6. Cut your prepared puff pastry into six equal pieces. (Puff pastry trimmings are just as good as you do not really want the pastry to rise in cooking.) Roll them out into six roughly shaped circles and leave to rest for a few minutes. This is important or the pastry will shrink away from the sides of the shell during cooking.

7. Make an egg wash: crack the egg into a bowl, pour in the milk, season with salt and pepper and whisk together thoroughly.

Cooking the vegetable garnish

8. Heat the fish stock in a shallow pan, then add the garlic and two of the tarragon leaves, and bring to the boil. Add the vegetable

julienne in order of cooking times: firstly the fennel; 2 minutes later the carrot; then the celery, and then the leek. The courgette should be left raw to retain its texture. This operation takes approximately 5 minutes.

9. Strain off the vegetables, pouring the fish stock into another pan. Lay the vegetable strips out on to a tray to cool quickly and evenly. Season them with salt and pepper.

Making the savoury butter

10. Peel and crush the garlic.

11. Melt the butter with the crushed garlic, thyme and bay leaf, then add a little salt, cayenne and lemon juice. Do not boil or burn this butter; it just wants to melt and take on some of the herb flavours. Strain.

Lining the scallop shells

12. Using a basting brush, coat the cleaned scallop shells with a good layer of the savoury butter. Allow to cool.

13. Cover the shells with the prepared baby spinach leaves, overlapping each leaf to completely cover the base. Add the prepared *julienne* strips of vegetables, placing them at the centre of each shell, and on top of this place the scallop corals. (I like to add a little fish quenelle or shaped fish mousseline, but this is purely an optional garnish.)

14. Arrange three scallops per shell (or per person) around the vegetables. Add some chervil and a tarragon leaf per shell for flavour. Season with salt and pepper.

Making the sauce

15. Return the vegetable cooking stock to the stove and slowly reduce by two-thirds of its original volume.

16. Peel the shallots and garlic. Finely slice the

former and crush the latter.

17. In another pan melt 30 g (1 oz) of the butter, and cook the shallots and garlic without colouring.

18. Add the remaining tarragon leaves, pour in the Noilly Prat and reduce the liquid until syrupy. Add the white wine and reduce by half. Add the reduced vegetable stock, bring to the boil and skim off all surfacing fat.

19. Pass the liquid through a fine-mesh conical strainer into another pan. Bring to the boil and, piece by piece, feed the sauce with the remaining butter. Check seasoning and add the lemon juice. Reduce the sauce to a fairly thick syrup consistency and remove from the stove to cool.

To finish and serve

20. Preheat the oven to 180°C (350°F) Gas 4.

21. Spoon the cooled sauce over the scallops, coating the whole dish with a fine layer.

22. With a basting brush carefully baste the outer rim of the scallop shells with the egg wash. Cover with the pastry tops and gently push down the edges of the pastry, slightly overlapping the shell. Be careful not to puncture the pastry, as the scallops cook by the steam created in cooking. Trim off any excess pastry with a knife (save for use in another dish). Egg wash the pastry.

23. Place the shells on a baking tray and cook in the preheated oven for approximately 9 minutes. Serve immediately.

With this dish I like to serve Butter Sauce for Fish, using chives (see p.231). This again is optional, but it does add another dimension to surprise your guests. Dill, parsley or chervil may be used instead of the chives.

GLAZED FILLETS OF SOLE IN A MUSHROOM AND PARSLEY SAUCE

SERVES 6

*T*his dish is probably a fairly well-known one in its French guise, *Filet de sole bonne femme*. However, it is a good dish for those people who like fish but not shellfish, and I have chosen it because it demonstrates one of the principal methods of handling fish sauces.

The sole used depends on your budget. For the less rich, substitute lemon sole for the Dover sole.

3 x 450 g (1 lb) Dover soles, filleted	180 ml (6 fl oz) dry white wine
salt and pepper	300 ml (10 fl oz) Fish Stock, strong-flavoured
Poaching liquor	and clear (see p.223)
6 shallots	*Sauce*
2 garlic cloves	1 bunch fresh parsley (flat or wild has the best
1 sprig fresh tarragon	flavour)
180 g (6 oz) white button mushrooms	180 ml (6 fl oz) whipping cream
juice of ½ lemon	3 egg yolks
90 g (3 oz) butter	lemon juice

Preparing the sole

1. Take the sole fillets and, starting at the thin (pointed) end, roll them and pierce them together with a cocktail stick. This ensures that the fillets are of one thickness and cook evenly. Season them with salt and pepper.

Preparing the poaching liquor

2. Peel and chop the shallots and garlic. Blanch the tarragon.

3. Wash the mushrooms and slice them. Squeeze and strain the lemon juice.

4. Melt the butter in a shallow ovenproof pan.

Add the shallots, tarragon and garlic, and cook gently until the shallots are opaque, with no colour.

5. Pour in the white wine, turn up the flame and reduce by half its volume.

6. Add the sliced mushrooms and the fish stock, and bring to the boil. (The mushrooms are added after the wine because the acid in the wine will keep them white.)

Cooking the fish

7. Preheat the oven to 180°C (350°F) Gas 4.

8. Place the sole fillets into the poaching liquor, cover with a butter paper and then a lid, and poach in the preheated oven for about 5 minutes only. It is very important to check the fish and to remove it from the liquor before it is completely cooked as it is still to be grilled.

9. Take the dish from the oven and remove the sole fillets. Place them on to your presentation dish or tray. Keep warm.

Finishing the sauce

10. Return the stock pan to the stove and reduce the cooking liquor until it becomes thick and slightly syrupy, a consistency which will coat the back of a spoon.

11. Preheat the grill.

12. Wash, drain and dry the parsley, then chop very finely.

13. Whip the cream to a peak. Do not over-whip or it will become granular and split the sauce.

14. Turn the egg yolks into the cream and gently fold them over until thoroughly mixed.

15. When the stock has reduced to the correct consistency, pour it into a bowl, using a spatula. Gently stir in the whipped cream and egg yolks. Check the seasoning and add a little lemon juice to bring up the flavours. Stir in the prepared chopped parsley.

CHEF'S TIP

Reducing the sauce to the correct consistency is an important part of the dish. If the liquor has not been sufficiently reduced, there will not be enough strength or natural gelatine to facilitate its glazing.

To finish and serve

16. Pour the sauce over the sole and, under the preheated grill, glaze the dish to a pale golden brown. Serve immediately.

As a personal preference, I like either to line the serving dish with blanched baby spinach leaves before glazing the fish, or to serve buttered spinach separately. Steamed or buttered new potatoes are also a great accompaniment. You'll need about two handfuls of baby spinach and 450 g (1lb) small new potatoes.

ICED MOUSSE NOUGATINE WITH A CARAMEL SAUCE

SERVES 8

This is a delicious iced mousse, lighter in texture than an ice cream. It's useful because it can be made well in advance and stored in the freezer. The sauce, too, can be made in advance.

Mousse	60 g (2 oz) Nougatine (see p.248)
8 egg yolks	**Caramel sauce**
120 g (4 oz) caster sugar	150 g (5 oz) caster sugar
60 g (2 oz) dark chocolate	30 ml (1 fl oz) Amaretto (an almond liqueur)
510 ml (17 fl oz) double cream	**Decoration**
30 ml (1 fl oz) Cognac	300 ml (10 fl oz) whipping cream
30 ml (1 fl oz) Armagnac	60 g (2 oz) toasted flaked almonds

Making the mousse

1. Boil a large saucepan of water as a bain-marie.
2. In a bowl that will fit over the pan, whisk the egg yolks and sugar together over the boiling water until pale in colour, thickened and forming a peak. Remove from the pan.
3. Chop the chocolate, place it in another similarly sized bowl and, again over the water (*not* boiling this time), gently melt it, stirring from time to time. Reserve aside.
4. In yet another bowl, whisk the cream to a stiff peak, the same consistency as the egg and sugar mixture.
5. At this stage add the chocolate to the egg and sugar sabayon mixture, and with a plastic spatula fold the two together.
6. Add the Cognac and Armagnac to the cream and gradually fold this in turn into the egg mixture. Do not *over*-mix.

CHEF'S TIP

It is important that the three processes outlined here be executed with the greatest possible care. The idea is to have a light frothy mousse. If you over-mix any of the bases, the mousse will collapse.

7. Crush the nougatine finely and sprinkle and fold into the mousse mixture.
8. Using a ladle, pour the finished mousse into eight dariole moulds or ramekins approximately 7.5 cm (3 in) high by 5 cm (2 in) wide. Very gently tap the base of the moulds to ensure that no air pockets are trapped in the mixture. Place on a tray and freeze for a minimum of 4 hours.

Making the sauce

9. Put the sugar and 60 ml (2 fl oz) water in a small pan. Over a fierce flame, boil and reduce the liquid until it thickens and turns a golden colour. Remove the pan from the heat.
10. Immediately add the Amaretto, stirring all the time. Allow the caramel to cool. If you find the sauce is too thick on serving, warm it on the stove and add a little more Amaretto.

To serve

11. In a bowl beat the whipping cream with a whisk to a firm peak. Do not over-whip or the cream will become granular and split. Place in a piping bag with a large star nozzle.
12. Remove the mousses from the freezer and unmould them. The best way to do this is to dip the moulds into hot water for a few seconds. Run a small knife around the inside of the outer edge of the mould. Turn the mousses upside-down into the centre of the dessert plates and lift off the moulds.
13. Pipe the tops of the mousses with a generous amount of cream and sprinkle this with toasted flaked almonds.
14. Finally, dip a large fork or spoon into the prepared cold caramel sauce and streak it across the desserts. Serve immediately.

As an option I like to serve almond tuile biscuits with this dish (see p.245).

CHEF'S TIP

When serving an iced dessert, it is always a good idea to chill the serving plates in the freezer first.

Winter Menu 5

ONION TART

LAMB CASSEROLE

A LIGHT CHOCOLATE TRUFFLE CAKE TOPPED WITH A COFFEE SABAYON MOUSSE

ONION TART

SERVES 6

This is a classical French first course, not to be confused with 'quiche', and it makes a good and fairly substantial winter dish.

350 g (12 oz) Shortcrust Pastry (see p.243)
Filling
2 large onions (or you can use shallots for added flavour)
1 garlic clove
2–3 sprigs fresh parsley
90 g (3 oz) Emmenthal (or Gruyère) cheese
30 g (1 oz) smoked bacon lardons

(see Chef's Tip)
60 ml (2 fl oz) olive oil
1 sprig fresh thyme
¼ bay leaf
90 ml (3 fl oz) dry white wine
90 g (3 oz) White Sauce (see p.228)
salt and pepper
1 egg yolk

Preparing the pastry cases
1. Preheat the oven to 180°C (350°F) Gas 4.
2. Divide the pastry into six even-sized pieces. Roll these out and use to line six tart moulds 10 cm (4 in) in diameter, 2 cm (¾ in) deep.
3. Fill with foil and baking beans and bake blind in the preheated oven for 10 minutes, or until the pastry is dry and golden in colour.
4. Carefully turn the cases on to a wire rack to cool.

Preparing the filling
5. Peel and finely slice the onions. Peel and chop the garlic. Pick the parsley leaves off the stalks, wash and dry them. Finely chop and reserve aside.
6. Grate the cheese into a bowl and reserve aside.

To prepare lardons, remove the rind from smoked rashers of bacon. Lay the rashers down on a board and, cutting against the grain of the meat, slice into thin strips or lardons. Blanch these in boiling water for about 1 minute, skimming off all the surfacing impurities. Strain through a fine-mesh conical strainer to remove the remaining impurities and most of the salt from the bacon. They are now ready to use.

7. On the stove heat a small frying pan until white hot. Add a little of the olive oil followed immediately by the bacon lardons. Stir until golden brown and remove from the pan on to a piece of kitchen paper to drain.

Cooking the filling

8. In a saucepan over a fierce flame heat the remaining olive oil and, as it begins to smoke, throw in the sliced onion, stirring all the time until golden brown. Add the thyme and bay leaf.

9. Pour in the white wine and reduce the liquid until the onions take on a syrupy consistency. Add the chopped garlic and the prepared lardons.

10. Add the white sauce to the mixture and stir to a smooth paste. Season with salt and pepper and sprinkle in the chopped parsley. Stir in the egg yolk. Do not re-boil the mixture.

To finish

11. Preheat the oven to 180°C (350°F) Gas 4, and preheat the grill.

12. Fill the cases with the onion mixture and top them with the grated cheese. Reheat in the preheated oven for 5 minutes then glaze under the preheated grill until the cheese is crisp and brown. Serve immediately.

LAMB CASSEROLE

SERVES 6

$\mathscr{T}$his is a hearty, warming winter dish and is reasonably inexpensive. It is one of those dishes that can be prepared in advance in anticipation of a house party, when it can be brought out and reheated without altering the finished product in any way.

There are two cuts of meat that can be used for this dish, depending on how much you want to spend. For the more expensive version we use cutlets taken from the best end of lamb. These are more tender, have a larger eye of meat, and present better. The less expensive cut should be taken from the middle neck of lamb, higher up nearest the head. The meat is tougher and the eye smaller, but the toughness does not matter too much as it is a braising dish. The cooking time will vary.

18 lamb cutlets or chops	***Beans***
450 g (1 lb) tomatoes	**180 g (6 oz) *haricots blancs***
1 onion	**2 garlic cloves**
½ carrot	**1 sprig fresh thyme**
1 leek	**½ bay leaf**
1 celery stalk	**180 g (6 oz) streaky bacon lardons**
8 garlic cloves	**(see Chef's Tip, p.196)**
salt and pepper	**100 g (3½ oz) fresh parsley**
about 210 ml (7 fl oz) cooking oil	***Garnishes***
30 g (1 oz) tomato paste	**1 courgette**
1 sprig fresh thyme	**2 carrots**
½ bay leaf	**1 celeriac**
3 litres (5½ pints) Chicken Stock (see p.225)	**1 leek**
	4 firm tomatoes

Preparing the beans

1. Soak the beans in plenty of cold water overnight.
2. The next day, drain, cover with fresh water (or stock), and bring to the boil. Skim off any surfacing scum. Add the garlic, thyme and bay leaf, and simmer until the beans are tender, which could take between 1 and 12 hours. Drain them when ready, and discard the flavourings.

Preparing the casserole vegetables

3. Squeeze and discard the seeds from each of the tomatoes over a sieve and bowl. Keep the juices.
4. Peel and chop the onion, carrot, leek and celery. Peel and chop the garlic.

Cooking the casserole

5. Lay out the cutlets and season with salt and pepper. In a large pan, heat a little of the oil and gently seal the cutlets on both sides until they are brown. Do this in batches, using about 1 tablespoon of oil per six cutlets, depending on the size of your pan. Lift them out into a casserole (see Chef's Tip), using a slotted spoon.
6. In the oil used to cook the cutlets, carefully cook the onion, leek, celery and carrot. Allow to brown evenly, stirring occasionally, then remove and add to the lamb.
7. In a bowl mix together the tomato paste and the squeezed tomatoes. Add this, along with the thyme, bay leaf, over half of the chopped garlic, and chicken stock, to the lamb and vegetables in the casserole.
8. Bring to the boil, skim and cover with a

tight-fitting lid. The casserole can either be cooked gently on top of the stove for 1½ hours or in a cool oven preheated to 120°C (250°F) Gas ½, for the same length of time, depending on which cut of meat you are using. Be careful not to *over*-cook the lamb or it will fall apart when reheated.

CHEF'S TIP
The cutlets do not have to lie flat while they are stewing, so the casserole used could be small, but tall – perhaps 25 x 20 cm (10 x 8 in) – with a lid.

Preparing the garnishes

9. Wash, peel and cut the courgette, carrots, celeriac and leek into batons of about 5 cm (2 in) thick, and 1 cm (½ in) long.
10. Skin, seed and cut the tomatoes into 1 cm (½ in) dice (see Chef's Tip, p.183).
11. For the bean garnish, brown the bacon lardons in a little oil. Wash, dry and chop the parsley finely.

Finishing the casserole

12. When the meat is cooked, carefully lift each cutlet out of the liquor and place on a tray or serving dish. Strain off the root vegetables and discard.
13. Skim the liquor well (see Chef's Tip), and put back on to a fast heat to boil. While reducing, add the remaining chopped garlic. Reduce by half. Taste and season if required.

CHEF'S TIP
Be sure to skim off all the fat before it boils into the sauce as it can alter the taste and make it cloudy. At this stage, I would recommend you pass the sauce through a clean piece of muslin to trap all the remaining sediments, which will leave the finished sauce bright, clear and a vivid red, rather than a cloudy, dull liquid.

To reheat and serve

14. Place the beans in a pan and add a small amount of the sauce. Heat through gently and check the seasoning. Add the lardons, tomato dice and parsley.
15. Cook the vegetable batons in boiling salted water for about 4 minutes, or until tender.
16. Reheat the cutlets in a little of the sauce.
17. Place a spoonful of the hot beans in the middle of each plate. Sprinkle around the hot vegetable batons. Lean three cutlets against each other, using the beans as a rest to gain more height. Quickly pour the finished sauce around and serve immediately.

CHEF'S TIP
When I want to use a lot of tomatoes for flavour, I buy over-ripe tomatoes from the greengrocer at practically giveaway prices. These I squeeze to get rid of the seeds – the only sour part of the fruit – and then use the flavourful tomato pulp and skin in the sauce or stock. This skin will later be sieved out.

A Light Chocolate Truffle Cake Topped with a Coffee Sabayon Mousse

SERVES 8

*Y*ou could serve this dish with a coffee egg custard sauce and almond tuile biscuits (see p.250 and p.245).

½ quantity Biscuit Sponge (see p.245), baked on 1 tray
150 g (5 oz) best dark chocolate
30 ml (1 fl oz) Tia Maria
sweetened cocoa powder
(*not* drinking chocolate)
Chocolate mousse
60 ml (2 fl oz) Stock Syrup (see p.249)

2 egg yolks
250 ml (8½ fl oz) whipping cream
Coffee sabayon mousse
1 gelatine leaf
1 egg yolk
10 g (⅓ oz) instant coffee powder
20 g (⅔ oz) caster sugar
150 ml (5 fl oz) whipping cream

Preparing the cake and chocolate mousse

1. Cut two discs from the biscuit sponge, one 20 cm (8 in) in diameter for the base, and a second 15 cm (6 in) in diameter for the centre of the dessert.
2. Chop the chocolate into small pieces and put it into a bowl. Place this over simmering water to melt. Be careful not to get any water into the chocolate as it will thicken and spoil.
3. When the chocolate has melted, spread some of it thinly over one side of each of the biscuit discs. Place them on a tray, and refrigerate.
4. Keep the remaining chocolate warm and liquid over the hot water while you prepare the mousse. Do not boil or overheat.
5. Bring the stock syrup to the boil in a small pan. Reserve aside.
6. Whip the egg yolks in a bowl, then add the prepared syrup. Whisk continuously until the yolks become light and fluffy.
7. In another bowl whisk the cream so that it thickens but not to a peak.
8. With a spatula carefully fold the warm liquid chocolate into the egg yolk sabayon, then fold this into the cream. As soon as the cream is incorporated stop mixing (over-mixing at this stage will cause the texture of the chocolate mousse to be dense and granular). We want the mousse to be as light as possible.

9. Place the larger disc of biscuit sponge, chocolate-side down, inside a 20 x 7.5 cm (8 x 3 in) cake ring on a tray. Brush the top of the sponge with half of the Tia Maria.
10. Take the chocolate mousse and, using a spatula, spread it into the cake ring over the sponge. In the centre of the ring gently press down the smaller biscuit sponge disc, again chocolate-side down. Brush this with the remainder of the Tia Maria. Place the tray and its contents in the refrigerator.

Preparing the coffee sabayon mousse

11. Soak the gelatine leaf in cold water to soften it.
12. Put the egg yolk, coffee powder, 30 ml (1 fl oz) water and the sugar in a clean bowl. Whisk together over a pan of simmering water until light and fluffy.
13. Squeeze the excess water from the gelatine leaf and whisk it into your sabayon until dissolved. Remove from the heat.
14. Whisk the cream until thick but not stiff, then fold this into your warm sabayon.
15. Pour this mousse mixture over the chocolate mousse cake in the ring and freeze for 2 hours. This is to set the mousses firm as they are extremely light.
16. Remove the cake from the freezer 2 hours before serving and allow to come round in the fridge.

To serve

17. Dust the top with the sweetened cocoa powder. Dip a fine knife in hot water and run this around the inside of the ring very carefully. Remove the ring. Do this at the very last moment.

18. Cut the cake, using a sharp thin knife, into eight wedges. Serve accompanied, if you like, by coffee egg custard sauce and almond tuiles.

Winter Menu 6

NEW POTATOES FILLED WITH SNAILS, MARROW, SHALLOT AND BACON, SERVED WITH A RED WINE SAUCE

BARON OF RABBIT COOKED IN VINEGAR, TOMATOES AND FRESH HERBS

GÂTEAU ST HONORÉ

NEW POTATOES FILLED WITH SNAILS, MARROW, SHALLOT AND BACON, SERVED WITH A RED WINE SAUCE

SERVES 6

I buy fresh snails but, as they are difficult to come by, this recipe uses already prepared, tinned snails.

18 x 60 g (2 oz) small new potatoes	*Filling*
salt and pepper	3 garlic cloves
Sauce	60 g (2 oz) parsley
4 shallots	36 baby cocktail onions
3 garlic cloves	36 snails, washed
1 sprig fresh tarragon	120 g (4 oz) bone marrow
240 g (8 oz) mushrooms	60 g (2 oz) clarified butter (see Chef's Tip, p.15)
30 g (1 oz) butter	120 g (4 oz) smoked streaky bacon lardons
1 sprig fresh thyme	(see Chef's Tip, p.196)
1 bay leaf	*Garnish*
60 ml (2 fl oz) ruby port	210 g (7 oz) *Choucroûte* (see p.237)
300 ml (10 fl oz) red Sancerre wine	180 g (6 oz) Parslied Breadcrumbs (see p.240)
300 ml (10 fl oz) Chicken Stock (see p.225)	

Preparing the potatoes

1. Wash and scrub the potatoes. Lay them on a board and make sure they do not roll. If they do, just take a very thin slice off the bottom to stabilise them. Lengthways, cut a quarter slice off the top of each potato. Discard these tops.

2. With a small scoop, take the potato flesh out of the larger piece of potato until you have the skin and 3 mm (⅛ in) thickness of flesh left. Keep the potato 'shells' in cold water.

3. In a large pan of boiling salted water simmer the potatoes until tender, about 3–4 minutes, depending on size. When cooked, remove with a slotted spoon and tip out any excess water.

Preparing the sauce

4. Peel and slice the shallots and garlic. Blanch the tarragon. Wash and slice the mushrooms.

5. Melt the butter in a pan, add the sliced shallots and garlic, and cook slowly. Add the blanched tarragon, thyme and bay leaf. Add the mushrooms and allow them to give off their water, then increase the heat and evaporate.

6. Add the port and reduce by half. Add the Sancerre and reduce by half. Add the chicken stock, bring to the boil, skim and simmer for 20 minutes. Strain and reduce by half. Season with salt and pepper and keep hot.

Making the 'filling'

7. Peel and crush the garlic. Wash, dry and finely chop the parsley. Peel and cook the onions in boiling salted water, about 10 minutes, depending on size.

8. Wash the snails. Dice the marrow.

9. Add a splash of clarified butter to a hot skillet pan and quickly crisp the bacon lardons. Add the cooked baby onions and allow to turn golden brown, a few minutes. Keep hot.

10. Into a separate red-hot pan, *without any fat in it*, quickly throw the diced marrow and the snails. Turn over and over rapidly for 1 minute, then add the bacon and onions. Off the heat, add the crushed garlic, chopped parsley, and some salt and pepper. Continue tossing until well mixed. Taste and adjust seasoning if necessary.

11. Quickly fill each potato with the snails, marrow, bacon and onions.

To serve

12. Preheat the grill.

13. Heat up the *choucroûte*, then place into six tall moulds (dariole moulds are fine). Keep hot.

14. Top each potato with some of the parslied breadcrumbs and brown under the preheated grill.

15. In the centre of each plate place a *choucroûte* mould. Place the potatoes around this, three per serving. Lift off the mould and spoon around the red wine sauce. Serve at once.

As an option, you could trickle on a little Butter Sauce for Fish (see p.231), and scatter the sauce with some tomato dice.

BARON OF RABBIT COOKED IN VINEGAR, TOMATOES AND FRESH HERBS

SERVES 6

*R*abbits are easily available and come in two forms – the more expensive French domestic rabbit, reared for the table, and the wild rabbit which has more depth of flavour. Ask your butcher to skin your rabbit and remove the head. He will also joint it for you (or see the Chef's Tip below).

In order to draw out the blood from a wild rabbit, it is best to cut the carcass into joints, remove the sinews and immerse the pieces in milk for 24 hours. After this the flesh becomes whiter and less acrid. The joints should be washed off under running water until the milk has gone, and then dried on kitchen paper or a cloth.

CHEF'S TIP

Jointing a rabbit:

With the rabbit on its back, rear legs nearest to you, turn it on to its side. Feel for the pelvic bone and cut along this, letting it guide you down the backbone. The cut is only 2–3 cm (about 1 in) deep, and the pelvis is on the leg joint rather than the saddle. Repeat on the other side and it should expose a ball and socket joint near the back. Lever the legs backwards and, with a heavy knife, chop through the remaining bone. You should now have two loose back legs. Place aside.

Facing you now is what is called the saddle. This consists of two tender fillets running along the back, up towards the shoulders and rib cage. Where the ribs start, count up four ribs and cut through the skin either side, then chop through the backbone. You should now have a loose saddle. Place aside.

Slip the knife under the shoulder blade and gently ease off the shoulders which do not seem to be attached at all!

There is a silvery skin or membrane on the meat, and it is best removed before soaking in the milk by gently inserting a sharp knife in between the membrane and flesh and easing it away. This takes time but is well worth it.

Then immerse the chopped and prepared meat in milk for 24 hours.

---

2 rabbits, skinned and jointed (see Chef's Tip)
510 ml (17 fl oz) milk
60 ml (2 fl oz) vegetable oil
salt and pepper
Sauce
500 g (18 oz) tomatoes
1 onion
½ carrot
1 leek
1 celery stalk
6 garlic cloves
210 ml (7 fl oz) white wine vinegar
60 g (2 oz) tomato paste

210 ml (7 fl oz) white wine
2 litres (3½ pints) Chicken Stock (see p.225)
1 sprig fresh thyme
1 bay leaf
To finish
4 tomatoes
2 shallots
a little fresh parsley, chervil, tarragon and chives
110 ml (3½ fl oz) whipping cream
60 g (2 oz) unsalted butter
juice of 1 lemon
2 teaspoons Dijon mustard

Making the sauce

1. Squeeze the tomatoes, to remove the seeds. Keep juice and flesh. Peel and chop the onion, carrot, leek, celery and garlic.

2. Chop the rib cage and rabbit trimmings into small pieces and roast in 2 tablespoons of the hot oil on top of the stove until golden brown.

3. Meanwhile, in a separate large pan, reduce

the white wine vinegar by half. Add the crushed tomatoes and tomato paste and continue to cook gently until a bright red paste or purée is formed, about 15 minutes.

4. Add the golden brown bones and mix thoroughly.

5. Pour off the remaining fat from the roasting pan and pour in the white wine. Scrape any sediments into the wine, then boil to reduce by half.

6. Add this to the bones and tomato pulp and cover with the chicken stock. Bring to the boil and skim.

7. In 1 tablespoon more of the oil, roast the onion, carrot, leek and celery until brown, then add to the stock with the garlic, thyme and bay leaf. Skim and simmer for 1 hour.

8. Pass through a conical strainer then strain through a piece of muslin. Set over heat to reduce by half.

Cooking the rabbit

9. Preheat the oven to 200°C (400°F) Gas 6.

10. Season the rabbit joints and seal in the remaining hot oil until brown. Tip off the excess fat and place in the preheated oven for 10 minutes, turning regularly. When firm to the touch, remove from the oven and allow to rest.

To finish and serve

11. Skin, seed and dice the tomatoes. Peel and chop the shallots. Wash, dry and finely chop the herbs (you want about a teaspoon of each). Mix together in a pan.

12. Reheat the rabbit joints and chop each one in half for presentation.

13. Add the cream to the reduced stock and boil. Whisk in the butter and taste for seasoning. Add salt, pepper and lemon juice as necessary.

14. Off the heat, whisk the mustard into the creamy stock and then strain on to the herb and tomato mixture.

15. Place the hot rabbit pieces around the plates and spoon the hot tomato and herb sauce   over each.

This is good served with fresh green pasta. I sometimes finish off the dish with scalded baby spinach leaves to add more colour and flavour to the dish.

GÂTEAU ST HONORÉ

SERVES 6-8

This is a well-tried traditional dessert. It's easy to prepare, and combines three classical base recipes: puff pastry, choux pastry and pastry cream.

500 g (18 oz) Puff Pastry (see p.242)	**(17 fl oz) milk (see p.249)**
flour for dusting	**6 egg whites**
1 egg	**Biscuit Sponge trimmings (see p.245)**
10 g (⅓ oz) caster sugar	**2 tablespoons Grand Marnier**
1 quantity Choux Pastry, using 4 eggs	**4 satsumas**
(see p.244)	*Garnish caramel*
Filling	**110 g (3½ oz) caster sugar**
1 quantity Pastry Cream, using 510 ml	

Preparing and cooking the pastry base

1. Preheat the oven to 220°C (425°F) Gas 7.

2. Roll out the puff pastry to 3 mm (⅛ in) thick approximately, and 25 cm (10 in) square. Lightly dust a baking sheet with flour and lay the pastry on it. With a fork, puncture the pastry all over (this stops it rising). Place in the refrigerator to rest, at least 20 minutes.

3. Crack the egg into a bowl and add the caster sugar. With a whisk, beat until smooth. This is

Sea Bass in Oyster and Champagne Sauce

New Potatoes Filled with Snails, Marrow, Shallot and Bacon, served with a Red Wine Sauce

Duck Legs Braised in Red Wine and Served on a Shallot Cream

Caramelised Bananas and Iced Pistachio Parfait

a sugar wash.

4. Make the choux pastry. Place in a piping bag with a 1 cm (½ in) plain nozzle.

5. Remove the puff pastry from the refrigerator and cut out a disc approximately 20–23 cm (8–9 in) in diameter. Lightly brush the outer edge of the disc with the sugar wash.

6. Pipe a ring of choux pastry around the outer rim of the puff pastry disc. On another baking sheet, this time lined with greaseproof paper, pipe the remaining choux into buns approximately the size of a walnut.

7. Bake the choux buns and pastry disc in the preheated oven until brown and dry, about 30 minutes. Remove and place on a rack to cool.

Making the filling

8. Make the pastry cream, and have it hot.

9. Pour the egg whites into an electric mixer bowl and whisk to a firm peak. Fold into the hot pastry cream. (This is the real secret of St Honoré.) Leave to cool.

10. Dice the biscuit sponge trimmings into cubes and place them in a bowl. Sprinkle with the Grand Marnier and gently, with a spoon, stir them until coated. Place these in the centre of the puff and choux pastry case, ensuring there are no gaps.

11. Peel the satsumas, break into segments, and arrange these over the top of the sponge.

12. Make a small hole in the bottom of each choux bun. Place the cold St Honoré cream in a piping bag fitted with a 5 mm (¼ in) nozzle and fill the choux buns.

Making the caramel

13. Fill a large bowl with cold water. In a small saucepan or copper sugar pan boil the sugar and 60 ml (2 fl oz) water together over a fast flame for the caramel. Reduce the liquid until a light caramel is obtained. Be careful not to overcook the sugar as it will blacken and give a bitter taste. To stop the sugar once the correct colour has been achieved, quickly take the pan and half immerse in the bowl of water. This will stop further cooking of the caramel and bring down its temperature. Hold it over the water for approximately 30 seconds.

14. Immediately, and piece by piece, dip the tops of your choux buns into the caramel. Be very careful at this point; remember the caramel is still very hot and can give a nasty burn.

15. Place the caramel buns around the outer edge of your dessert. Pipe the remaining St Honoré cream into the centre. Present to your guests first, then cut in wedges and serve.

Optional Spun Sugar Garnish

For added appearance, I like to decorate this dish with spun sugar, using the caramel left over.

1. Take the pan containing the caramel to the stove and over a gentle flame warm it through again until it takes on the consistency of treacle.

2. Dip a large fork into the caramel and wave it up and down vigorously over a sheet of greaseproof paper. Repeat this process several times until enough spun sugar is obtained (i.e. when everything in the kitchen is covered in sugar!). It should look like candy floss.

3. Form the spun sugar into a loose ball and place this on top of your Gâteau St Honoré.

Winter Menu 7

Hot Mousse of Jerusalem Artichoke with a Watercress Coulis

Duck Legs Braised in Red Wine and Served on a Shallot Cream

Apples in a Walnut Caramel

Hot Mousse of Jerusalem Artichoke with a Watercress Coulis

SERVES 7

*T*his dish is a comparatively simple one and is very inexpensive. It makes a good alternative to a fish or meat hors-d'oeuvre, and can be used to start any menu.

Artichoke mousse
450 g (1 lb) small Jerusalem artichokes
120 g (4 oz) unsalted butter
2 eggs
2 egg yolks
110 ml (3½ fl oz) double cream
salt and pepper
Cooking liquor
270 ml (9 fl oz) water
juice of 1 lemon
40 g (1½ oz) plain flour
1 small garlic clove
Watercress coulis

3 bunches hot peppery watercress
1 bunch fresh parsley, about 110 g (3½ oz)
1 small potato
1 leek
2 shallots
1 garlic clove
90 g (3 oz) unsalted butter
1 small sprig fresh thyme
1 small piece bay leaf
90 ml (3 fl oz) white wine
150 ml (5 fl oz) Chicken Stock (see p.225)
60 ml (2 fl oz) double cream

Preparing the cooking liquor

1. Pour the water into a saucepan, and add the lemon juice through a strainer. Season with salt and pepper and add the flour, whisking vigorously until fully dissolved. Peel and add the clove of garlic for extra flavour.

2. Put the pan on to boil, stirring all the time so that the flour does not catch at the bottom of the pan. Bring to the boil and reserve aside. The cooking liquor is now ready.

CHEF'S TIP

Jerusalem artichokes are treated much the same way as for new potatoes. If they are first crop, small and very firm, they can be scraped; if older, they should be peeled. The most important thing in their cooking is to keep them a nice white colour. The lemon and flour in the cooking liquor help this.

Preparing and cooking the artichoke mousse

3. In a pan gently melt half the butter. Do not colour. With a brush, coat the insides of seven ramekins (roughly 6.5 cm/2½ in in diameter and 3.5 cm/1¼ in in depth containing 60 ml/2 fl oz) with a good layer of the butter and refrigerate to set. Cut out seven small round discs of greaseproof paper, using the bottom of an empty ramekin dish for the size, and line the bottom of each dish. Refrigerate.

4. Preheat the oven to 180°C (350°F) Gas 4.

5. Wash, peel or scrape and re-wash the artichokes. Put them directly into the cooking liquor. It is important to note that, like new potatoes, Jerusalem artichokes are high in vitamin C and can easily break up in cooking if started from cold. Cook for approximately 10 minutes. To check if they are ready, pierce with the point of a sharp knife. If they fall off the knife, they are cooked.

6. Strain the artichokes through a colander and turn them out on to a baking sheet. Remove the garlic clove. Place them in the preheated oven for about 3 minutes for all the steam to evaporate from them. Remove them, then reduce the temperature of the oven to low, 120°C (250°F) Gas ½.

7. Place the artichokes into a liquidiser or processor. Beat them to a pulp or purée.

8. In a pan, melt the remaining butter and cook to a nut-brown colour. As it begins to foam and colour, pour it very quickly into the artichoke purée in the machine. Add the eggs and egg yolks, and continue beating. Check the seasoning.

9. Finally add the cream. If you have carried out the procedures for cooking the artichokes correctly, the purée should not be too wet. If you have not, do not add all the specified cream. And, if the purée is of a good, smooth consistency, it should not be necessary to sieve it. If still a little rough, strain the mixture through a sieve, with the aid of a plastic pastry scraper.

10. With a ladle, pour the purée into the prepared ramekins. Fill to the top. Place them in a bain-marie (a shallow roasting tray of water just below boiling point). Make sure the water is as high up the dishes as possible for even cooking. Also make sure the water is *not* boiling and the oven *not too hot* or the mousse will bubble or, at the very worst, 'soufflé' and take on a scrambled or beaded consistency.

11. With the point of a knife, make several small incisions evenly spaced in two butter papers. Place these over the mousses and carefully put the bain-marie in the low oven. Cook for 20 minutes or until set. (It is important to make these holes in the paper to allow the steam to escape evenly.)

Preparing the watercress coulis

12. Wash the watercress and pick off the leaves (keep a handful back in another bowl to use for garnish). Wash and pick off the parsley leaves. Wash and peel the potato and dice into small pieces. Wash, trim and dice the leek. Peel and chop the shallots. Peel and crush the garlic.

13. In a pan melt half the butter, and add the leek and shallot dice, the thyme and bay leaf. Cook until opaque. Add the potato dice and continue cooking over a moderate flame for approximately 5 minutes. Add the white wine and crushed garlic. Boil to reduce the liquid by half of its original volume, then add the chicken stock.

14. Bring the liquid to the boil and with a ladle

remove all surfacing scum and fat. Turn down the flame and continue cooking for a further 5 minutes. Season with salt and pepper.

15. Add the watercress and parsley. Bring back to the boil and immediately pour the liquid into a liquidiser. Purée until completely smooth, then pass the finished sauce through a conical strainer. With the back of a ladle, force all the liquid through, pressing against the sediments and the strainer.

16. Pour the sauce into a pan. Check seasoning. With a whisk stir in the remaining butter, piece by piece, until fully dissolved. Stir in the cream. Keep warm.

To serve

17. Remove the mousses from the oven. They should be set and firm to the touch. Edge round the dishes with the point of a sharp knife and turn the mousses out on to the centre of each plate. With a spoon, carefully place the finished sauce around the mousses.

As an option and for a more appealing presentation, you can heat a little butter, water, salt and pepper and scald the remaining watercress leaves in this. With a fork, remove and arrange them in three equal piles around the edge of the plate. I also like to cover the tops of the mousses with a little *beurre blanc* (butter sauce) for added effect; the recipe for this is on p.231.

DUCK LEGS BRAISED IN RED WINE AND SERVED ON A SHALLOT CREAM

SERVES 6

*T*his is an excellent dish for those cold winter months, and is relatively inexpensive. It can be prepared two or three days in advance as the cooking time is quite long. It will keep very well, covered in a refrigerator. The ducks we use at the restaurant are Gressingham ducks, as they yield more meat than other ducks and are less fatty.

We always have duck legs in the restaurant because we buy the ducks whole and remove the breasts. You *can* buy duck legs, but I suggest every time you cook duck you remove the legs and freeze them until you have enough for this dish.

12 duck legs	**1 sprig fresh thyme**
cooking oil	**1 bay leaf**
salt and pepper	**1 quantity *Mirepoix* (see p.239)**
6 garlic cloves	***Garnish***
30 ml (1 fl oz) red wine vinegar	**1 quantity Shallot Purée (see p.235)**
1 bottle of Beaujolais or similar red wine	**about 180 g (6 oz) vegetables, mixed and**
60 ml (2 fl oz) ruby port	**cooked to taste (see Chef's Tip)**
1.5 litres (2¾ pints) Chicken Stock (see p.225)	

Preparing the duck legs

1. Trim off all excess fat from around the duck legs, but leave one side with the skin intact.

2. Heat a little cooking oil in a heavy pan on the stove. Season the legs and place them in the pan, skin-side down. They should sizzle right away but not too fast, as you wish to

melt off as much of the fat remaining on the legs as possible before they get too brown.

3. Once browned, turn the legs over and seal the other side. This operation should take 10 minutes. When they are browned on both sides, remove with a slotted spoon to a suitable casserole.

Cooking the duck legs

4. Peel and chop the garlic.

5. Tip the remaining fat out of the frying pan and, whilst still on the heat, pour in the red wine vinegar. This should bubble up. With a wooden spoon, all the sediments on the bottom of the pan can easily be lifted off into the vinegar.

6. When the vinegar is reduced to almost nothing, add the red wine and boil to reduce by a third. Add the port, boil once, then pour over the duck legs in the casserole pan.

7. Cover with the chicken stock, add the garlic, thyme and bay leaf, and bring to the boil.

8. Meanwhile, in a frying pan in a little more hot oil, brown the *mirepoix* vegetables, about 5 minutes, and add to the stock.

9. Bring the liquid back to the boil and skim off all surfacing fat, turn down the flame and simmer. This dish can either be cooked very gently on the stove or in the oven, preheated to 110°C (225°F) Gas ¼, for 3 hours. The timing can vary: some legs are bigger and tougher than others, so it could take more or less time. Check periodically until they are tender.

10. When cooked, the flesh should be tender but not falling off the bones, as this can be tricky to serve. If the legs are for the same day, remove from the stock to a warm plate or tray, cover and keep warm. (If not, remove from the stock, gently place into a container and strain the stock over them. Allow to cool completely, then refrigerate.)

To serve

11. If using immediately, strain the stock and skim off all fat. This is important, as it could cloud the finished sauce. Place on a fast gas in a shallow open pan and boil to reduce by half. (At the restaurant we enrich the stock at this stage with a spoon of meat glaze, but it is only an optional extra.)

12. Heat through the shallot purée and cook the chosen vegetables in boiling salted water.

13. Place a spoonful of the shallot purée in the middle of each serving plate, and around the perimeter the warm crisp garnish vegetables.

14. On top of the purée, place one leg and the other on top of the first.

15. Check the sauce for final seasoning and consistency, then strain it over each plate, taking care not to disturb the shallot purée. (A garlic *croûton*, one end dipped in chopped parsley, can be added for extra texture, see Chef's Tip, p.138.) Serve at once.

CHEF'S TIP

As accompaniment in the restaurant, we use vegetables all 'turned' – cut and shaped – to the same size. We use potatoes, carrot, celeriac and courgette usually, but in the winter you can use vegetables such as turnip, parsnip or swede.

APPLES IN A WALNUT CARAMEL

SERVES 6

*N*othing goes better with hot caramelised apples than walnuts. This is one of my favourite winter sweets.

1 quantity Puff Pastry (see p.242)	**240 ml (8 fl oz) single cream**
1 egg, beaten	**60 g (2 oz) unsalted butter**
a little icing sugar	**60 g (2 oz) shelled walnuts, skinned (see p.30)**
3 dessert apples	***To serve***
juice of 1 lemon	**110 g (3½ oz) caster sugar**
150 ml (5 fl oz) dry cider	**1 quantity Vanilla Ice Cream (see p.248)**
Sauce	**6 sprigs fresh mint**
110 g (3½ oz) caster sugar	

Preparing and baking the pastry cases

1. Roll out the puff pastry to 3 mm (⅛ in) thick, and cut out twelve discs with a 7.5 cm (3 in) circular pastry cutter.
2. To make a pastry case, sandwich together two discs, using a little water. Using a 4 cm (1½ in) cutter, cut through the top disc only. Do the same with the other ten discs. Place on a baking sheet. Brush the tops with a little beaten egg, and place in the freezer for 20 minutes to harden.
3. Preheat the oven to 220°C (425°F) Gas 7, and preheat the grill.
4. Remove the baking sheet from the freezer and score the inside discs in a fan shape with a sharp knife. These will become the lids of the pastry cases.
5. Bake the pastry cases in the preheated oven until golden in colour and crisp, about 20 minutes.
6. Dust with icing sugar and caramelise under the hot grill.
7. Carefully cut out the lids with a sharp knife. With a fork, and whilst the pastry cases are still hot, hollow out the cases, discarding all the glutinous uncooked pastry.

Preparing the apples

8. Peel, core and halve the apples. Brush the cut surfaces with a little of the lemon juice to prevent discoloration.
9. Bring the cider and remaining lemon juice to the boil together. Add the apple halves and remove from the heat as soon as the liquid comes back to the boil. Cover with cling film. The apples will continue cooking gently in the trapped steam.

Making the sauce

10. Gently melt the sugar in a saucepan over a very low flame, to a golden amber colour. At this point add the cream. Stir the sauce back to the boil.
11. Remove from the heat, stirring continuously. Add the butter and stir until completely dissolved, then add the skinned walnuts.

To finish and serve

12. Preheat the oven to 160°C (325°F) Gas 3.
13. For a caramel, in a small pan over a fierce flame melt the sugar with 60 ml (2 fl oz) water. Reduce and cook until the sugar starts to turn a golden colour and caramelise. Reserve aside.
14. Reheat the puff pastry cases in the warm preheated oven, and reheat the apples in their cider syrup in a small pan.
15. Gently warm the walnut caramel sauce in another pan, then spoon this on to your serving plates. In the centre of these plates place the warm pastry cases.
16. Top the open cases with a ball of vanilla ice cream, and in turn top these with the warm half apples.
17. Coat each apple with the prepared caramel, and quickly replace the pastry lids. Garnish with a sprig of mint and serve immediately.

Winter Menu 8

MULLIGATAWNY SOUP

BREAST OF PHEASANT COOKED IN SHALLOTS AND WINE, WITH CHICORY AND GAME CHIPS

CARAMELISED BANANAS AND ICED PISTACHIO PARFAIT

MULLIGATAWNY SOUP

SERVES 6

*T*here are countless English versions of this Indian soup. Here is mine, and I have included it in the book because it is one of my favourite soups.

2 litres (3½ pints) Oxtail Stock (see p.227)	½ bay leaf
400 g (14 oz) onions	1 sprig fresh thyme
1 large leek	a handful of parsley stalks
1 large carrot	60 g (2 oz) plain flour
1 celery stalk	60 g (2 oz) tomato purée
1 large eating apple	30 g (1 oz) sultanas
2 garlic cloves	salt and pepper
1 lemon	*Garnish*
60 ml (2 fl oz) olive oil	60 ml (2 fl oz) single cream, coconut milk or
30 g (1 oz) butter	coconut water (see Chef's Tip)
60 g (2 oz) Madras curry paste	60 g (2 oz) plain basmati rice, cooked
1 clove	

Preparing the vegetables

1. Peel the onions and dice them into 1 cm (½ in) cubes. Wash and peel the leek and discard

the outer leaf. Cut off the dark green bitter top and discard. Dice as for the onion. Peel and dice the carrot. Wash the celery and again dice

215

it into 1 cm (½ in) cubes. Reserve aside in
a bowl.

2. Peel, core and dice the apple, and keep
apart from the vegetables.

3. Peel the garlic cloves and crush them with
the back of a knife.

4. Peel two strands of lemon zest from the
lemon. In a shallow pan of boiling water cook
for about 2 minutes to remove the bitterness.
Drain and refresh in cold water. Repeat the
process. Drain and reserve aside.

Cooking the soup

5. Heat a large heavy-bottomed saucepan over
a fierce flame. Add the oil and when smoking
add the butter, followed immediately by the
diced vegetables. Cook for about 5 minutes,
stirring from time to time until light brown
but not burnt.

6. Add the curry paste, clove, bay leaf, thyme,
parsley stalks and blanched lemon zest.

7. Add the flour and stir the base together
thoroughly until all the flour has mixed in
with the vegetables. Cook for a further 3
minutes and then add the tomato purée and
crushed garlic. Turn down the flame and stir
the mixture together. Cook for a further 2
minutes but do not allow the ingredients to
catch or burn on the bottom of the pan.

8. Add the diced apple, sultanas and the
prepared oxtail stock or broth. (I like to use
oxtail rather than just the traditional chicken
or veal stock because it gives a richer flavour
and more depth to the soup.) Bring the liquid
to the boil and with the aid of a ladle skim off
all the surfacing fats and sediment. Turn down
the flame and gently simmer the soup for an
hour. Stir from time to time to ensure that the
vegetables do not stick on the bottom of the
pan during cooking. Skim if necessary.

CHEF'S TIP

The meat still remaining on the oxtails after straining the
stock can be picked off the tails, diced and used as part of
the garnish in finishing the soup.

9. When cooked, strain the soup through a
conical strainer into another pan. Return this
to the stove and reheat.

10. Add the juice of half the lemon to the
soup, and check the seasoning, adding salt and
pepper to taste. Finally stir in the cream. When
possible use fresh coconut milk instead, or
alternatively coconut water (see Chef's Tip) in
place of half the quantity of stock.

CHEF'S TIP

To make coconut water, soak 240 g (8 oz) grated coconut
in 1.2 litres (2 pints) boiling water for approximately 1
hour. Strain 1 litre (1¾ pints) of this into the soup at the
same time as the stock or broth is used. Remember to use
a half quantity of the stock.

To serve

11. Lay out your warm soup plates. In each
put approximately 1 dessertspoon of cooked
basmati rice and 1 dessertspoon of the cooked
oxtail meat (if using). Carefully, with a ladle,
pour in your finished mulligatawny soup, and
serve immediately.

BREAST OF PHEASANT COOKED IN SHALLOTS AND WINE, WITH CHICORY AND GAME CHIPS

SERVES 6

*P*heasants make a super winter dish. They are light to eat, full of flavour and readily available. The most succulent are the hen birds with yellowish fat and skin. Avoid, if you can, the large male birds with sharp spurs (spurs are found behind the foot, high up the ankle). These birds can be dry and tough as they have been around for a while.

In this recipe we use only the breast meat. The legs will be used in other dishes.

3 pheasants	½ quantity *Mirepoix* (see p.239)
cooking oil	½ bottle dry white wine
salt and pepper	1.3 litres (2½ pints) Chicken Stock (see p.225)
Sauce	*Garnish*
400 g (14 oz) shallots	3 heads of Belgian endive (chicory)
6 garlic cloves	6 rashers streaky bacon
40 g (1½ oz) unsalted butter	1 potato
lemon juice	720 ml (24 fl oz) Chicken Stock (see p.225)
1 sprig fresh thyme	6 baby cabbages or Brussels sprout tops
1 bay leaf	vegetable oil for deep-frying

Preparing the pheasants

1. Remove the legs, wishbones and backbones from the pheasants, leaving the breasts on the rib cages. Set the legs aside for another dish. Chop the remaining bones, including the wing tips.

Preparing the sauce

2. Peel and coarsely chop the shallots. Peel the garlic.
3. Place the shallots in a shallow pan and barely cover with water. Add the butter, a few drops of lemon juice, half the thyme, a third of the bay leaf and 1 garlic clove. Bring to the boil and cook until the shallots are tender and most of the liquid has evaporated. Remove and discard the bay leaf and thyme.
4. In a liquidiser, blend until the shallots are smooth, then set aside.
5. Brown the chopped pheasant bones evenly in hot oil on top of the stove, turning often. Remove with a slotted spoon to a large saucepan.
6. Brown the *mirepoix* vegetables evenly in the oil remaining in the pan, then add to the

bones, again using a slotted spoon.
7. Pour off the oil remaining in the pan, but leave the bits stuck to the bottom (if any). Pour in the white wine which should bubble up. Scrape off the sediment with a wooden or plastic spoon, then reduce the wine by half. Add to the bones, along with the reserved shallot mixture.
8. Cover the bones and other ingredients with the chicken stock, bring to the boil, skim and simmer for 1 hour. Add also, at this stage, the remaining garlic, thyme and bay leaf.

Cooking the pheasant breasts

9. Preheat the oven to 230°C (450°F) Gas 8.
10. Season the pheasant breasts with salt and pepper. In a roasting pan or tray, heat up a little oil. Carefully place each pheasant breast into the tray, on one side, and sauté until golden brown. Turn on to the other side and repeat the process until the breasts look evenly golden. This should take about 3–4 minutes.
11. Bring the bird upright, place into the preheated oven, and roast for 12–15 minutes, depending on size. The breasts, when roasted,

should feel firm but not hard. It is nice to keep the flesh slightly pink to retain a little moisture. Allow to relax for a few minutes out of the oven. Reduce the temperature of the oven to 150°C (300°F) Gas 2.

Preparing and cooking the garnish
12. Remove the first one or two leaves of the endive, then cut each endive in half. Cut the rind from the bacon. Wash, peel and wash the potato. Cut *very finely* into game chips (potato crisps) and keep in cold water.
13. Wrap each endive half round with a rasher of bacon, holding the ends in place with a cocktail stick. Put into a small shallow pan, season and barely cover with the chicken stock. Bring to the boil and simmer until tender, about 5 minutes. Keep warm in the cool oven.
14. Cook the baby cabbages in boiling salted water until tender, about 3 minutes. Drain and keep warm in the cool oven.

15. Drain the potato slices and pat dry. Heat the oil in a pan, and deep-fry the potato slices, a few at a time, until brown and crisp. Drain on kitchen paper and season with salt. Keep warm in the cool oven.

To finish and serve
16. Strain the sauce, pass through a fine-mesh sieve or muslin cloth, then boil to reduce by half. Season to taste.
17. Remove the pheasant breast meat from the carcass, following the contours of the breast and rib bones. The joint should come off in one.
18. Place an endive in the centre of each warm plate, not forgetting to remove the cocktail sticks if used. At the top of each plate place a hot baby cabbage. Sprinkle the game chips around.
19. Carve the pheasant breast, across the grain at an angle, four or five times, and lie across the endive. Quickly strain the reduced sauce over, and serve.

CARAMELISED BANANAS AND ICED PISTACHIO PARFAIT

SERVES 8

*D*uring the winter months it is very difficult to buy any decent quality red fruits. Our season for red berries is the summer, subsequently any fruit that you see in the markets at this time will be imported. In my experience a lot of it will look good, but most will have very little taste. Bananas, on the other hand, are always available, and are an excellent fruit to use in a dessert at this time.

8 bananas	*Vanilla cream*
Pistachio parfait	150 g (5 oz) Pastry Cream (see p.249)
90 ml (3 fl oz) Stock Syrup (see p.249)	½ vanilla pod
2 egg yolks	150 ml (5 fl oz) whipping cream
270 ml (9 fl oz) double cream	*To serve*
30 ml (1 fl oz) Crème de Banane (banana liqueur)	24 x 7 cm (2½ in) *Langue de Chat* discs (see p.246)
80 g (2¾ oz) shelled and peeled pistachio nuts	icing sugar
Rum caramel	400 ml (13½ fl oz) Lemon Egg Custard Sauce (see p.250)
450 g (1 lb) caster sugar	8 sprigs fresh mint
110 ml (3½ fl oz) Stock Syrup (see p.249)	
110 ml (3½ fl oz) dark rum	

Making the pistachio parfait

1. Lay out eight 6 x 2 cm (2½ x ¾ in) ring moulds on to a tray lined with greaseproof paper and reserve.

2. Place the stock syrup in a pan, and put on to the stove to boil.

3. Place the egg yolks in a mixing bowl, and whisk the boiling syrup into them. Continue whisking until the egg yolks become a thick and white sabayon. Reserve aside.

4. Add the cream to another bowl and whisk until thick and peaked. Fold in the banana liqueur, then fold in the sabayon. Pour the mixture into the eight ring moulds.

5. Add the peeled pistachio nuts, dropping them into the parfait. Place the parfaits into the freezer and freeze for 4 hours or until needed.

Making the rum caramel

6. Place the caster sugar and 210 ml (7 fl oz) cold water in a saucepan. Mix together with a spoon, then bring to the boil. Boil the syrup until it caramelises to a deep golden brown.

7. Remove from the heat and stir in the stock syrup, then the rum. Reserve aside.

Making the vanilla cream

8. Whisk the pastry cream until smooth. Split the vanilla pod lengthways and scrape the vanilla seeds into the pastry cream. Whisk them together.

9. In another bowl whisk the cream until firm and peaked. Fold the cream into the pastry cream until fully incorporated. Reserve in the refrigerator.

Finishing the dessert

10. Place eight of the *langue de chat* discs on to a tray and dust them liberally with icing sugar.

Heat a metal skewer over a naked flame until it glows red hot. Scorch the sugared biscuits in criss-cross lines with the skewer. These will be the tops of the desserts.

11. Place the rum caramel back on to the stove to warm. Peel the bananas and slice each into ten equal pieces. Place them into the caramel to warm. Do not boil as the bananas will go 'pulpy' and lose their appearance and texture.

To serve

12. Spoon the lemon egg custard sauce into the centre of each of eight large plates, leaving a 4 cm (1½ in) border, and place a 'plain' *langue de chat* biscuit into the centre of each puddle of sauce.

13. Remove the parfaits from the freezer. Rub the ring moulds in the palms of your hands and gently push the parfait out on top of the *langue de chat* biscuit on the plate. Place another 'plain' biscuit disc on top of the parfait.

14. Using a fork, place five slices of warm banana around the outside of the lemon sauce. Repeat for the other plates.

15. Put another five slices of warm banana on top of the *langue de chat* biscuit. Place a spoonful of vanilla cream into the centre of the bananas and top with the sugared, criss-cross *langue de chat* disc.

16. Spoon a little more caramel around the banana slices on the plate and place a sprig of mint into the side of the dessert. Serve immediately.

CHEF'S TIP

When assembling the dessert, I would advise you to complete two at a time only, as the parfait will not stand for long when in contact with the warm bananas and caramel.

The Basics

VEGETABLE STOCK

MAKES ABOUT 750 ML (1¼ PINTS)

This is an essential stock which I use all the time when reheating prepared vegetables, or actually making the emulsions when cooking certain types of root vegetables. It is not necessary to use whole vegetables in the construction of the stock: in fact in my restaurant I just use the trimmings from the day's preparation.

white of 1 medium leek	**60 g (2 oz) unsalted butter**
1 onion	**1 sprig fresh thyme**
1 small carrot	**½ bay leaf**
1 celery stalk	**750 ml (1¼ pints) water**
90 g (3 oz) white mushrooms	**30 g (1 oz) parsley stalks**
4 garlic cloves	**15 g (½ oz) each of chervil and tarragon stalks**
15 g (½ oz) white peppercorns	**1 lemon**
40 ml (1½ fl oz) olive oil	**salt and pepper**

1. Trim off most of the dark green, bitter top leaves from the leek and discard. Cut the leek into 1.5 cm (¾ in) dice. Wash, drain and dry. Peel and cut the onion, carrot and celery into similar dice.

2. Wash and slice the mushrooms. Peel and chop the garlic. Crush the peppercorns.

3. Heat the oil in a thick-bottomed saucepan. When hot, add the butter and immediately stir in the diced vegetables. Cook for 3 or 4 minutes but do not colour.

4. Add the garlic, peppercorns, thyme and bay leaf. Stir the mixture and continue cooking for a further 2 minutes.

5. Cover with the water. Bring the liquid to the boil, removing all surfacing fat with a small ladle. Turn down the heat and gently cook the stock at a simmer for 10 minutes.

6. Add the herb stalks to the stock. Re-boil the liquid and again skim off any surfacing sediments.

7. Add the lemon in slices, and take the pan off the stove. Pour into a clean bowl to cool and when cold refrigerate for 24 hours.

CHEF'S TIP
During this 24-hour resting process, the vegetables and herbs will impart all their flavours to the stock.

8. Strain the liquid into another bowl and discard the vegetables. Season to taste, and keep in the fridge until required. Cold, this stock will keep for a couple of days.

FISH STOCK

This recipe is essential for the make-up of most of the hot fish dishes included in this book. For simplicity's sake I have listed quantities which will produce 2 litres (3½ pints) of finished stock. The best bones for a fish stock are the flat fish ones such as sole, turbot and brill. If these are not available at the fishmonger's, choose white fish bones if possible. Halibut is a good substitute but a little oily for the perfect stock.

2 kg (4¼ lb) fish bones	**1 large sprig fresh thyme**
12 shallots	**a handful of parsley stalks**
3 garlic cloves	**½ teaspoon dried fennel seeds**
60 ml (2 fl oz) olive oil	**240 ml (8 fl oz) Noilly Prat**
60 g (2 oz) butter	**375 ml (12½ fl oz) dry white wine**
1 bay leaf	**1.5 litres (2¾ pints) water**

1. Preheat the oven to 180°C (350°F) Gas 4.
2. Wash the fish bones thoroughly and with a good strong pair of fish scissors trim off any dark fins and remove the gills from any of the fish heads. This is essential because nothing must discolour the stock. Cut the bones into manageable pieces and re-wash them.
3. Peel and slice the shallots. Peel and crush the garlic.
4. In a deep casserole heat the olive oil, throw in the butter and before it colours add the shallots, bay leaf, thyme and parsley stalks. Stir and cook until the shallots are opaque but not coloured.
5. Add the fennel seeds and Noilly Prat and reduce the liquid until it becomes syrupy. Do not allow the shallots to burn or colour.
6. Add the garlic and white wine, and boil to reduce by half.
7. Add the water and bring to the boil. With a ladle, skim off any surfacing fat or scum, then bring to the boil again and add the fish bones. Bring the liquid back up to the boil yet again,

skimming off any surfacing fat or scum. The water should just cover the bones, not drown them.
8. Cover the casserole with greaseproof paper and a lid, then cook in the preheated oven for 12 minutes.

CHEF'S TIP
I cook my fish stock in the oven, not on the stove, so that the heat is even, gentle and all-round, not just from the bottom of the pan.

9. Remove the fish stock from the oven. Take off the lid and paper, and pour, bones and all, into a colander with a large bowl underneath to trap the liquid.
10. Strain again through a fine-mesh conical strainer lined with a muslin cloth into another bowl. This will trap all but the finest sediment and ensure a clear fish stock, essential for your fish cookery.
11. When cold, refrigerate. This can be kept for several days and used as and when required.

COURT BOUILLON OR NAGE FOR SHELLFISH

MAKES 2 LITRES (3½ PINTS)

A good *court bouillon* is essential for the boiling of shellfish such as lobster, crab or langoustines.

1 large onion	2 star anise
1 large carrot	15 g (½ oz) dried fennel seeds
1 celery stalk	15 g (½ oz) white peppercorns
3 fennel bulb leaves	60 ml (2 fl oz) white wine vinegar
1 large leek	120 ml (4 fl oz) dry white wine
1 whole garlic bulb	2 litres (3½ pints) water
60 ml (2 fl oz) olive oil	30 g (1 oz) salt
60 g (2 oz) parsley stalks	1 lemon

1. Peel the onion and cut into large dice of about 2.5 cm (1 in). Wash and peel the carrot and celery, then dice finely. Dice the fennel bulb leaves. Repeat the process for the leek.

2. Cut the garlic bulb in two and reserve aside. It is not necessary to peel the cloves.

3. Heat a large saucepan on the stove over a fierce heat. Add the oil and as it starts to smoke, add the vegetables. Reduce the heat and cook for about 5 minutes, stirring from time to time. Do not colour them.

4. Add the parsley stalks, star anise, dried fennel seeds and peppercorns. Stir.

5. Pour in the white wine vinegar and reduce until a syrup. Add the white wine and boil to reduce its volume by half.

6. At this stage, add the water and garlic. Bring to the boil and with a ladle skim off all the surfacing fat and scum. Cook for a further 5 minutes, again skimming if necessary. Turn down the *court bouillon* to simmer for 10 minutes.

7. Add the salt. Slice the lemon and add to the *court bouillon*. Remove from the stove to cool, and use when required.

CHEF'S TIP
After cooking a crab, lobster or langoustines in the court bouillon, *you can strain the liquid through a fine-mesh conical strainer into a bowl. When cold, refrigerate (or freeze) and it can be used again.*

BASIC FISH MARINADE

MAKES 300 ML (10 FL OZ)

*T*his marinade is used for all fish and shellfish to be grilled. You can vary the herbs and seasoning according to the item you wish to marinate – for no longer than a day.

300 ml (10 fl oz) good virgin olive oil	2 sprigs fresh basil
1 orange	2 shallots
2 sprigs fresh thyme	3 garlic cloves
1 bay leaf	1 teaspoon white peppercorns
a pinch of dried fennel seeds	

1. Pour the olive oil into a deep tray.
2. Take the orange, and with a peeler remove the orange zest. With a knife carefully cut away all the white pith from the underneath of the orange zest.
3. In a small pan of boiling water blanch the orange zest for about 3 minutes. Refresh in cold water and repeat this process twice. This will remove all the bitterness in the zest, leaving just the orange flavour. Dry the zest on kitchen paper and add to the olive oil.
4. Add the thyme, bay leaf, fennel seeds and basil.
5. Peel and slice the shallots. Peel the garlic. Add these to the oil.
6. Crush the peppercorns and add to the marinade, which is now ready for use.

CHICKEN STOCK

MAKES 3 LITRES (5¼ PINTS)

*T*ogether with veal stock, this is an essential base for sauces in most meat cookery. Do take care to achieve a good end product: if your base stock is not good, your finished sauce won't be either.

2 kg (4¼ lb) raw chicken bones	**20 black peppercorns**
1 onion	**8 garlic cloves**
½ carrot	**1 sprig fresh thyme**
1 leek	**1 bay leaf**
1 celery stalk	**a handful of parsley stalks**

1. Wash the bones and place in a large tall saucepan. Cover with water, about 4 litres (7 pints), bring to the boil and carefully skim off all fat and scum.
2. Meanwhile, peel and roughly cut up the onion, carrot, leek and celery. Crush the peppercorns. Peel the garlic.
3. Add the vegetables to the bones, along with the peppercorns, thyme, bay leaf, washed parsley stalks and garlic.
4. Bring back to the boil, skim and set to simmer for 3–4 hours, still skimming off the fat as it surfaces to ensure a good, clear stock.
5. When cooked, strain through a fine sieve and allow to cool before refrigerating. It can be kept like this for a couple of days. It can also be frozen, of course.

WHITE VEAL STOCK

MAKES ABOUT 4 LITRES (7 PINTS)

This is a stock I keep readily available. It takes a while to cook but is used in various meat sauce preparations where a cream sauce or juice without any colour is required.

Ask your butcher to chop up the bones, which should include some knuckle joints because these have a high gelatine content.

2 kg (4¼ lb) veal bones	½ celery stalk
2 raw chicken carcasses	1 garlic clove
1 pig's trotter	20 white peppercorns
2 onions	60 g (2 oz) parsley stalks
1 carrot	1 sprig fresh thyme
1 leek	1 bay leaf

1. Peel and halve the onions, carrot, leek, celery and garlic. Crush the peppercorns.
2. Place all the bones and the pig's trotter in a large pan, cover with water and bring to the boil. The water will throw up a lot of impurities, which should be skimmed off as the water begins to boil.
3. Tip the bones into a colander, strain off and discard the liquid.
4. Place the blanched bones into a clean pan, and once again cover with cold water. You want to have at least 4.25 litres (7½ pints). Bring to the boil and skim off any surfacing fat and impurities.
5. Add all the remaining ingredients, skim once again, and set to simmer for 5 hours.
6. Once cooked, carefully strain through a fine-mesh sieve and allow to cool.
7. Once cold, any remaining fat will have set, and can be scraped off the top. This stock can be frozen in suitable sized quantities, or saved in a good refrigerator for up to a week.

MEAT GLAZE (GLACE DE VIANDE)

MAKES APPROX. 900 ML (1½ PINTS)

This concentrated veal stock is expensive and takes a long time to make but is well worth it as it lends a brilliant sheen to finished sauces, as well as enhancing the flavour. You'll need a proper tall stock pot, the smallest of which holds 10.75 litres (19 pints).

2.5 kg (5½ lb) veal bones, sawn or chopped	1 quantity *Mirepoix* (see p.239)
500 g (18 oz) chicken bones	1 sprig fresh thyme
350 g (12 oz) shin of beef	1 bay leaf
350 g (12 oz) shin of veal	½ whole garlic bulb
75 ml (2½ fl oz) cooking oil	45 g (1½ oz) tomato paste
10 black peppercorns	60 g (2 oz) parsley stalks
3 tomatoes	30 g (1 oz) tarragon stalks
120 g (4 oz) open cap mushrooms	60 ml (2 fl oz) dry Madeira

1. Preheat the oven to 220°C (425°F) Gas 7.
2. Heat some of the cooking oil in a large roasting tray. Carefully put in the veal bones and brown evenly on top of the stove.

3. In a smaller pan repeat with the chicken bones.

4. Place the veal bones in the preheated oven and continue to roast until the bones are brown all over, about 30 minutes. *Do not burn.* Turn them occasionally.

5. Crush the peppercorns. Squash the tomatoes to get rid of the pips. Wash and coarsely slice the mushrooms.

6. In your tall stock pot (big enough to take all the bones, vegetables and water) heat a little more oil and add the *mirepoix*. Brown evenly.

7. Add the peppercorns, thyme, bay leaf, garlic and tomato paste. Be careful at this stage because the paste can catch and burn, so reduce the heat and stir often.

8. When the bones are ready, remove from the oven and place them on top of the vegetables. Cover with cold water – you'll need at least 9 litres (15 pints) – and bring to the boil. Skim very well, then reduce the heat to a simmer.

9. Add the tomatoes and parsley and tarragon stalks.

10. Brown the shins of beef and veal well in a little oil and lower gently into the simmering stock. It is advisable to tie string around the meat, and lower it into the stock, keeping hold of the string which you tie on to the handle. It is then easier to remove the meats after their 3 or 4 hours' cooking before they start to disintegrate.

11. Simmer the stock for 7–8 hours, skimming off the surfacing fat frequently. When cooked, carefully strain through a coarse strainer.

12. Place back on the stove and bring back to the boil. The stock will throw up a lot of scum and fat which should be skimmed off thoroughly.

13. Add the mushrooms to the stock, and skim. Reduce the stock by ten times its volume, i.e. from that initial 9 litres (15 pints) of stock you should end up with 900 ml (1½ pints) of meat glaze. The stock should change colour to a glossy dark brown and the bubbles surfacing should no longer be fine but larger, and the stock should look thicker.

14. Add the Madeira, boil and skim.

15. Strain through a fine strainer and allow to cool. The stock is now ready. Once cold it will keep in the fridge for up to one week or it can be frozen in handy blocks.

OXTAIL STOCK

MAKES 1.5 LITRES (2¾ PINTS)

*T*his can be made as a soup base – for Mulligatawny Soup (see p.215), or as a stock for a main-course oxtail dish (see p.41). Save the meat from the stock-making to use in the soup. Clarified, this makes an excellent consommé for the cold winter months. It sets hard because of all the gelatine, so can store in the fridge for up to a week, or in the freezer.

1 oxtail or 2 kg (4¼ lb) oxtail	**10 black peppercorns**
1 onion	**salt and pepper**
1 leek	**about 60 ml (2 fl oz) vegetable oil**
1 celery stalk	**1 sprig fresh thyme**
½ carrot	**1 bay leaf**
4 garlic cloves	**2 litres (3½ pints) Chicken Stock (see p.225)**

CHEF'S TIP
In the restaurant we buy six oxtails to make this stock. We cut the thin ends of the tails off and use them for the *stock; the thick ends are saved for other dishes, like the braised oxtail on p.41.*

1. Place the oxtail on a chopping board and cut straight through the joints. Soak in cold water for 24 hours to remove the blood.
2. Peel and chop the onion; chop the leek, celery and carrot; peel and halve the garlic. Crush the peppercorns.
3. Drain the oxtail pieces well, dry on kitchen paper, and season with salt and pepper.
4. In a saucepan heat the oil and brown the pieces of oxtail on all sides. When nicely caramelised, lift them out with a slotted spoon into a large casserole pan.
5. In the same saucepan, brown the chopped vegetables until golden, and add to the oxtail. Add the thyme, bay leaf, garlic and peppercorns.
6. Cover with the chicken stock and bring to the boil. Skim off all the surfacing fat and scum. Simmer very gently for 4–5 hours, or until the meat falls away from the bone.
7. Strain off the pieces of oxtail and sieve the stock. It is now ready for use.

WHITE SAUCE (BÉCHAMEL)

MAKES ABOUT 300 ML (10 FL OZ)

In classic cookery this is one of the fundamental base sauces that you need to know how to make when learning how to cook. It is used less often today than it used to be, but still makes an excellent base when a fairly neutral sauce is wanted. It is also a lot cheaper than cream.
This sauce is essential to the home cook for dishes such as onion tarts or cauliflower cheese, and in vegetarian cookery where milk is not a problem.

450 ml (15 fl oz) milk	1 sprig fresh thyme
1 small onion	grated nutmeg
1 clove	60 g (2 oz) unsalted butter
¼ bay leaf	60 g (2 oz) plain flour, sieved

1. Peel the onion, and stud it with the clove.
2. Pour the milk into a saucepan and add the onion, bay leaf, thyme and grated nutmeg. Bring to the boil, then turn down the flame and simmer.
3. In another pan melt the butter over a moderate heat and when melted stir in the flour. When thoroughly mixed and just as it begins to take colour, gradually add the milk, straining it through a fine-mesh conical strainer to trap the flavourings.
4. Cook the sauce for approximately 30 minutes over a low flame. Pass the finished sauce through a conical strainer into a bowl. To stop the sauce from forming a skin, place one or two small pieces of extra butter on top of it while still hot.

LAMB SAUCE BASE

MAKES 750 ML (1¼ PINTS)

*W*ithin the recipes below there is scope to make a number of different tastes and sauces by substituting various herbs or base ingredients, to produce a good variety of ideas.

1.5 kg (3¼ lb) raw lamb bones
2 onions
½ carrot
1 leek
1 celery stalk

10 garlic cloves
90 ml (3 fl oz) cooking oil
2 litres (3½ pints) Chicken Stock (see p.225)
1 sprig fresh thyme
1 bay leaf
1 lemon

1. Peel and coarsely chop the onions, carrot, leek and celery. Peel and chop the garlic.
2. Chop the lamb bones into small pieces and roast in hot oil in a heavy pan on top of the stove until brown all over.
3. Remove with a slotted spoon to a large saucepan, and cover with the chicken stock.
4. Roast the vegetables in the same oil until brown, about 5 minutes, then lift out with a slotted spoon and add to the bones.
5. Bring to the boil, skim, then add the thyme, bay leaf and chopped garlic. Simmer for 1 hour.
6. At this stage you may add various ingredients to flavour your sauce – see Chef's Tips.

CHEF'S TIPS

If a **thyme sauce** *is required, increase the thyme to 2 sprigs, and add after bruising the leaves with the flat of a knife. If a* **rosemary sauce** *is required, add the original amount of thyme but include as well a large sprig of chopped or bruised fresh rosemary, reserving a little aside to add to the finished reducing stock to perfume it more. If a* **tomato sauce** *is required, then in a separate pan cook to a pulp 6 soft tomatoes and 60 g (2 oz) double concentrated tomato paste, and add to the simmering stock. This addition not only gives a delightful flavour but also a subtle pink colour. The addition of about 90 ml (3 fl oz) port to the pan creates a super stock with a lovely deep colour (recommended with lamb sweetbreads!).*

7. After the hour's simmering, strain the sauce through a fine sieve and boil to reduce by half. (It is best to strain the tomato version through a muslin first, before reducing, as it is difficult to remove the tomato pulp *after* the sauce is reduced.)
8. During this reduction, more of the various flavours can be added, i.e. a sprig of thyme, some chopped rosemary or, especially, some chopped garlic. A little lemon juice helps to bring out the flavours and cut the sweetness from some lamb sauces.

RED WINE SAUCE FOR FISH

MAKES 1 LITRE (1¾ PINTS)

I have included this sauce because it makes an ideal accompaniment for grilled or roasted fish such as sea bass, sole, etc. It may be kept in the fridge for up to a week to use as and when required.

The best bones for this, as for the fish stock, are flat fish bones such as turbot and sole, but red mullet and bream bones can give an extra depth of flavour. Ask your fishmonger to save the bones from his filleting during the course of a day. (You can freeze them until you have enough to use.)

2 kg (4¼ lb) fish bones and trimmings (see above)	a handful of parsley stalks
1 large fennel bulb	2 star anise
3 garlic cloves	180 ml (6 fl oz) Noilly Prat
12 shallots	1 bottle red wine (choose an inexpensive bottle but not a poor-quality one, which would ruin the sauce)
225 g (7½ oz) button mushrooms	
500 g (18 oz) ripe tomatoes	
60 ml (2 fl oz) olive oil	1.5 litres (2¾ pints) water
60 g (2 oz) butter	1 sprig fresh basil
1 bay leaf	salt and pepper
1 large sprig fresh thyme	30 ml (1 fl oz) Meat Glaze (optional, see p.226)

1. Preheat the oven to 180°C (350°F) Gas 4.
2. Trim all the fish bones and remove and discard all the fins. On a chopping board cut up the bones into manageable pieces and wash them thoroughly under running cold water. Drain in a colander.
3. Wash the fennel. Cut off the top and remove the first two layers. Keep the heart of the fennel, as this is the best part for use in salads or a hot fennel dish. Chop or slice the top and outer leaves for use in the sauce.
4. Peel and crush the garlic. Peel and slice the shallots. Wash and slice the mushrooms. Halve the tomatoes and squeeze out the pulp and seeds.
5. In a deep ovenproof pan heat the olive oil, then add the butter. Before it colours, stir in the shallots, bay leaf, parsley stalks, star anise and chopped fennel trimmings. Cook for 3–4 minutes without colouring the shallots.
6. Add the Noilly Prat, and boil to reduce the liquid until it becomes syrupy.
7. Add the garlic and red wine. Boil to reduce the wine by half its volume.

8. Add the fish bones to the reduced wine, and cover with the water. Bring to the boil, and with a ladle skim off all the surfacing fats and impurities.
9. Add the mushrooms and the sprig of basil. Cover with greaseproof paper and a lid, and cook in the preheated oven for approximately 20 minutes.
10. When cooked, remove the stock from the oven. Take off the lid and paper, and pour the bones and liquid into a colander with a bowl underneath to trap all the draining liquid.
11. Strain this liquid through a fine-mesh conical strainer into another saucepan. Return the stock to the stove and bring it to the boil – again remove all sediments and fats which come to the surface. Turn down the flame and simmer for about half an hour or until the stock has reduced by half its volume.
12. As it is reduced the stock will thicken. Check seasoning and finally add the meat glaze if using, which will enrich the finished sauce.
13. Strain the sauce again slowly through a muslin cloth in a conical strainer over a bowl. Leave to cool and when cold refrigerate.

CHEF'S TIP
It is important to get rid of the seeds and pulp of the tomatoes as they are too acidic and if added they would cloud the finished sauce.

BUTTER SAUCE FOR FISH

MAKES ABOUT 300 ML (10 FL OZ)

*D*ill, parsley or chervil may be used instead of the chives.

240 g (8 oz) unsalted butter

2 shallots

1 sprig fresh tarragon

1 garlic clove

1 teaspoon white peppercorns

1 sprig fresh thyme

¼ bay leaf

30 ml (1 fl oz) white wine vinegar

30 ml (1 fl oz) white wine

30 ml (1 fl oz) double cream

salt

lemon juice to taste

2 tablespoons chopped chives

1. Peel and chop the shallots. Blanch the tarragon. Peel and crush the garlic. Crush the peppercorns.

2. In a pan melt 30 g (1 oz) of the butter. Add the shallots, thyme, tarragon, bay leaf, garlic and peppercorns. Cook gently for about 3 minutes without colouring.

3. Pour in the white wine vinegar and reduce the liquid to a syrup. Repeat the process for the white wine.

4. Turn up the flame and add the cream. Boil, stirring all the time with a whisk.

5. Chop up the remaining butter into small pieces and, turning down the flame, gradually add, whisking and stirring all the time.

6. Season the sauce with salt and add lemon juice until the required acidity is achieved.

7. Pass the sauce through a fine-mesh conical strainer and keep warm above the stove until required.

8. Just before use, the chives can be added, but not before or they will lose their colour and go brown.

CHIVE CREAM SAUCE

MAKES 600 ML (1 PINT)

I have used this sauce as an accompaniment to the terrine of artichokes on p.67, but it can also be served with smoked fish dishes, especially salmon. It's a green, fresh-tasting sauce.

½ cucumber, about 120g (4 oz), peeled and cut in half lengthways

30 g (1 oz) table salt

270 ml (9 fl oz) whipping cream

90 g (3 oz) horseradish relish, or 60 g (2 oz) fresh grated horseradish

60 g (2 oz) Dijon mustard

150 g (5 oz) natural yoghurt

60 g (2 oz) chives, washed and chopped

juice of 1 lemon

salt and cayenne pepper

1. With a spoon, remove all the seeds from the cucumber and discard them. Sprinkle the flesh with the salt and leave for 10 minutes to marinate. The salt will draw all the impurities and most of the water out of the cucumber.

2. Wash the cucumber under cold water to remove all the salt, then dry thoroughly.

3. Place the cream, horseradish, Dijon mustard, yoghurt and cucumber into a liquidiser bowl. Liquidise for 2 minutes.

4. Add the chives and lemon juice and season to taste with salt and cayenne. Liquidise for a further 30 seconds.

5. Strain the finished sauce through a clean conical strainer into a clean container, and refrigerate for up to three days.

TOMATO SAUCE

MAKES ABOUT 100 ML (1 PINT)

*T*his versatile tomato sauce or coulis can be used to accompany a hot or cold fish dish. It can be used in the construction of certain meat dishes, and served hot or cold as a sauce for a vegetarian plate.

If you liquidise together some cooked tomato sauce, the same quantity of blanched raw tomato pulp and a little stock syrup and the necessary seasonings, you can make an excellent tomato sorbet which is a great dish in the summer months.

1 kg (2¼ lb) ripe plum tomatoes	60 g (2 oz) tomato purée (concentrate)
1 carrot	90 ml (3 fl oz) white wine vinegar
2 celery stalks	30 g (1 oz) caster sugar
1 large onion	120 ml (4 fl oz) white wine
2 garlic cloves	1 sprig fresh basil
10 g (⅓ oz) white peppercorns	a handful of parsley stalks
90 ml (3 fl oz) olive oil	300 ml (10 fl oz) Chicken Stock (see p.225)
1 sprig fresh thyme	a bacon bone (smoked)
1 bay leaf	salt

1. Peel and dice the carrot and celery. Peel and slice the onion. Peel and crush the garlic. Crush the peppercorns. Dry the diced vegetables and onion well.

2. In a deep saucepan, preferably with a thick bottom, heat the olive oil until you see a slight film rising from the pan.

3. Throw in the vegetables and fry them to a light golden colour, but do not burn.

4. Add the crushed peppercorns, thyme and bay leaf.

5. Add the tomato purée and cook, stirring continually with a spoon, for 3–4 minutes. Again, do not allow the tomato purée to burn or discolour.

6. In a separate shallow saucepan, bring the vinegar to the boil and add the sugar. Reduce this liquid down until most of the vinegar has evaporated and a light golden syrup is obtained. Remove from the stove and reserve aside. This is called the 'gastric' and when added will help to bring up the flavours of the sauce.

7. Deglaze the vegetables by adding the white wine and cook for a further 5 minutes, reducing the wine volume by half.

8. Add the garlic, basil, parsley stalks and chicken stock. Using a spatula, add the 'gastric'.

9. Cut the fresh ripe tomatoes in half, and squeeze out and discard the seeds and pulp. These are acidic and not required for the sauce. Dice the tomato flesh and add this to the pan.

10. Bring the liquid to the boil and with a ladle remove all the surfacing scum and fat.

11. Add the bacon bone and turn down the heat. Gently simmer the sauce for approximately 1 hour, from time to time stirring and removing all surfacing sediment and fat.

CHEF'S TIP

If possible, ask your butcher for a large bacon bone, preferably smoked, or if you buy your bacon on the bone, cut out the bone and add this to the sauce. It really makes a difference to the finished taste of the sauce.

12. When ready, remove the bone and discard it. Pour the sauce into a large, strong conical strainer and with the aid of a ladle crush and squeeze all the liquid into a bowl.

13. Return this liquid to the stove in another pan. Boil and again remove the surfacing fats and scum. Check the seasoning and reduce the sauce to your required consistency and flavour.

14. Again strain the sauce, this time through a fine-mesh conical strainer to trap all but the smallest of the sediment. The sauce is now ready.

WALNUT VINAIGRETTE

MAKES 360 ML (12 FL OZ)

This dressing is particularly good with a salad of *mâche* (corn salad), red trevisse (or radicchio), escarole, lollo rosso and nasturtium leaves. Peeled walnuts are a delicious addition.

70 ml (2½ fl oz) sherry vinegar
1 teaspoon lemon juice
salt and white pepper

150 ml (5 fl oz) groundnut oil
150 ml (5 fl oz) walnut oil

1. Place the sherry vinegar, lemon juice, salt and white pepper into a bowl.
2. Mix the oils together and with a whisk stir them into the vinegar.

3. Bottle the vinaigrette, using a small funnel. I store my vinaigrette in bottles with airtight tops. This way they will keep for days. Shake the bottle vigorously before use.

HAZELNUT VINAIGRETTE

Make in exactly the same way, substituting hazelnut oil for the walnut oil.

GROUNDNUT VINAIGRETTE

Make this in exactly the same way, but using 210 ml (7 fl oz) groundnut oil to 90 ml (3 fl oz) walnut or hazelnut oil.

TARRAGON VINAIGRETTE

MAKES ABOUT 630 ML (21 FL OZ)

This dressing is good on salads made with yellow frisée, chicory, Little Gem and iceberg lettuces, rocket and all the mild flat lettuces. A suggested addition would be chopped shallots and chives.

2 garlic cloves
juice of ½ lemon
120 ml (4 fl oz) white wine vinegar

salt and white pepper
500 ml (17 fl oz) best virgin olive oil
30 g (1 oz) fresh tarragon sprigs

1. Peel the garlic.
2. Put the lemon juice, vinegar, salt and pepper into a bowl.
3. Whisk in the oil.

4. Using a small funnel, bottle the vinaigrette, and add the garlic and tarragon sprigs. These will impart their flavour through the vinaigrette if kept for a week or so.

MAYONNAISE

MAKES 300 ML (10 FL OZ)

This recipe is useful in a variety of ways. Home-made mayonnaise is 100 per cent more delicious than bought.

2 egg yolks
30 g (1 oz) French or Dijon mustard
60 ml (2 fl oz) malt vinegar
30 g (1 oz) caster sugar

150 ml (5 fl oz) olive oil
150 ml (5 fl oz) vegetable oil
salt and white pepper
lemon juice to taste

1. Place the egg yolks in a stainless-steel mixing bowl. Add the mustard, and whisk together.
2. Pour the vinegar into a small pan, add the sugar and over a fierce flame melt the sugar. Reduce the liquid until the sugar caramelises and becomes syrupy. Remove from the stove to cool. This is the 'gastric', or flavouring element.
3. Mix the two oils together and *very slowly* pour into the egg yolks, whisking vigorously and continuously. Make sure the oils are not too cold or the sauce will split.
4. When half of the oil is thoroughly mixed into the yolks, and the mayonnaise has started to thicken, add the 'gastric'.
5. Continue slowly pouring in the oil, mixing continuously until a smooth paste is obtained. If the mayonnaise is too thick add a little warm water to dilute it.
6. Season with salt and pepper and squeeze in a little lemon juice for acidity.
7. Store in the refrigerator until needed, covered with cling film, for up to a week.

RÉMOULADE SAUCE

This sauce goes well with a variety of dishes. To a quantity of mayonnaise, add 1 teaspoon each of chopped capers and gherkins, 2 anchovy fillets squashed to a paste, and 1 teaspoon each of chopped parsley and chervil.

SHALLOT OR ONION PURÉE

MAKES ABOUT 300 ML (10 FL OZ)

This has many uses, mostly as a base to accompany meat or fish. However, with the addition of some stock or cream, it can be used as a sauce or as a thickening agent to flavour a sauce.

One of my favourite dishes, not given in this book, is a veal kidney roasted in its fat, served with a shallot purée and a rich red wine sauce. Shallots make the better purée, because they have a better flavour.

180 g (6 oz) shallots or baby onions
150 ml (5 fl oz) clear Chicken Stock (see p.225)
10 g (⅓ oz) caster sugar
¼ bay leaf
1 sprig fresh thyme
120 g (4 oz) unsalted butter
salt and pepper
120 ml (4 fl oz) whipping cream

1. Preheat the oven to 180°C (350°F) Gas 4.
2. Peel and wash the shallots, and place in a shallow pan.
3. Cover with the chicken stock, and sprinkle with the sugar. Add the bay leaf, thyme, half the butter, and salt and pepper to taste.
4. Bring to the boil, cover with a butter paper and cook in the preheated oven for approximately 15 minutes or until all the liquid has evaporated and the shallots are tender and soft.

5. Pour the shallots into a liquidiser and blend to a smooth paste or purée. Check the seasoning.
6. Pour the purée into another pan. Add the cream and remaining butter and gently cook on top of the stove for a few minutes, stirring the mixture so that it does not catch on the bottom of the pan.
7. Cool and store in the fridge until required, no longer than a day. *Never* freeze.

GAZPACHO

MAKES 450 ML (15 FL OZ)

*T*his base appears in one form or another in the make-up of several of my dishes. It's particularly useful as a base for the scallops on p.13. I like to make this more interesting by adding just a little shellfish consommé (see p.55). This not only helps to thin the gazpacho, but also introduces another taste, which I think improves the dish.

You can also use gazpacho, on its own, as a cold soup.

1 cucumber	3 sprigs fresh parsley
30 g (1 oz) table salt	60 ml (2 fl oz) white wine vinegar
2 large red peppers	15 g (½ oz) caster sugar
1 fresh chilli	120 ml (4 fl oz) Tomato Sauce (see p.232)
1 celery stalk	lemon juice to taste
6 ripe plum tomatoes	a splash of Worcestershire sauce
1 garlic clove	salt and white pepper
3 shallots	30 ml (1 fl oz) virgin olive oil

CHEF'S TIP

'Purging' the cucumber is essential as it removes all its impurities, leaving it firmer in texture and generally tastier. Do not leave the cucumber in the salt for more than 10 minutes because beyond this point, instead of extracting the impurities from the cucumber, the reverse will occur and it will begin to absorb *all the salt.*

1. Peel the cucumber, slice it down the middle and with a small spoon remove and discard the seeds. Cut each half in two and sprinkle with the table salt. Leave for approximately 10 minutes while you prepare the other vegetables.

2. Peel the peppers with a potato peeler. Slice each pepper into quarters. Remove and discard the seeds and core. Scald the peppers for 2 minutes in a pan of boiling salted water. Drain off the water and refresh them under running cold water until completely cold. Drain them again and dry on a clean kitchen towel.

3. Halve the chilli and remove the seeds. In another pan of boiling salted water cook until tender, then cool down, drain and dry as for the peppers.

4. Remove the strings from the celery and blanch as for the peppers.

5. Blanch and skin the tomatoes. Cut them into quarters and remove the seeds. We use only the flesh.

6. Peel the garlic and shallots, and finely chop the latter. Wash the parsley, then remove the leaves and chop finely.

7. Put the vinegar and sugar in a small pan, and over a fierce flame boil and reduce until it thickens and turns a light golden colour (the thickness and colour of golden treacle). Remove the pan from the stove and set aside to cool. This is the 'gastric' and is added to the gazpacho to bring out the flavours of all the ingredients.

To finish

8. Wash all the salt off the cucumber under cold running water and dry.

9. Put all the vegetables, apart from the shallots and parsley, in a liquidiser bowl. Add the tomato sauce and blend for 2–3 minutes to a smooth soup.

10. When completely smooth, stop the machine and add the 'gastric'. Liquidise for a further 30 seconds.

11. Add the lemon juice, Worcestershire sauce, salt and pepper to taste, and the virgin olive oil, and liquidise again for 10 seconds to fully mix in the seasonings.

12. Pour the gazpacho out of the liquidiser into a clean container and finally add the shallots and parsley. Stir. It is now ready to serve or use.

CHOUCROÛTE

MAKES ABOUT 450 ML (15 FL OZ)

This is not a traditional *choucroûte*: it is freshly green and crisp, and can be used as an accompaniment for either meat or fish dishes. With the addition of various Continental sausages, it could be a main course by itself.

60 g (2 oz) parsley (flat or wild is the best)
120 g (4 oz) smoked bacon in the piece
1 small Savoy cabbage, about 450 g (1 lb) in weight
salt and pepper
4 shallots

1 garlic clove
1 teaspoon white wine vinegar
120 ml (4 fl oz) white wine (preferably a Gewürztraminer, Riesling or Sylvaner)
60 g (2 oz) unsalted butter

1. Wash the parsley, pick off the leaves and wash again. Dry it on a clean kitchen cloth and chop finely.

2. Remove the rind from the bacon. Cut into four equal rashers approximately 5 mm (¼ in) thick. Lay these flat on the chopping board and, cutting against the grain of the meat, slice them into strips (lardons). Blanch as described in Chef's Tip on p.196.

3. Peel off the outer leaves of the cabbage (they are usually dark green, marked and too bitter), and discard them. With a knife, cut the cabbage into four. Turn each quarter on its side and cut away all the middle stalk and white core. Separate the remaining leaves and wash them thoroughly in a sink of cold water. Remove and drain in a colander.

4. Half fill a saucepan of salted water and bring to the boil. Add the cabbage, put a lid on the pan and when the water has re-boiled, remove the lid. It is important not to leave the lid on any longer than necessary or the cabbage will lose its colour. Cook it for only about 3 minutes. (It must retain its texture as it is going to be cooked again.) Strain off the water, pouring the cabbage into a colander, and refresh it immediately in cold water. Strain again and turn it out on a kitchen cloth. Gently dry it.

5. Peel and chop the shallots and garlic.

6. Put the chopped shallots, garlic and vinegar into a shallow pan. Take the pan to the stove and, over a fierce flame, reduce the vinegar until a syrup. Add the white wine and reduce the liquid by two-thirds of its volume. Do not colour.

7. Transfer to a larger pan. Add the butter and, when melted and fully blended with the shallots, add the lardons and fry the mixture until syrupy.

8. With a sharp knife, cut the cabbage into fine shreds about 5 mm (¼ in) thick and add to the mixture. Stir the '*choucroûte*' thoroughly over a fierce heat for about 2 minutes and finally sprinkle with the chopped parsley. Serve immediately.

ARTICHOKE HEARTS

FOR 20 ARTICHOKE HEARTS

*Y*ou can serve artichokes whole, of course, but the hearts are useful in a number of dishes, most notably the terrine on p.67.

20 large artichokes	1 onion
1 lemon	1 whole head garlic
Cooking liquor	1 sprig fresh thyme
270 ml (9 fl oz) lemon juice (or the juice from 8 lemons)	1 bay leaf
	30 g (1 oz) salt
60 g (2 oz) plain flour	1 teaspoon white peppercorns, crushed
3 litres (5¼ pints) water	110 ml (3½ fl oz) olive oil

Preparing the artichoke 'blanc'

First prepare the artichoke cooking liquor, in French called the '*blanc*'. The main thing to remember when preparing artichokes is that, to preserve their colour, a good blanc is essential.

1. Pour the squeezed lemon juice into a large saucepan and add the flour. With the aid of a whisk, mix together to form a smooth paste. Gradually pour in the water, whisking all the time to ensure that there are no lumps.

2. Peel the onion, and cut the head of garlic into two. (It is not necessary to peel the garlic.) Add these to the liquid.

3. Add the thyme, bay leaf, salt and crushed peppercorns, whisk, and finally add the oil.

4. Take the saucepan to the stove and over a fierce flame bring the *blanc* to the boil. Stir the mixture from time to time to ensure that the flour does not catch or burn on the bottom of the saucepan. This is very important: if it starts to burn, transfer it immediately to another pan. A burnt *blanc* is useless! Turn down the flame and it is now ready for your prepared artichokes.

Preparing the artichokes

5. Turn one artichoke on its side and with the aid of a sharp, serrated knife cut off the stalk at its base. Cut the lemon into two and quickly rub the base with a ½ lemon to stop discoloration.

6. Half-way down the artichoke, saw through the leaves horizontally with the serrated knife again. Rub the cut leaf tops with lemon.

7. Peel off and discard any outside leaves which can be pulled off. Put the artichoke, leafy side down, into the *blanc*. (Any remaining leaves and the heart can be removed after cooking.)

8. Repeat this process for the rest of the artichokes, then cover them with greaseproof paper, and cook gently in the *blanc* for about 20 minutes, or until tender. The cooking time really depends on the size and age of the artichokes. Test by gently pricking the artichoke bases with a fork.

9. Take the saucepan from the stove and reserve aside, allowing the artichokes to cool down in the *blanc*.

10. When cold, remove the artichokes and strain the *blanc* into a stainless-steel bowl. Trim off the remaining leaves (keep any edible tender bits, these can be used). With the aid of a spoon carefully pull off the fine hair-like inner choke and discard. Be careful not to break the artichoke hearts. Return the artichokes to the strained *blanc* and leave overnight to whiten or blanch.

MIREPOIX

Mirepoix – the French word for a mixture of chopped root vegetables – is used a great deal in sauce cookery. It enhances an already flavoursome stock and gives more depth to sauces. This should be enough to flavour 3 litres (5¼ pints) stock.

1 large leek
2 medium onions

1 small carrot
½ celery stalk

1. Remove the dark bitter leaves from the leek. Split the leek down the middle and wash under running water. Cut it straight across into 2 cm (½ in) strips.
2. Peel and cut the onions into eighths. Peel and cut the carrot straight across into 2 cm (¾ in) slices.
3. Cut the celery into 2 cm (¾ in) pieces.
4. Mix all well together and use as required.

CHICKEN MOUSSE

MAKES 600 G (1¼ LB)

This recipe is used in at least two or three dishes in the book, and again its versatility is virtually limitless.

With the addition of more cream, and scented with truffles or spiked with wild mushrooms, then piped into a sausage skin and poached, this mixture can be used for an excellent chicken sausage.

300 g (10 oz) chicken flesh, skin and fat removed
1 sprig fresh tarragon
2 garlic cloves

salt and pepper
40 ml (1½ fl oz) white wine vinegar
90 ml (3 fl oz) Chicken Stock (see p.225)
300 ml (10 fl oz) whipping cream

1. Blanch the tarragon. Peel and finely slice the garlic.
2. Roughly chop the chicken and place it in a food processor. Process until the flesh is a smooth paste. *Do not allow the chicken to get too warm.*
3. Stop the machine, add salt and pepper to taste and 3 tarragon leaves and process again. The mixture should turn into a firm ball. Place in the refrigerator for 15 minutes.
4. Boil the vinegar in a small pan with the remaining tarragon and the garlic. Reduce until the vinegar has almost evaporated.
5. Add the chicken stock, bring to the boil and reduce until the stock becomes sticky.
6. Add a dash of the cream, mix and strain.

Allow to cool. Keep the remaining cream cool.
7. Return the chicken to the machine and slowly add half the remaining cream. Stop and, with a knife or spatula, scrape down the sides of the bowl, especially the corners where the blade does not quite reach.
8. Add the remainder of the cream and the cooled sticky stock more quickly to the machine while still turning. Mix well.
9. Pass through a fine-mesh sieve to trap all the sinews, etc. It is always best to test it for seasoning and texture: take a small spoonful and drop it in very hot but not boiling water. If the mixture is too firm, it may need more cream to lighten it.

PARSLIED BREADCRUMBS

MAKES 180–240 G (6–8 OZ)

*T*hese can be used in a number of ways to enhance a dish, be it lamb, chicken, snails or mushrooms. They not only give the dish a different texture but also add to flavour and appearance. Stale white bread makes the nicest breadcrumbs but brown may also be used. The crumbs may be moistened in several ways but in this recipe we use either bone marrow or olive oil.

They are best sprinkled on foods after they are cooked, and quickly grilled to crisp them up and turn them golden brown.

90 g (3 oz) fresh white breadcrumbs
90 g (3 oz) parsley
1 sprig fresh thyme
½ bay leaf
3 garlic cloves

olive oil to moisten (approx. 60 ml/2 fl oz), or 2 pieces bone marrow, 30 g (1 oz) total weight
salt and pepper

1. Wash, dry and finely chop the parsley. Wash the thyme and pick off the leaves. Crush the bay leaf, and peel and crush the garlic.
2. Place the breadcrumbs in a food processor or large mixing bowl, and add the parsley, thyme, bay leaf and garlic. Mix in the machine, or vigorously by hand, until all the ingredients are well combined.
3. Slowly add the oil, mixing all the time, while moistening the crumbs but not bringing them together in a ball. The finished crumbs should be loose, moist and bright green. If they are still white or pale green, then more parsley should be added. Finally, season with salt and pepper to taste. The garlic should be quite prominent.
4. If using the marrow, then feed it through the machine apparatus, to moisten the crumbs. Season and use as above.
5. The crumbs can be kept for a couple of days in the refrigerator, but are best used on the same day.

GREEN (HERB) PASTA

MAKES 500 G (18 OZ)

I have included white or green pasta as a garnish for several dishes in the book. I find it a great alternative to potatoes: its excellent texture and fairly neutral taste is an ideal accompaniment for fish and white meats such as veal and chicken. There are various thicknesses and shapes you can achieve when preparing pasta, but all of them follow a fairly rigid basic recipe.

Tightly wrapped in cling film, so that it is airtight, the pasta will store in the fridge for 3 days.

90 g (3 oz) parsley leaves, washed
45 g (1½ oz) each of basil, chervil and tarragon leaves, washed
salt

Pasta base
4 whole eggs
5 egg yolks
½ teaspoon salt
1 teaspoon good olive oil
500 g (18 oz) plain flour, sieved

1. Half fill a large saucepan with water and season with salt to taste. Bring to the boil.
2. Throw in first the parsley and boil for approximately 3 minutes. Add the tarragon and 30 seconds later the basil and chervil. Cook for a further minute. Strain into a fine strainer and refresh under cold running water.
3. Turn the herbs out on to a clean kitchen cloth and over the sink squeeze out all the excess water. This is important: too much water in the herbs and the pasta is ruined.
4. In a liquidiser cut the herbs to a smooth paste.
5. To the herbs still in the liquidiser, add the eggs and egg yolks. Add the ½ teaspoon salt and the olive oil and again cut the mixture to a smooth paste, ensuring that the eggs have been fully mixed with the herbs.

6. Pour the sieved flour into the bowl of an electric mixer, and add the herb paste gradually, using a beater, not a cutter. Beat until you have a smooth green dough.
7. Remove from the machine, and wrap in cling film so that it is airtight. Leave for at least 20 minutes to relax before use. (If you attempt to roll it immediately after making, it will be too elastic and too tough.)
8. Roll out as thinly as you can (a machine is very useful), and cut into the shape required: into long thin strips for fettucine or tagliatelle, wider strips for pappardelle, or broad rectangles for lasagne.
9. Either cook immediately, for 1 or 2 minutes only, in boiling salted water, or leave to dry a little. Dried home-made pasta will take a few minutes longer to cook.

PASTA FOR RAVIOLI

MAKES 500 G (18 OZ)

This recipe is a base which can be used for any type of ravioli or tortellini, fish or meat. The only variation is the actual filling. It will keep in the fridge, made airtight by wrapping in cling film, for up to 3 days.

2 eggs	**30 ml (1 fl oz) olive oil**
3 egg yolks	**500 g (18 oz) plain or pasta flour, sieved**
30 ml (1 fl oz) water	**1 teaspoon table salt**

1. Crack the whole eggs into a bowl, then add the egg yolks. Beat them together with a whisk until smooth. Reserve aside.
2. In a measuring jug, mix the water and the oil together, and stir.
3. Put the flour and salt in an electric mixer bowl and, on a very low speed, mix together. Add the eggs and beat to a smooth paste.
4. Gradually add the water and oil mixture. Turn up the speed of the machine and beat to a smooth dough for about 2 minutes.
5. Remove the ravioli paste from the machine

and wrap in cling film so that it is airtight. Leave the pasta for at least 20 minutes to relax before use. If you attempt to roll it immediately after making it, it will be too elastic and too tough.
6. Roll out by hand or machine and cut and fill as required, moistening the edges well so that the pasta adheres to itself and the filling doesn't fall out.
7. Allow to dry a little before cooking in boiling salted water for about 4–5 minutes, according to size.

PUFF PASTRY

MAKES ABOUT 1.25 KG (2¾ LB)

*A*lthough complicated and rather lengthy in its construction, I have included this recipe for the adventurous amongst you. All chefs have their own special puff pastry recipe: some add a little lemon, to achieve an acidity; some substitute that with vinegar; others use no acid at all. This is the recipe that works best for me and in my opinion, when considering a dish that uses puff pastry, you should always make your own to achieve the best result. The flavour and texture are 100 per cent better.

Puff pastry can be made in bulk in advance, then cut into blocks, and stored in the freezer until required. Defrost for 6 hours before using. Do not store for more than 2–3 days in the fridge, as the pastry will break down and discolour.

500 g (18 oz) plain flour
10 g (⅓ oz) salt
475 g (17 oz) unsalted butter

240 ml (8 fl oz) cold water
1 tablespoon lemon juice

1. Place the flour and salt in a bowl or on to a clean working surface. Rub 120 g (4 oz) of the butter in until the texture resembles breadcrumbs.
2. Add the cold water and lemon juice, and mix to form a good dough.
3. Wrap in cling film and leave to rest in the fridge for 6 hours. The pastry needs plenty of time to relax.
4. Remove from the fridge and mould the dough into a ball. Cut a cross on the top. Roll the corners out to form a rough square, making these corner `flaps' thinner than the centre.
5. Beat the remaining butter to soften but not melt it, and form it into a square.
6. Place the butter in the centre of the dough and fold over each corner flap, completely enveloping the butter. Rest in the fridge for an hour, so that the pastry and butter are at the same temperature.
7. Roll out on a lightly floured surface, rolling *away* from you, to a rectangle about 50 cm (20 in) long and 25 cm (10 in) wide.
8. Mentally divide this rectangle into three lengthwise. Fold the bottom third up over the middle third, then fold the top third down over both. Give the block a half turn from 12 o'clock to 3 o'clock, and roll out again and fold again into three. Press the edges lightly

together and rest for an hour in the fridge.
9. Remove from the fridge and repeat this rolling out to a rectangle, folding, rolling and folding and chilling twice more. The pastry needs a total of six 3-fold turns.
10. Leave to rest for 2 hours in the fridge before use.
11. Roll out to no thinner than 1 cm (½ in) and cut cleanly (pressed edges will not rise). Bake as described in individual recipes, but the best temperature is about 220°C (425°F) Gas 7.

CHEF'S TIP

Making puff pastry cases:
For round cases or vol-au-vents, cut as described on p.47. For square or rectangular cases, cut the shape out cleanly, then moisten the top edges with water. Cut strips from the remaining pastry and press lightly in place to fit. Prick the 'bottom' of the case if you do not want it to rise as much as the sides.

CHEF'S TIP

Certain things like vol-au-vents, which you want to rise well, require virgin puff pastry. Other things, however, can use the scraps, not requiring height when cooked. Puff pastry is too valuable in ingredients and time ever to be thrown away. Store any and all puff pastry trimmings in the freezer, well wrapped.

Faults in puff pastry making:

1. *Uneven rolling technique.*
2. *Insufficient resting between turns.*
3. *The dough getting too warm, melting the butter.*
4. *Insufficient rest before baking.*
5. *Rolling out too thinly (this gives a poor lift).*
6. *Too cold an oven.*

A THREE-FOLD TURN

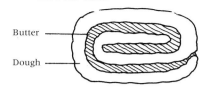

Butter

Dough

TURNING THE DOUGH A HALF TURN BETWEEN EACH
THREE-FOLD TURN

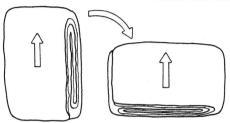

SHORTCRUST PASTRY

MAKES ABOUT 700 G (1½ LB)

Like all base pastries, there are 101 different recipes. This is the one that I find the nicest. It can be used in the construction of most savoury pies, such as steak and kidney or quiche Lorraine. With the addition of grated cheese, it can be rolled out and cut for simple cheese straws, to precede a meal. It freezes well.

375 g (13 oz) plain flour
15 g (½ oz) salt
225 g (7½ oz) unsalted butter

1 egg, beaten
60 ml (2 fl oz) cold water

1. Sieve the flour and salt into a bowl.
2. Dice the butter, approximately 1 cm (½ in) square, and add to the flour and salt.
3. Using your fingers, gently rub the butter into the flour until it resembles breadcrumbs.
4. Add your beaten egg and cold water. Gently bind together until you can press it into a ball.

5. Wrap in cling film and refrigerate for at least 2 hours before use.
6. When ready to use, allow to come back to room temperature for about 10 minutes, then roll out and bake as described in individual recipes. A good temperature is 220°C (425°F) Gas 7.

CHOUX PASTRY

MAKES ABOUT 600 G (1¼ LB)

*T*his is one of my favourite pastries. It has enormous versatility when filled with variously flavoured pastry creams. It is used in the construction of éclairs or profiteroles, and Gâteau St Honoré. A savoury choux filled with sauce makes a delicious canapé to precede any meal. Mixed with puréed potato or cooked semolina, choux pastry can be used in the construction of gnocchi.

110 g (3½ oz) unsalted butter
1 teaspoon caster sugar
1 teaspoon salt

270 ml (9 fl oz) water
120 g (4 oz) plain flour
4 eggs, beaten

1. Place the butter, sugar, salt and water in a saucepan and bring to the boil.
2. Immediately remove from the heat, and beat in the flour to make a smooth paste.
3. Return to a gentle heat and cook out, stirring until the mixture leaves the side of the pan.
4. Turn out into the bowl of a mixer or blender (or similar).
5. On a high speed, gradually beat in the eggs.
6. Place the mixture into a piping bag fitted with a nozzle according to the shape you desire, and pipe on to a non-stick tray or a well-greased one. (The mixture should be soft but retain its shape.)
7. Bake as instructed in individual recipes, but a good average temperature for choux is 220°C (425°F) Gas 7.

CHEF'S TIP
Choux pastry can, of course, be made entirely by hand, but in smaller quantities than here.

SWEET PASTRY

MAKES ABOUT 1 KG (2¼ LB)

*T*here are hundreds of sweet pastry recipes. This is mine, and I use it in the construction of most sweet tarts, pies and flans. It is the one which works best for me.

Wrapped well in cling film, it can store in the fridge for a couple of days. It freezes well, for up to a month.

300 g (10 oz) unsalted butter
110 g (3½ oz) icing sugar

110 g (3½ oz) shelled eggs (approx. 2 x size 3 eggs)
500 g (18 oz) soft plain flour

1. Beat the butter and icing sugar together in a bowl until white and fluffy.
2. Add the eggs, one at a time, and beat to a smooth paste.
3. Sift the flour into the eggs and butter, and mix until it comes away from the sides of the bowl.
4. As soon as the dough comes together, mould into a ball. Wrap in cling film and place in a refrigerator, preferably overnight but for at least 2–3 hours.
5. Remove from the fridge, and roll out on a floured surface. Keep the pastry as cold as possible, working quickly and not overhandling it.
6. Rest the pastry in the fridge before baking, otherwise shrinking or collapsing of the sides may occur.
7. Bake as outlined in individual recipes, but the pastry should be cooked in a moderate oven – 200°C (400°F) Gas 6 – until golden.

BISCUIT SPONGE

This I use mainly as a base for mousses, whether fruit or chocolate. It has a two-fold advantage in dessert construction: it adds another texture to a dessert; and it can be soaked in various syrups and alcohol to give another flavour. It is also useful because it prevents your mousse or charlotte from sticking to the bottom of the pan!

150 g (5 oz) icing sugar
150 g (5 oz) ground almonds
3 whole eggs
90 g (3 oz) egg yolks

275 g (9 oz) egg whites
110 g (3½ oz) caster sugar
120 g (4 oz) plain flour, sieved

1. Preheat the oven to 220°C (425°F) Gas 7, and line two Swiss roll tins with silicone paper.
2. Sieve together the icing sugar and ground almonds.
3. In a bowl, whisk the eggs and yolks together, then whisk in the icing sugar and almonds until pale and thick.
4. Whisk the egg whites to a peak in a separate bowl then add the sugar slowly. Fold into the eggs and almonds.
5. Gently fold in the sieved flour.
6. Divide between the two lined Swiss roll tins, then level with a palette knife, and bake in the preheated oven for 12–14 minutes.
7. When cooked, carefully lift the biscuit sponge on to a wire tray, still on its paper to keep it in one piece, and leave to cool. When cold, wrap in cling film and then use as required. It will keep for up to three days in the fridge. Do *not* freeze.

ORANGE AND ALMOND TUILES

MAKES 20-40, DEPENDING ON SIZE

These make an excellent accompaniment for ice creams, or you can serve them with coffee. The tuiles can be any size you want – small or large – but you must remember to leave them plenty of space to spread (by two to three times) on the tray while baking.

The quantity given is large, but the recipe doesn't work so well when smaller. You can take out and bake as many tuiles as you like, then freeze the remainder of the mixture for another time. The mixture also keeps well in the fridge, for up to 2 weeks.

250 g (8¼ oz) nibbed almonds
250 g (8¼ oz) caster sugar
75 g (2½ oz) plain flour

210 g (7 oz) unsalted butter
zest and juice of 1 orange

1. Mix the almonds, sugar and flour together in a bowl.
2. Melt the butter in a saucepan and add the juice and finely grated zest of the orange. Add this to the flour mixture.
3. Make sure all ingredients are thoroughly mixed together then refrigerate for 1 hour.
4. Preheat the oven to 220°C (425°F) Gas 7.
5. Grease a non-stick baking tray with a little extra melted butter. Place five balls of the 'tuile' mixture the size of walnuts (or whatever size tuile you want to make) on to the tray, allowing room for spreading when cooking.
6. Place in the preheated oven and bake until

golden brown, about 10–12 minutes. Ideally go by the colour as ovens vary so much.

7. Remove from the oven and leave to cool slightly on the baking tray, then carefully remove with a palette knife and place over a rolling pin or the side of an empty milk bottle.

Leave to cool. The tuile will bend and then go brittle and fragile.

8. Repeat with the remaining mixture to make more tuiles.

9. Serve on the same day, keeping them in an airtight container.

GLUCOSE BISCUITS

MAKES ABOUT 20

This is just another example of a basic tuile biscuit. In the book this recipe is used in the construction of a strawberry dessert. By themselves, the biscuits have a multitude of different uses, or can be served plain to accompany your coffee after a meal.

150 g (5 oz) unsalted butter
150 g (5 oz) caster sugar

150 ml (5 fl oz) liquid glucose
150 g (5 oz) plain flour

1. Gently melt the butter, sugar and liquid glucose in a saucepan over a low heat, stirring all the time.

2. Gently beat in the flour and remove from the heat. Put the mixture in a clean bowl and refrigerate for 1 hour before using.

3. Preheat the oven to 230°C (450°F) Gas 8.

4. On a greased non-stick tray place six small balls of the glucose mixture (about the size of a walnut), leaving space between each for spreading. Gently press down, flattening them slightly.

5. Bake in the preheated oven until golden in colour, about 10–12 minutes. Remove the tray from the oven and leave to cool slightly.

6. Whilst still warm cut out the tuiles using a plain 8 cm (3¼ in) cutter. Remove them from the tray using a wide palette knife. Store in an airtight container for four to five days.

CHEF'S TIP
The uncooked mixture can be kept for at least a fortnight if covered and placed in the refrigerator.

7. Repeat the baking and cutting with the rest of the mixture.

LANGUE DE CHAT BISCUITS

MAKES ANY NUMBER, DEPENDING ON SIZE

These biscuits are primarily used as a garnish for ice creams, *petits-fours*, or as an accompaniment to a dessert. For some recipes you will require round *langue de chat* biscuits and to make these you will need a stencil. If a stencil is not available cut holes to the required size in the plastic lid of a biscuit tin: you want to 'smear' the mixture into the hole to the thickness of the lid, then remove the 'lid stencil' to leave a perfect circle.

100 g (3½ oz) unsalted butter, melted
210 g (7 oz) icing sugar
150 ml (5 fl oz) egg whites (approx. 5 eggs)

120 g (4 oz) plain flour
2 teaspoons vanilla sugar

1. Place the melted butter in a bowl and gradually beat in the icing sugar.
2. To avoid curdling the mixture add, alternately, 1 egg white then 1 tablespoon of flour at a time, whisking constantly until both ingredients are used up and a smooth paste is obtained.
3. Beat in the vanilla sugar, then refrigerate until needed. (This mixture will keep for up to a week in the refrigerator or can be stored in the freezer.)
4. Preheat the oven to 220°C (425°F) Gas 7.
5. Either spread or pipe on to a greased baking tray. Bake in the preheated oven until the edges go brown, no longer than 10–12 minutes.
6. These biscuits can be shaped, twisted or curled while still warm. Roll them up into cigar or cigarette shapes (particularly effective and delicious with one end dipped into melted chocolate), or make into handkerchief tuiles: fold a disc in half and then in half again like the handkerchief you might put in your top pocket! Store in an airtight container.

ITALIAN MERINGUE

MAKES 350 G (12 OZ)

*M*ost good cooks know about the beauty of a good meringue. I use Italian meringue – one with cooked sugar – as a base for several mousses and dishes included in this book.

120 g (4 oz) egg whites (approx. 4 eggs)
240 g (8 oz) caster sugar

60 ml (2 fl oz) water

1. Heat 210 g (7 oz) of the sugar and the water together to 118°C (245°F), using a copper pan if available.
2. Stiffly beat the egg whites, adding the remaining sugar gradually.
3. Still whisking, add the boiled syrup to the egg white in a steady stream. Do this carefully so that the syrup does not fly out.
4. Continue whisking until the meringue is firm. The meringue will keep for a few hours if placed in an airtight container in the fridge.

CHEF'S TIP
When the meringue is firm it can be flavoured. Simply stir in some unsweetened fruit purée, a little essence, some chopped nuts or some crushed nougatine.

NOUGATINE

MAKES ABOUT 1.3 KG (4 LB)

I have included this recipe as, when crumbled, it is an excellent addition to mousses, ice creams and pastry creams. It can also be used to make tuile biscuits. Hazelnuts could be used instead of the almonds.

400 g (14 oz) nibbed almonds

400 ml (14 fl oz) liquid glucose

500 g (18 oz) caster sugar

120 g (4 oz) unsalted butter

1. Preheat the oven to 140°C (275°F) Gas 1.
2. Warm the almonds through in the preheated oven for 3–4 minutes to colour them slightly.
3. Stir the glucose and sugar together in a saucepan over a gentle heat until mixed.
4. Raise the temperature and cook until caramelised, or amber in colour.
5. Stir in the warm almonds and add the butter. Remove from the heat.
6. Turn on to a greased tray, and help it to cool by turning it over a few times with a palette knife as it cools. It is now called *croquant*.
7. Crush the desired amount of *croquant* with a rolling pin, making it into nougatine.
8. The *croquant* which is left can be stored for future use for up to a month. Keep as whole as possible in an airtight container.

VANILLA ICE CREAM

MAKES ABOUT 1.5 LITRES (2¼ PINTS)

*V*anilla ice cream, made from fresh eggs, Jersey double cream and the blackest of vanilla pods, is simplicity at its best.

600 ml (1 pint) milk

600 ml (1 pint) double cream

60 ml (2 fl oz) liquid glucose

1 vanilla pod

210 g (7 oz) egg yolks (approx. 7 eggs)

240 g (8 oz) caster sugar

1. Put the milk, cream and glucose in a saucepan, and scrape the inside of the vanilla pod into it. Bring to the boil.
2. Whisk the egg yolks and sugar together until white and thick in texture.
3. Whisk the boiling liquid into the yolks and sugar, and transfer to a clean pan.
4. Stir the mixture continuously over a low heat until it coats the back of the spoon. *Do not boil.*
5. Pass the mixture through a fine sieve, then leave to cool.
6. Churn in an ice-cream machine until frozen, then store in the freezer. The ice cream is best eaten on the day it has been made.
7. If you do not have an ice-cream machine, place in a suitable container and freeze, taking out and mixing at hourly intervals, until frozen.

CHEF'S TIP

For a simple but spectacular dessert interspace balls of ice cream with round langue de chat *biscuits as in the drawing. Dust the top, handkerchief-shape biscuit with icing sugar and serve immediately.*

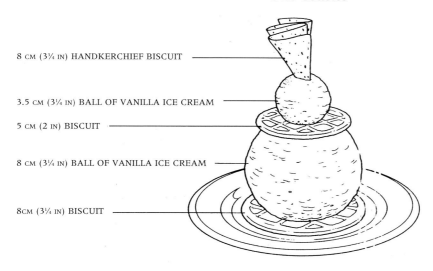

8 CM (3¼ IN) HANDKERCHIEF BISCUIT

3.5 CM (3¼ IN) BALL OF VANILLA ICE CREAM

5 CM (2 IN) BISCUIT

8 CM (3¼ IN) BALL OF VANILLA ICE CREAM

8 CM (3¼ IN) BISCUIT

STOCK SYRUP

MAKES ABOUT 1 LITRE (1¾ PINTS)

I have included stock syrup as a basic recipe as it is used to poach the fruits in much of my dessert cookery. Poured over a fruit salad it will add sweetness, but also stop the oxidisation and discoloration of the fruit. In various sugar degrees – i.e. depending on the amount of sugar in the liquid – it is used as a base in all sorbet construction. It is the dessert equivalent to chicken stock!

510 ml (17 fl oz) water

650 g (1lb 6 oz) caster sugar

1. Pour the water into a large saucepan and add the sugar.
2. Place on the stove and bring to the boil. Turn off the heat when it has boiled and the sugar has dissolved.
3. Transfer to a suitable container with a lid and, when cooled, use as directed. Keep for as long as you like!

PASTRY CREAM

MAKES 800 G (1¾ LB)

*I*n France this is called *crème pâtissière*, and the French, even more than the Brits, use this like we use whipped cream when constructing pastries and cakes. Like the French, I use this as a base to a lot of dessert cookery, and even as a base for soufflés.

600 ml (1 pint) milk
1 vanilla pod
30 g (1 oz) cornflour

30 g (1 oz) plain flour
6 egg yolks
120 g (4 oz) caster sugar

1. Bring the milk to the boil in a saucepan with the vanilla pod.
2. Mix the flours together.

3. Whisk the egg yolks in a bowl with the sugar until pale and thick. Then add the mixed flour and cornflour, and mix in carefully.

4. Gently pour approximately one-third of the boiling milk over the yolks and sugar, mix together until smooth, and add back to the milk in the saucepan.

5. Bring back to the boil, whisking all the time. When it has boiled and thickened, using a spatula, pour into a clean bowl and put cling film over the top. When cold, reserve and refrigerate for up to three days.

EGG CUSTARD SAUCE (CRÈME ANGLAISE)

MAKES 600 ML (1 PINT)

*T*here are a great many possible variations on this recipe. The sauce has a very limited life, and it will only keep for two days in the fridge.

510 ml (17 fl oz) milk

6 egg yolks

100 g (3½ oz) caster sugar

1. Bring the milk to the boil in a saucepan, then remove from the heat.

2. Whisk the egg yolks and sugar together in a bowl until white.

3. Pour the milk, little by little at first, over the yolks and sugar, mixing them together.

4. Transfer the mixture to a clean saucepan and, stirring all the time, cook the mixture over a low heat until it thickens slightly – it should coat the back of a spoon. *Do not boil* as this will cause the mixture to curdle.

5. When cooked, pour the custard through a fine-mesh sieve into a bowl and leave to cool.

Vanilla Egg Custard Sauce
Add a split vanilla pod to the milk at the beginning of cooking.

Lemon Egg Custard Sauce
Remove the zests from two lemons and add to the milk at the beginning of cooking. Discard the zest when straining the custard.

Coffee Egg Custard Sauce
Add 10 g (⅓ oz) instant coffee powder to the milk at the beginning of cooking.

CHOCOLATE SAUCE

MAKES ABOUT 600 ML (1 PINT)

I have included this recipe because it has been used several times when dressing a plate. Served hot it is great poured over home-made vanilla ice cream.

120 ml (4 fl oz) water

120 g (4 oz) caster sugar

40 g (1½ oz) cocoa powder

240 ml (8 fl oz) whipping cream

1. Place the water, sugar and cocoa powder in a saucepan. Bring to the boil, whisking occasionally.

2. Pour in the whipping cream and bring back to the boil. Boil for 2 minutes then remove from the heat.

3. Pass the sauce through a fine sieve. Cover with cling film, allowing this to touch the sauce so it does not form a skin. Refrigerate when cold, for up to a week. Serve at room temperature.

Index

NOTE: Page references in *italics* indicate chef's tips; those in **bold** type indicate photographs of finished dishes.

R

rabbit
  baron, cooked in vinegar, tomatoes and fresh herbs 203–4
  jointing *203*
  leg and saddle with Bayonne ham **39**, 62–3
  terrine with bacon and crisp baby vegetables **130**, 141–2
raspberries
  glazed, with white chocolate mousse **76**, 101–2
  with iced honeyed nougat and dried apples **94**, 112–13
  jellied terrine with quinces 133–4
  in queen of pudding tartlets 81–2
  sauce 87, 139–40
  vacherin with apricots 87
ratatouille 109–10
ravioli
  of lobster 97–9
  pasta for 241
rhubarb
  biscuit 71–2
  sauce 71–2
rice, wild *117*
rillettes 77–9

S

sabayon *59*
  in chocolate charlotte 153–4
  coffee 199–200
  in gratin of pear, chocolate and nuts 164
saffron *174*
salads
  avocado pear with crab and pink grapefruit 103–4
  breast of guinea fowl with lime glaze 114–15
  grilled, of scallops 13–14, **17**
  hot calf's tongue **96**, 126–7
  orange 189
  pigeon with pine kernels in red wine sauce 181–2
  skate with soya vinaigrette **75**, 88–90
  and walnut vinaigrette 233
  see also mayonnaise; vinaigrette
salmon
  carpaccio 172–3
  dry-grilled with red cabbage and chicory 60–61
  marinading *61*
  smoked with oysters in English wine jelly **132**, 155–6
  smoked salmon mousse 49–50
  wild, steamed fillet 79–81
salt crust pastry, sea bass in **74**, 85–6
samosas, curried lamb 135–6
sauces
  savoury
    Béarnaise 122–3
    Béchamel 228
    brandy and port 162–3
    butter 231
    champagne 183–4
    chive butter 79–81, 190–92
    chive cream 49–50, 231
    cider 176–7

gazpacho as 13–14, **17**
    herb butter **131**, 145–6
    honey 105–6
    lamb (base) 229
    parsley and mushroom 192–3
    port 15–16
    port, tarragon and mustard **95**, 116–17
    red wine 111, 127–8, 147–9, 181–2, 201–2, 230
    reducing *193*
    rémoulade 126–7, 235
    rosemary *229*
    shallot and white wine 217–18
    soya vinaigrette 89–90
    squid ink 25–7
    thyme *229*
    tomato 137–8, *229*, 232–3
    tomato and anchovy 86
    tomato and fennel 99
    tomato and herb 203–4
    tomato and parsley 177–8
    white 228
    white wine and shallot 121–2
  sweet
    apricot 87
    caramel 193–4
    chocolate 250
    clementine 180
    egg custard 250
    plum 144
    raspberry 87, 139–40
    rhubarb 71–2
    rum caramel 218–19
    strawberry 107
    walnut caramel 213–14
sausage, chicken 239
scallops
  forcemeat with grilled squid 25–7
  grilled salad 13–14, **17**
  preparing *13*
  in puff pastry with chive butter sauce 190–92
sea bass
  in oyster and champagne sauce 183–4, **205**
  in salt crust with tomato and anchovy sauce **74**, 85–6
sea bream, royal, with shallot cream and red wine sauce 127–8
shallots, purée 235
shellfish
  cockles 177–8
  court bouillon 224
  crab 44–5, 103–4
  langoustines 55–6
  lobster 69–71, **73**, 97–9
  mussels **151**, 160–61
  oysters **131**, **132**, 145–6, *145*, 155–6, 183–4
  scallops 13–14, 25–7, 190–92
shortbread, strawberry tartlets 21–2
shortcrust pastry 243
shrimps, grey *32*
skate, salad with soya vinaigrette **75**, 88–90
snails, new potatoes filled with 201–2, **206**
sole, glazed fillets in mushroom and parsley sauce 192–3